MANDELSTAM:
THE LATER POETRY

MANDELSTAM:
THE LATER POETRY

JENNIFER BAINES
Lecturer in Russian, University of Durham

CAMBRIDGE UNIVERSITY PRESS

CAMBRIDGE
LONDON · NEW YORK · MELBOURNE

Published by the Syndics of the Cambridge University Press

The Pitt Building, Trumpington Street, Cambridge CB2 1RP

Bentley House, 200 Euston Road, London NW12DB

32 East 57th Street, New York, NY 10022, USA

296 Beaconsfield Parade, Middle Park, Melbourne 3206, Australia

First published 1976

Printed in Great Britain

at the University Printing House, Cambridge

(Euan Phillips, University Printer)

Library of Congress Cataloguing in Publication Data

Baines, Jennifer.
   Mandelstam: the later poetry.

   1. Mandel'shtam, Osip Emil'evich, 1891-1938 -
Criticism and interpretation.
PG3476.M355Z56   891.7'1'3   76-8515
ISBN 0 521 21273 1

CONTENTS

ACKNOWLEDGEMENTS

I should like to acknowledge my immense debt to Nadezhda
Yakovlevna Mandelstam, who provided invaluable source
material and practical help.

I am particularly grateful to Professor Dmitri Obolensky
for his advice, assistance and meticulous attention to my
manuscript; and to Professor John Baines.

PREFACE

Whenever Mandelstam's name is mentioned in the West, it is
the Mandelstam of *Камень* and *Tristia* whom the speaker
usually has in mind. Of the scholarly attention given to him
by modern commentators most has been devoted exclusively to
the years when he was working on his first three collections, 1908-25. Before the appearance of Clarence Brown's
book, *Mandelstam*[1], although this also is only the poet of
the first three collections, there was very little of interest or value written about Mandelstam. Professor Brown's
study is the major contribution to the subject and will
remain a standard work for some time to come.

   The poetry of Mandelstam's fourth and subsequent
collections comprises over two-thirds of his poetic output:
yet this poetry, like a good deal of his prose writing after
1920, is very little known. Only recently have the impressive
and invaluable memoirs of Mandelstam's widow, Nadezhda
Yakovlevna, appeared[2]. The biographical information which
they give about him is integrated with more general
recollections and revelations about life in the Soviet
Union from the early twenties to the present day, but in
particular from the time of Mandelstam's first arrest in
1934 to his death in 1938. The memoirs contain random
comments on the poems themselves, but little in the way of
systematic commentary to facilitate interpretation. I have

---

[1] CUP, Cambridge 1973.

[2] See *Text sources and Abbreviations*.

been most fortunate in being given access by Nadezhda
Yakovlevna to her own typescript of Mandelstam's poetry and
to her written and verbal comments on it, which are the
source material for a large proportion of this book.

The conventional wisdom that Mandelstam's later work is
obscure and significantly weaker than his early poetry still
seems to be widely accepted, and the need to explode this
myth has inevitably conditioned my approach. The result
represents an exercise in ground-clearing for future
scholars rather than a definitive account. While I attempt
to provide a continuous narrative of the events which formed
the background to the writing of the 1930-7 poetry, my
chief aim has been the understanding and interpretation of
that poetry. I originally intended to examine it through
the normal methods of analysis - a discussion of his themes,
his imagery, his metres and so forth - but it soon became
clear that such an analysis would be premature, since its
essential precondition, a minimal appreciation of the basic
meaning of the poems, did not exist among readers of
Mandelstam; and to examine, for instance, the metrical
structure of poetry which made no sense to the reader
seemed a foolish activity.

When Mandelstam arranged his poems into collections
(whether they were actually published or not) he almost
invariably placed them in the chronological order in which
they were written down for the first time - an order which
was not necessarily that of their composition in all cases.
This order, clearly very deliberate, has been followed here.
By this means the relationship of Mandelstam's life to his
poems, and the relationship of the poems to each other, can,
I believe, be most conveniently demonstrated.

It is essential that the *Note* and the *Appendix* should
be consulted for the correct order and dating of the poems.

A detailed knowledge of the American and Soviet editions of
Mandelstam's work is assumed throughout, as is an acquaintance
with both volumes of Nadezhda Yakovlevna's memoirs[1] and with
Clarence Brown's study. I have not, however, included a
bibliography. There is so much that is misleading, both as to
fact and as to interpretation, in recent work on the later
poetry that it cannot be recommended for further reading.

I have retained the spelling of Mandelstam's name used by
Professor Brown in order to avoid inconsistency. Other names
are given in the form most generally found in works of literary criticism (e.g. Andrei Bely), rather than in conformity
to a system.

1976   J.B.

---

[1] See *Text sources and Abbreviations.*

TEXT SOURCES AND ABBREVIATIONS

I О.Э.Мандельштам: *Собрание сочинений в трех томах*, том первый, издание второе, под редакцией Г.П.Струве и Б.А.Филиппова, Вашингтон 1967.

II О.Э.Мандельштам: *Собрание сочинений в трех томах*, том второй, издание второе, под редакцией Г.П.Струве и Б.А.Филиппова, Нью Йорк 1971.

III О.Э.Мандельштам: *Собрание сочинений в трех томах*, том третий, под редакцией Г.П.Струве и Б.А. Филиппова, Нью Йорк 1969.

S О.Мандельштам: *Стихотворения*, составление, подготовка текста и примечания Н.И.Харджиева, Ленинград 1973, второй завод 1974.

N.Ya.I Надежда Мандельштам: *Воспоминания*, Нью Йорк 1970.

N.Ya.II Надежда Мандельштам: *Вторая книга*, Париж 1972.

N.Ya.III refers to Nadezhda Yakovlevna's personal typescript copy of Mandelstam's poems, together with additional biographical information and her own comments on the poetry which accompany the texts.

NOTE

The order and dating of the last five collections of Mandelstam's poetry

When Mandelstam broke his poetic silence - between January 1925 and October 1930 he composed no serious poetry - he gave his new poems a name which demonstrates his usual lack of interest in titles: *Новые стихи.* Between 1930 and 1937 he wrote, but could not publish, two books of *Новые стихи*: the two Moscow collections (1930-4) and the three Voronezh collections (1935-7). The original autographs of many poems in the first book were lost during or after the police search at the time of his first arrest, in May 1934, and it was only on one of Nadezhda Yakovlevna Mandelstam's journeys from Voronezh to Moscow in search of work for them both that some copies of the lost poems were found. Meanwhile Mandelstam had been attempting to resurrect various of them from memory, and so it would happen that two different poems arose from the same source, as in the case of 'Ариост' (I Nos.267 & 268). Mandelstam, hoping for their eventual publication, copied and ordered these two collections of Moscow poems in separate school notebooks - hence their domestic name of 'тетрадь'. In Voronezh the three new collections which he composed there were similarly put into their final versions and order in three notebooks, thus becoming the so-called *Первая воронежская тетрадь, Вторая воронежская тетрадь* and *Третья воронежская тетрадь.* Typescript and manuscript copies of all five collections were made at various times and given to friends for safe-keeping, most of these authorised by Mandelstam himself. Within these copies, however, there are

variant versions of the text; where the texts diverge in the
American edition and the incomplete Soviet edition it will
be as a result of these variant versions.

In Nadezhda Yakovlevna Mandelstam's personal typescript
of the 1930-7 poetry each poem is dated and accompanied by
her own commentary and explanation of the background to the
groups of poems within each collections. This is the order
and dating which are reproduced in the *Appendix* here. The
order is definitive, since it is that of Mandelstam himself.
The dates are in all cases to be preferred to those in the
American edition, where they conflict, and in most cases to
those in the Soviet edition. Although Khardzhiev, its editor,
has made use of copies from personal archives, Nadezhda
Yakovlevna will have had a wider range of just such sources
on which to draw in determining a date, as well as her own
recollection. An example of why total credence cannot be
given to Khardzhiev is the poem 'Нет, не мигрень, но подай
карандашик ментоловый' (I No.317, S No.152). This poem of
July 1935 was written, *faute de mieux,* on the back of one of
the rescued 1931 autographs of the rough drafts of 'Волк'
(I No.227, S No.149). Khardzhiev, on this evidence alone,
and in spite of repeated protests from Nadezhda Yakovlevna,
dates the poem to April 1931. The content and style alone
disprove this dating.

For the sake of consistency the titles or first lines of
poems are given here in the form shown in the American
edition, since this edition is the more complete, although,
because of the difficulties inherent in the *samizdat* method
of circulation, the texts which reached the editors of this
otherwise excellent edition will inevitably be more liable
to inaccuracy than those in the Soviet one. Again, however,
there are examples of apparently wilful distortion in the
latter, such as the printing of an earlier version of the

the first line of 'Вехи дальнего обоза' (I No.340, S No.193)
as though it were the final version.

Where poems feature in both the editions I have normally
given only the number of the poem in the American edition,
since the selection of post-1930 poetry in the Soviet edition
is so incomplete. Corresponding numbers for the poems which
can be found in the Soviet edition are given in the *Appendix*.

1. *НОВЫЕ СТИХИ:*
ПЕРВАЯ МОСКОВСКАЯ ТЕТРАДЬ
October 1930 - October 1931

Mandelstam's letters of 1925-6 and 1930 to his wife, Nadezhda
Yakovlevna, are on two subjects: her health and his constant
struggle to find and keep commissions for translation work
and children's poetry, as well as a roof over their heads
(Letters No.10-48, 50-3, III pp.203-55, 256-62). Nadezhda
Yakovlevna had always been fragile; in a letter to her mother
in 1921 Mandelstam reassures Vera Yakovlevna that he is taking
every precaution to safeguard her daughter's health (Letter
No.7, III pp.199-200), which was to become a constant worry
to him. In spring 1925 they were living at the former Tsarskoe
- now Detskoe - Selo.[1] They spent the summer in Luga, and then
Mandelstam sent her to Yalta, in the hope that the Crimean
climate would arrest, perhaps cure, the tuberculosis from
which she was suffering. Meanwhile he had to support them both,
including provision for consultations with doctors and a spec-
ially devised invalid diet for her. This meant endless running
around editorial offices, endless negotiations, the careful
calculation of every rouble, and the unbearable separation
from Nadezhda Yakovlevna.

Mandelstam's 1925-6 poems for children (I Nos.396-415),
delightful though they are, gave him no more satisfaction
than any other work written to order. Only the publication
of *Шум времени* in 1928 did so. It came out with the newly

---

[1]   А.А.Ахматова, *Сочинения*, (2 vols., 2nd edn. of vol. 1,
   Washington, 1967-8), p.176.

written *Египетская марка* and with a new edition of *Камень*
and *Tristia* which, with the 1921-5 poems, appeared under the
title *Стихотворения* (its appearance being due entirely to
the good offices of Bukharin [N.Ya.I p.20]), and also with
the publication of selected articles on literature under the
title *О поэзии*, both in 1928. Mandelstam's position, however,
remained unaltered by these reminders to the official world
of his continued existence. The rest of the second half of
this decade is a nightmarish scurrying all over the Soviet
Union: spring 1926 in Tsarskoe, summer in Kitaiskaya Derev-
nya and Kiev, autumn in Koktebel, winter in the Lycée in
Tsarskoe - all this in an attempt to reconcile the conflicting demands of Nadezhda Yakovlevna's health, which limited
acceptable places to live, and the need to find work. The
'commuting' between the North and the Crimea continued
throughout 1928 and was followed by a homeless winter and
summer, when friends and relatives in Moscow had to come to
their aid. Then in 1929 came the sordid 'Eulenspiegel affair'
- a deliberately planned campaign to discredit Mandelstam on
the part of official literary hacks such as David Zaslavsky
- which made them decide to make their move to Moscow a
permanent one.[1] Only the unexpected gift of their journey to
Armenia in April-November 1930 (again the benevolent
influence of Bukharin at work) gave some respite from their
precarious Moscow existence, and ended the period of silence

---

[1] For an account of this affair see:
  a) The introduction by Clarence Brown to his translation
     of 'Четвертая проза', *Hudson Review* (Spring 1970),
     49-50.
  b) The translator's footnote in Nadezhda Mandelstam, *Hope
     against hope*, transl. Max Hayward (New York, 1970),
     p.178.
  c) N.Ya.I p.186.
  d) Editorial commentary in II p.604.

in his poetry.

His prose work of this period had played an equally important role in the return of poetry. Of *Египетская марка*, completed during the winter of 1927-8, and 'Четвертая проза' of 1930, the first sets out the problem facing Mandelstam while the second demonstrates its solution. The brilliant surrealism of *Египетская марка* does not conceal the gravity of the question: to what extent was Mandelstam to be identified with Parnok, the hypersensitive failure standing at the end of a long line of 'лишние люди', from Pushkin's Evgeny in *Медный всадник* and Dostoevsky's Golyadkin onwards:

> Господи! Не сделай меня похожим на Парнока! Дай мне силы
> отличить себя от него.   (II p.24)

All Parnok's efforts to save his fellows from mob brutality meet with as little success as his bid to save his morning-coat - like Akaky Akakievich's overcoat, the symbol of his individuality, his soul almost - from the clutches of his successful 'double', Captain Krzhizhanovsky. Mandelstam saw himself as just such a pathetic figure, invariably on the losing side, unable to answer force with force or indeed to find any ground on which to counter-attack. In the Petersburg mob of the Kerensky summer all the repulsive traits of the mob of Leningrad party hacks who were turning on him can be discerned. The significance of 'Четвертая проза' is aptly summarised by Nadezhda Yakovlevna:

> Именно эта проза расчистила путь стихам, определила
> место О.М. в действительности и вернула чувство правоты.
> В 'Четвертой прозе' О.М. называл нашу землю кровавой,
> проклял казенную литературу, сорвал с себя литературную
> шубу и снова протянул руку разночинцу – 'старейшему
> комсомольцу – Акакию Акакиевичу... '   (N.Ya.I p.185)

Naturally this gives no idea of the remarkable qualities of 'Четвертая проза' which, according to Anna Akhmatova,[1] has now begun to receive due acclaim from the younger generation

---

[1] Ахматова, vol.2, p.181.

in the Soviet Union. However, at the time it served its
function as, in the words of Clarence Brown, 'a desperate act
of self-therapy... an explosion, a scream, a howl of his
injured humanity - and whatever else it may have accomplished,
it cleared his lungs.'[1] The fact of having defined his position in Soviet society as that of the outcast and untouchable
gave him strength to maintain his moral stand, and put an end
to the period of self-doubt which had caused the total silence
in his poetry between 1925 and 1930.

The journey to Armenia therefore completed a cure already
well under way. The Mandelstams' route lay through Sukhumi,
vividly described in the later 'Путешествие в Армению' (II
pp.156-9), and Tiflis. The significance of Armenia for Mandelstam cannot be overstated and is again best expressed by
Nadezhda Yakovlevna:

> Это было живое любопытство к маленькой стране, форпосту
> христианства на Востоке, устоявшей в течение веков
> против натиска магометанства. Быть может, в эпоху кризиса
> христианского сознания у нас Армения привлекла О.М. этой
> своей стойкостью.   (N.Ya.I p.245)

The historical, geographical and religious similarities
between the South, especially Armenia, and the Mediterranean,
especially Italy and the Holy Land, exercised a strong fascination over him. Hence his attempts, repeated during these
years, to arrange an official visit for himself (II p.183)
to the land which he called on this occasion 'младшей сестры
земли иудейской'. It is noteworthy that Mandelstam had come
to accept Judaism not because he was himself Jewish, but
through the medium of culture, for it is on cultural grounds
that he asserts his kinship with his racial group in his
attack on the tribe of writers:

> Я настаиваю на том, что писательство в том виде, как оно
> сложилось в Европе и в особенности в России, несовместимо

---

[1] Brown, *Hudson Review*, 52.

с почетным званием иудея, которым я горжусь. Моя кровь,
отягощенная наследством овцеводов, патриархов и царей,
бунтует против вороватой цыганщины писательского племени.
(II p.187)

This was the same 'чужое племя' against whom he had revolted
six years previously in his poem '1 января 1924' (I No.140),
and with whom he was now engaged in a full-blooded feud.
Armenia, by reminding him of a world where different values
prevailed, gave him back his self-confidence and his inspiration. Poetry returned to him in Tiflis, on the journey back
from Armenia, in the shape of his first genuine poem since
1925, 'Куда как страшно нам с тобой' (I No.202). With this
poem the first section of Tiflis and Moscow poems, whose
private name in their household, 'новые стихи', later came
to include all the poetry written after 1930, begins.

The opening poem

Mandelstam noted the form of the opening poem with some
satisfaction: he thought it fitting that the work which
marked the beginning of a new phase, in his life as in his
work, should have seven lines, a mystical number of favour-
able significance. Its mood was carefree and joking, as was
the event which occasioned it, the celebration of Nadezhda
Yakovlevna's name-day on 30 October 1930. They were staying
in Tiflis's Hotel Oriant, on the way back to Moscow, and her
aunt brought to the hotel a home-made nut 'торт', the
'ореховый пирог' of 'Куда как страшно нам с тобой' (I No.202)
(N.Ya.III). That the poem is addressed to Nadezhda Yakovlevna
is clear from the second line: 'Товарищ большеротый мой!'.
Nadezhda Yakovlevna still considers that the size of her
mouth ruined any pretensions to beauty she may have had.
Mandelstam, on the other hand, obviously found it as
endearing as her high forehead. Both are mentioned in terms of
great affection in his letters: 'Целую большой ротик' (Letter
No.22, III p.218) and 'Я на ночь целую тебя в лобик' (Letter

No.27, III p.227). It may seem incongruous that the formal 'товарищ' and the apparently insulting 'дурак', both referring to her, should find their way into the same poem. But 'товарищ', as she recounts (N.Ya.I p.343), was the accepted mode of address between husband and wife in the pre-Revolutionary underground, where the relationship of comrade was considered far more important than the marital relationship. That it still survived and should recently have been heard on the lips of Ezhov's wife amused Mandelstam, who remarked to his wife, with some truth, that it was more applicable to themselves. The masculine gender of 'дурак', seemingly inappropriate in a poem of which she is the addressee, is explained by considering its natural alternative - 'дура'. This would be not only coarse but positively insulting, whereas 'дурак', used in this way of a woman, is merely affectionate banter. Mandelstam often spoke or wrote to her in this way as in, for example, 'Родная моя, глупышка' (Letter No.23, III p.218). At the end of the first five-year plan, and as a result of the advent of kulak liquidation, hunger and appalling conditions were beginning to make themselves felt in Moscow. Obtaining food became a nightmare, and the Mandelstams were horrified by the greenish pallor of the half-starved children in the city. In Tiflis, however, the markets were full of food: only processed goods and cigarettes had disappeared from the stalls. They hunted round Tiflis for cigarettes and eventually found small boys selling them at a considerably higher price than usual - later the same cigarettes reappeared at a much higher, government, price. To compensate for this, it was possible to buy the loose tobacco available, not the best Caucasian, but the dried-up tobacco rejected by the manufacturers as substandard. It did indeed crumble: 'Ох, как крошится наш табак' (I No.202) (N.Ya.III). Although the date underneath the poem is later than many in the 'Armenian' group, Mandelstam said that 'Щелкунчик' (its

domestic name) actually came first and 'awoke' the rest. Its
completion came only with the producing of the 'ореховый
пирог'. The last lines epitomise his mood: life is terrible,
yet how marvellous it would be to be able to whistle through
it, to indulge oneself in it as in the luxury of a nut
gâteau. And how impossible: 'Да, видно, нельзя никак' (I No.
202). His lively dreams of frivolity are brought to an
abrupt end by the realisation that the return from Armenia
to Russia is a return to grim reality after a delightful
interlude. Perhaps he wrote at such length about Armenia
partly because he understood at the time its significance
as an untypically carefree respite and wanted to preserve
its memory in prose as well as verse. The dominant impulse
is sheer joy at the return of poetry in abundance, but seen
always against this background.

The Armenian group

Nadezhda Yakovlevna notes how the twelve poems which make up
the Armenian group (she calls it a 'подборка' rather than a
cycle), are not arranged in chronological order, unlike the
great majority of Mandelstam's poems, thereby acquiring the
character of a lyrical diary (N.Ya.I p.201). The correct
order and dating of these twelve (not thirteen, as in I) are
given in the *Appendix*. In addition to the main group there
are six other poems, all closely related, which complete the
poetry of the Armenian period (Nos. 201, 216, 217, 220, 218
§ 219, in that order). Between them they form a composite
picture of this 'historical' country - its landscape, its
people, their speech and their religion. The overriding
image is that of a wild beast. Armenia is said to nurture
'зверушек-детей' (I Nos. 205 § 206), the Armenian language
is likened to a wild cat (I Nos. 216 § 218), even the religion of the country is described as 'звериного и басенного
христианства' (I No.220). The people seem able, with no

apparent effort, to reconcile within a sort of 'двоеверие'
two extremes of worship:

> Примирившие дьявола и Бога,
> Каждому воздавши половину   (I No.212)

In the same way the country happily combines the austerity
of its stark red and ochre landscape and the animal splendour
of its women with symbols of tenderness and beauty, like the
rose of Hafiz (I No.204), and with the country's long cultural history. The interweaving of imagery shows how inseparable from one another these seemingly contradictory characteristics are:

> Скорей глаза сощурь,
> Как близорукий шах над перстнем бирюзовым,
> Над книгой звонких глин, над книжною землей,
> Которой мучимся как музыкой и словом.   (I No.215)

The vivid red clay of bare Armenian mountain slopes is
inextricably linked through the idea of layers of rock
accumulating down the ages with the advent of Christian
culture, relatively early in Armenia's history, its civilis-
ing influence gaining strength with time. It produces the
same strong and disturbing impact as do poetry and music.
The very stones are the bearers of an almost biblical
authority - 'Орущих камней государство' (I No.209) - which
is essential for a country in Armenia's geographical position among the pagans. Persia, in the rose of Hafiz, the
short-sighted Shah and the sun's 'Персидские деньги' (I No.
209), seems to have made more impression on Mandelstam as
being the nearest heathen country than, say, Turkey, in fact
a much more menacing neighbour. However, the magnetism of
the East is hard to resist, and nearby Asia, warlike though
it may be, exerts its own influence, in the translated
quotation from Catullus: 'К трубам серебряным Азии вечно
летящая' ('Ad claras Asiae volemus urbes') (I No.209); but
however strong the attraction the Christian country still
steadfastly turns its face from the barbarian cities of the

East:

> И отвернулась со стыдом и скорбью
> От городов бородатых востока   (I No.207)

The uniqueness of its Christianity is well expressed in its
churches, earthy and indomitable:

> Плечьми осьмигранными дышишь
> Мужицких бычачьих церквей.   (I No.204)

Armenia's famous pink tufa provides the only colouring - the
clay itself, a dark red-brown, and the paler pink of the
houses and churches, adding to the impression of wild
splendour:

> Ты красок себе пожелала -
> И выхватил лапой своей
> Рисующий лев из пенала
> С полдюжины карандашей.   (Cf.S p.286)   (I No.205)

Apart from the 'хриплая охра' there is only the water - the
chill melt-water of Lake Sevan, on the snow-line, and the
water in the villages:

> Снега, снега, снега на рисовой бумаге,
> Гора плывет к губам.   (I No.211)

> Какая роскошь в нищенском селенье, -
> Волосяная музыка воды!
> Что это? пряжа? звук? предупрежденье?
> Чур-чур меня! Далеко ль до беды!   (I No.213)

Both have ominous associations more in keeping with life in
Russia than with the Armenian landscape. Even the trout in
the lake are seen in terms of their counterparts at home:

> Сытых форелей усатые морды
> Несут полицейскую службу
> На известковом дне.   (I No.211)

These are the equivalents of the Russian pike which had
figured in Mandelstam's poems of the early twenties -
predators, here on surveillance duty.

The word 'пенал', used here in connection with the
artistic lion, produced an off-shoot of the Armenian group
which, although its subject-matter differs entirely from the
rest of the group, should be taken as an integral part of it.

'Не говори никому' (I No.201) was the result of reminiscences of Mandelstam's childhood in the North of Russia, evoked by the reminder of his 'Детский чернильный пенал' (I No.201). As a town child the only chance he had of contact with the country-side was the dacha holiday. His family spent its holidays somewhere in Vyritsa, where the landscape of pine forests and marshes is that described here. From an early age these pine forests inspired a particular awe in him: this intensified the horror of the journey to his first place of exile in Cherdyn, described in the poem 'День стоял о пяти головах' (I No.313). His attachment to this landscape lay in his conviction that this is where he 'проснулся и начал жить' - although it was not, surprisingly, his mother, but one of the long line of French maids she employed who noticed the awakening of the instinct for poetry in the boy, during one such vacation (N.Ya.III). Mandelstam's references to the scenery were to be elucidated in 'Путешествие в Армению':

> Мелкая хвойная дрожь...
> Или чернику в лесу,
> Что никогда не сбирал.   (I No.201)

> В детстве из глупого самолюбия, из ложной гордыни я
> никогда не ходил по ягоды и не нагибался за грибами.
> Больше грибов мне нравились готические хвойные шишки...
>   (II p.150)

His childhood differed radically, as he had pointed out in *Шум времени*, from that of the happy generations of Tolstoys and Aksakovs, whose novels, in their capacity as family chronicles, included such childhood pursuits as berry-gathering expeditions (II p.99). In general, this poems concerns various stages of his life, seen in retrospect, which would perhaps best be forgotten in the present circumstances:

> Все, что ты видел, забудь -
> Птицу, старуху, тюрьму.   (I No.201)

His chequered career of arrests by both sides during the Civil War accounts for the reference to prison; the old lady may well be the draconian landlady who tormented Nadezhda

Yakovlevna during her enforced convalescence in Yalta,
thereby causing Mandelstam much distress (Letters No.19, 23
& 30a, III pp.213, 220 & 232), or it may have been his own
landlady of earlier years in the quarantine quarter of Feodosiya, who viewed her lodgers as birds of passage, to be maintained according to the normal requirements of birds: she
changed their food and water and cleaned their cages from
time to time - hence the title 'старухина птица' which Mandelstam applies to himself when describing his stay there (II
pp.116-18). Within the context of the other poems, dealing
with Armenia, the northern poem stands alone, depending for
its effect partly on this contrast.

Nadezhda Yakovlevna considers that the Armenian group,
the northern poem and the remaining poems on the subject of
Armenia have more resemblance to a cycle than the Armenian
group on its own. Certainly there are themes in addition to
Armenia and the North, for example the uncouthness and
ignorance of the new type of Soviet official, portrayed with
some virulence:

> Страшен чиновник - лицо, как тюфяк, -
> Нету его ни жалчей, ни нелепей...
>
> Пропадом ты пропади, говорят,
> Сгинь ты навек, чтоб ни слуху, ни духу   (I No.218)

The Mandelstams met these products of the new regime everywhere in Armenian hotels and restaurants, and were amazed at
the contrast between these people and their predecessors
such as Shopen, author of the famous *Камеральное описание
Армении*. These had been men of education and perception, with
a lively interest in their surroundings and a true appreciation of, for instance, the cultural identity of Armenia.
Mandelstam has a very clear image of such travellers as
Shopen, perhaps combined with the memory of Pushkin and the
journey to Erzerum:

> Чудный чиновник без подорожной
> Командированный к тачке острожной   (I No.220)

These lines contrast sharply with similar ones of quite
different import in the earlier poem:

> Командированный - мать твою так!
> Без подорожной в армянские степи.   (I No.218)

Elaboration on the theme of the boorish official led to an
attack in the last Tiflis poem on the officials of the literary world, and their pen-pushing activities:

> Звезды поют - канцелярские птички
> Пишут и пишут свои рапортички.   (I No.219)

Thus the rising stars of RAPP, the newest constellation in
the black velvet of the Soviet night. True bureaucrats, with
their 'заявленье' and 'разрешенье', their only purpose in
life is to permit the continuance of 'мерцанье, писанье и
тленье'. The degeneration of literature is entirely their
work. Not only do they issue permits for mediocrity, but
even their connections are of the shadiest: 'На полицейской
бумаге верже' (I No.219). All that these connections might
imply about the officially recognised literature is implied
here.

The Leningrad poems

Mandelstam came into contact with and, needless to say, into
conflict with a more sophisticated type of such officialdom
on his return to Leningrad, via Moscow, in November 1930,
most notably in the person of Tikhonov. Unsuccessful in his
efforts to find a place to live and some means of livelihood,
Mandelstam appealed for assistance in both matters to him,
and met not only with non-cooperation but with active opposition - 'Мандельштам в Ленинграде жить не будет, комнату ему
мы не дадим' (N.Ya.I p.250). Opposition soon became outright
persecution, although not without due warning being given.
Nadezhda Yakovlevna recounts a conversation in the editorial
office of *Известия* between Mandelstam and a representative of
the paper who had read his barbed 'Я вернулся в мой город'

(I No.221) and pronounced this succinct verdict: 'А знаете,
что бывает после таких стихов? Трое приходят ... В форме...'
(N.Ya.I p.289). Amazingly enough, the poem was published in
the edition of *Литературная газета* for 23 November 1932. With
its graphic imagery it imparts a sense of revulsion and a fear
of Leningrad, in inverse proportion to the strength of Mandelstam's past feeling for Petersburg. The anapaestic metre
in which it is written is a new feature of his work; from now
on ternary metres, previously a very rare phenomenon in his
poetry, characterise the products of a particular, recurring
mood. They are to be found whenever Mandelstam is contemplating his past life, summing up his achievements and present-
ing a final account of himself - a mixture of the autobiographical and the testamentary. Here he recalls his childhood
Petersburg, 'знакомый до слез', his expression for emotions
most deeply felt, as in the 'клятвы крупные до слез' of '1
января 1924' (I No.140). He grasps avidly at familiar sights
seen again through childish eyes - 'Рыбий жир ленинградских
ночных фонарей' (I No.221) and the black-and-yellow city of
his memories 'Где к зловещему дегтю подмешан желток' (I No.
221). The city's menacing aspect has not diminished in its
hostility, even though the Imperial standard - a black eagle
on a yellow field - has vanished. Its association with the
exercise of power and the consequent pageantry had frightened
him as a child, and he denies all connection with it:

С миром державным я был лишь ребячески связан,
Устриц боялся и на гвардейцев смотрел изподлобья.
(I No.222)

In the same way that the Armenian pencil-box had conjured
up this northern past, so a children's picture of Lady Godiva
which he came across at this time seemed to strike a chord
in him. He saw a resemblance between the treatment of Lady
Godiva at the hands of the conquerors of her city and his own
victimisation by the literary victors of Leningrad. The city

still maintained its hold over him, provoking a childish
fear and sense of inferiority in him. It had become even more
degenerate than when he last saw it, as he recounts in the
exasperated tones of one to whom the city is nevertheless
dear and necessary:

> Он от пожаров еще и морозов наглее
> Самолюбивый, проклятый, пустой, моложавый!   (I No.222)

In the chapter of *Шум времени* entitled 'Ребяческий империал-
изм' (II pp.49-52) he illustrates the curious nature of his
relationship with Petersburg-Leningrad: fascinated by the
splendour of the city, he nevertheless realised how inappropriate such feelings were in one from his own background:

> Весь этот ворох военщины и даже какой-то полицейской
> эстетики... очень плохо вязался с кухонным чадом средне-
> мещанской квартиры, с отцовским кабинетом, пропахшим
> кожами, лайками и опойками, с еврейскими деловыми разго-
> ворами.   (II p.52)

Even in the South, where he was driven by premonitions of
evil to come - 'грядущие казни' - the city was able to
torment him through its daughters, who had taken the culture
and *moeurs* of their city to the Crimea, to such fashionable
spots as the Voloshin household at Koktebel. These 'нежные
европеянки' are described with some amusement by Anna
Akhmatova, who felt that she herself might have been one of
the ladies concerned.[1] However, Mandelstam's childish love
of spectacle and his humiliation at the hands of the modish
young ladies of Petersburg belong strictly to the past. The
city still retains its hold over his thoughts and feelings,
but the present relationship is one of fear and a sense of
persecution alone:

> Петербург! я еще не хочу умирать:
> У тебя телефонов моих номера.   (I No.221)

As always, he protested and fought back through his poetry.

---

[1]Ахматова, vol.2, pp.170-1.

He claims sardonically that he has addresses; but only the voices of dead friends - Gumilev and others from the old world - can be traced through them. He waits for the nocturnal visit of his 'гостей дорогих, Шевеля кандалами цепочек дверных' (I No.221). Their brutality and crudity are emphasised in the contrast between the delicate door-chain and the heavy chains ascribed to his guests by the poet's imagination. Yet the setting is realistic enough:

> Я на лестнице черной живу, и в висок
> Ударяет мне вырванный с мясом звонок. (I No.221)

After their month at the 'Дом Отдыха' working for 'Цекубу' the Mandelstams were residing, very much on sufferance, at the flat of Evgeny Emilevich Mandelstam, and the above detail is an accurate description of his defective doorbell (N.Ya. III). The idea that retribution from those hostile to Mandelstam was envisaged in the context of Evgeny Emilevich's flat caused Mandelstam's cowardly younger brother to create a family scene, demanding his instant removal from the flat. In spite of all that Mandelstam had done for him - interceding for him when he was arrested in 1922 on a trumped-up charge and, through Bukharin, securing his release - he was ungrateful to the point of forbidding them the house (N.Ya.I pp.122 -3). He even tried to demand that Mandelstam should go to the Writers' Union to ask for food for the whole family. Later, during Mandelstam's years in exile, he tried repeatedly to force him to take their father away to live in Voronezh (N.Ya. I p.331). In January 1931 he himself started work in the organisation of eating-places for writers, and the Mandelstams were allowed to stay on.

This was a period of complete isolation. Mandelstam was deeply hurt at being ostracised by society. Only Shostakovich greeted him normally in public, and the fact that Anna Akhmatova, with whom there was a joyful reunion at this time, shared this particular humiliation did little to console him.

Her account of the respect accorded him by Leningraders
reads strangely in the light of the January poems, and may
well have become distorted in recollection.[1] In one of the
most terrifying poems of this period, consisting of three
lines, the agony which he was enduring is movingly summarised.
He concealed its existence from Nadezhda Yakovlevna, whose
first knowledge of it came only after the end of the war,
presumably to spare her the terror he was feeling. Here he
beseeches God to help him survive through the night:

Я за жизнь боюсь - за Твою рабу -
В Петербурге жить - словно спать в гробу.   (I No.223)

The agony lay in a very real fear for his life. Since the
Eulenspiegel affair, his enemies had made every attempt to
erase him from the literary world, and appeared to be on the
point of success. Rejected by friends, colleagues and his
family, he saw nothing but betrayal and submission to expediency on all sides. His new Petersburg existence was a living
death, and the light, spacious city seemed as dark and
confined as a coffin in which he was buried alive, rather like
Raskolnikov in his coffin-like room. One of the chief pre-
conditions for poetic composition - human contact, the re-
assuring presence of people around him - had vanished.

In the form of the January 1931 poems and in those written
in Moscow during March there is an unusual variety, with no
settled preference for binary or ternary metres, four- or
five-footed lines. 'Помоги, Господь, эту ночь прожить' (I No.
223) is written in slow, heavy trochaics, with the unstressed
syllables at the end of the third and sixth feet omitted, thus
creating a feeling of effortfulness and difficulty with continuing, and giving an air of finality to each half-line.
However, the preceding (see *Appendix*) poem, 'Мы с тобой на
кухне посидим' (I No.224), is in complete contrast. The sense

[1] Ахматова, vol.2, pp.178-9.

of persecution is felt here equally acutely in the desire
for human warmth and refuge in the bustle and anonymity of a
station 'Где бы нас никто не отыскал' (I No.224). Yet the
rest of the poem could almost be described as a domestic
idyll. Mandelstam's favourite room in any house was the
kitchen (N.Ya.I p.266). He loved the hours spent sitting
quietly there, surrounded by familiar objects - here a sharp
knife, bread, the primus stove - and watching Nadezhda Yakovlevna at one of the tasks which necessity had led her to make
peculiarly her own, the plaiting of wicker baskets to carry
their belongings from one temporary lodging to another:

А не то веревок собери
Завязать корзину до зари   (I No.224)

It was the last poem in the cycle. Life at Evgeny
Emilevich's flat had become intolerable to both sides, and
Mandelstam moved to stay with his other brother, Aleksandr,
his wife Leleya and their son Shurka, while Nadezhda Yakovlevna went to her own brother, Evgeny Yakovlevich.

The 'Волк' cycle

One of the better results of the move was the 'Волк' cycle
(named after its master poem), about whose evolution and
meaning Nadezhda Yakovlevna has written in detail (N.Ya.I
pp.201-4). The ideas and feelings embodied in these poems
stayed with Mandelstam for some time, and although the
matrix and high point of the cycle is clearly the poem they
dubbed 'Волк' - 'За гремучую доблесть грядущих веков' (I No.
227), and the tone is correspondingly serious, this cycle
includes several humorous pieces - 'Я скажу тебе с последней'
(I No.226), 'Жил Александр Герцович' (I No.228), 'Я пью за
военные астры, за все, чем корили меня' (I No.233), plus an
unrelated poem on the subject of a concert, 'Рояль' (I No.
234). The circumstances in which the cycle was written are
aptly summed up in the phrase 'запрещенная тишь' (I No.225);

the chaos of the family life around him precluded any possibility of serious work on writing out completed poems during
this period of composition, March to early May (N.Ya.II p.
603). He wrote them practically in darkness, the original
manuscript being in red pencil. The next morning he would
take them round to Nadezhda Yakovlevna to be copied and
distributed to trustworthy friends for safe-keeping. The
other feature of this period, his deteriorating health, was
by now obtruding itself on his notice to the extent that he
could no longer pretend to ignore it. The cardiac disease
which had mercifully exempted him from conscription in 1914
was now serious. He was uncomfortably aware of shortness of
breath and racing heartbeats:

> После полуночи сердце ворует
> Прямо из рук запрещенную тишь   (I No.225)

His heart pounds as though in a young lover's breast -
'Любишь - не любишь' - and he is disturbed by the way it
flutters and quivers: 'Так почему ж как подкидыш дрожишь?'
(I No.225). In this and succeeding poems the beginning of a
new, rather breathless style is seen, characterised by very
short phrases, many commas and dashes, frequent hiatus - an
obvious reflection of the difficulty in breathing which was
affecting him. The last lines of the poem should read:

> Что по полуночи сердце пирует
> Взяв на прикус серебристую мышь?   (N.Ya.III)

The interrogative tone is important here. Like Pushkin on
his night of sleeplessness, Mandelstam is trying to ascertain
the meaning of the nocturnal sounds on which his heart is
feasting here. Pushkin's 'жизни мышья беготня'[1] and the
noises in Mandelstam's ears are equally mysterious, but

---

[1] А.С.Пушкин, 'Стихи, сочиненные ночью во время бессонницы'
in *Собрание сочинений в десяти томах* (10 vols., Moscow,
1974-), vol.2, p.248.

whereas Pushkin feels the scurrying to be vain and useless, Mandelstam sees in it his creative material, the stuff of life, to be transmuted into poetry - hence the idea of the heart feasting on it.

To produce humorous poems in these circumstances was something of a feat. 'Я скажу тебе с последней' (I No.226) was written in the 'Зоологический музей' during a party in the room of Kuzin, one of the keepers in the Moscow museum. A bottle of wine had been smuggled into the building - the best, Georgian, wine - in a briefcase, together with various 'закуски'. Mandelstam interrupted the proceedings by rushing up and down the room composing this poem, which Nadezhda Yakovlevna took down to dictation in the museum building (N.Ya.I p.188). Although its lively, joking tone is proof that Mandelstam had not lost his resilience, the subject-matter is basically as grim as that of the other contemporary poems. The 'sherry-brandy' of the poem - 'Все лишь бредни, шерри-бренди' (I No.226) - is a joke, dating from his youth. He had been staying with S.P.Kablukov in Finland at the time when the latter was secretary of the Religious-Philosophical Society in St Petersburg, and this word acquired a private connotation for them as a synonym for 'чепуха' (N.Ya.III). The notion that life, with all its misery, is trifling nonsense, not to be taken seriously, is an attractive one, attractively expressed. The succeeding stanzas do much to dispel the lightness of touch. Mandelstam contrasts himself with the Greeks in their honourable quest for Helen, as he remembers his own attempts to win the 'нежные европеянки' of his youth. The 'красота' which led them on and the salty foam on their lips as they traversed the waves are a far cry from the 'срамота', 'пустота' and 'нищета' which had been and would be his own fate. In place of the beautiful Helen he is saddled with 'ангел-Мэри' - Nadezhda Yakovlevna takes this humorous reference to apply to herself, although its implications are distinctly derogatory. Mary is the lady of doubtful virtue who is constantly enjoined to sing by the guests in Pushkin's 'Пир во время чумы'.[1] Mandelstam, however, exhorts her to drink: 'Ангел Мэри, пей коктейли' (I No.226). It is the situation of the Pushkin poem which is of relevance here. Mandelstam's own times did seem similar to a period of plague, when normal human communication ceased, men feared one another and the common enemy, who was liable to strike suddenly and indiscriminately. In the 'Волк' cycle proper this imminent catastrophe is accepted as inevitable.

The rough drafts of 'За гремучую доблесть грядущих веков' (I No.227) have been preserved and show how the poem formed the matrix of the whole 'convict' cycle (N.Ya.I, pp.201-2). There are no exact dates for them, but they are of great importance for the understanding not only of the central poem but of those which developed from it to form a cycle. When Mandelstam read the poem aloud these new variants would appear, to such an extent that Nadezhda Yakovlevna is not certain which ones he himself would have chosen had he been compiling a book for publication. In their typewritten version which was made during his lifetime they appear in the follow-ing formulation (N.Ya.III):

1.= I No.242 (VI), whose first two lines should read as follows:

> Не табачною кровью газета плюет,
> Не костяшкою дева стучит –

2.= I No.244 (VIII), first four lines only

3.= I No.243 (VII)

4.= I No.244 (VIII), last two lines only

5.= I No.245 (IX)

6.= I No.246 (X)

7.The words 'Реплика' and 'певцу' are written at the side of the stanza:

---

[1] Пушкин, *Собрание сочинений*, vol.4, pp.320-9.

Уведи меня в ночь, где течет Енисей,
И слеза на ресницах как лед,
Потому что не волк я по крови своей
И во мне человек не умрет.   (Cf.S p.288)

8. Уведи меня в ночь, где течет Енисей,
Отними и гордыню и труд –
Потому что не волк я по крови своей
И за мною другие придут...   (Cf.S p.288)

9. In her book (N.Ya.I p.202) Nadezhda Yakovlevna also quotes:

А не то уведи, да прошу поскорей,
К шестипалой неправде в избу.   (Cf.S p.288)

The background to the poem and the cycle is far from being
concealed - 'Смысл этого цикла – отщепенство, непризнанный
брат' (N.Ya.I p.204). It is, she remarks, devoted to Mandelstam's preparation for the inescapable fate arising from his
position, exile in the forests of Siberia and the 'нары, срубы
... Материал этого цикла – дерево: плаха, бадья, сосна,
сосновый гроб, лучина, топорище, городки, вишневая косточка.'
(N.Ya.I p.204). 'Волк' is a magnificent affirmation of principle and human dignity under threat of annihilation by the
forces of evil. The anapaestic metre here is that of the poem
'Ленинград' (I No.221) and reflects a similar mood of defiance
and the determination on the part of their author to make his
position clear. In the first stanza there is a solemn renunciation of present acclaim in favour of future glory. Denied
the honour due to him, his rightful place in the pantheon of
writers, even his happiness, he parades his integrity and
his refusal to participate in anything dishonourable, as
shown through the gesture which so strongly reminded Nadezhda
Yakovlevna of Akhmatova (N.Ya.I p.197):

Человеческий жаркий искривленный рот
Негодует и "нет" говорит   (I No.242 [VI])

It is the same twisted mouth, 'грозящий, искривленный', which
in the sixth variant (I No.246) recalls him to the shame of
his present way of life, the disrespect and humiliation
accorded to an outcast in the alien tribe of his own people.

His achievement would be appreciated and honoured only by
the 'высокое племя людей' of the future; meanwhile he had to
remain a silent voice to his contemporaries, as little heeded
by them and as meaningless to them as his time, of which only
charred ruins would soon be left:

> Замолчи! Ни о чем, никогда, никому -
> Там в пожарище время поет...   (I No.245 [IX])

The characteristic features of his own society are summarised
in the first variant lines:

> Не табачною кровью газета плюет
> Не костяшкою дева стучит -   (I No.242 amended)

In company with many of his fellow-writers he had suffered
from the vindictive denunciations which the press had spat
at him. These bilious attacks, so vividly conveyed in the
'tobacco-coloured blood' image, presumably refer to the
Eulenspiegel affair, which still rankled. His undiminished
contempt and fear of official writers lead here to the
comparison of their outbursts with the noise made by a girl
tapping on something with a bone - a simile reminiscent of
Dostoevsky's prostitute figure in *Записки из подполья*,[1] who
had also featured in '1 января 1924' (I No.140) as a symbol
of integrity violated and the acceptance of lower moral
standards. That Mandelstam had this earlier poem in mind is
borne out by the presence in the second stanza of 'Волк' of
its most striking image, the 'век-волкодав'. Mandelstam had
previously seen his century as a beast, fatally wounded. Now
it had revealed its nature and had revived in all its new
strength and menace to hurl itself from behind onto his
defenceless shoulders. Interestingly, Mandelstam had not
ceased in his attempts to analyse the way in which the bright
hopes of the Revolution had been thus debased. In the second
and third variants there are allusions to the October days

---

[1]   Ф.М.Достоевский, *Собрание сочинений в десяти томах*,
(10 vols., Moscow 1956-8), vol. 4, p.218.

themselves, in the image of the lorry at the gates of the
city and the 'труда чернецы' with their grim determination
and sense of purpose in destroying the old order, recording
themselves and their actions for ever on the pages of history:

> И по улицам шел на дворцы и морцы
> Самопишущий черный народ   (I No.244 [VII])

Far from delighting in the metamorphosis of the beast, Mandelstam firmly dissociates himself from all that it implies:

> Потому что не волк я по крови своей
> И во мне человек не умрет.   (I No.227 variant 7)

Since he does not share the vicious and rapacious character
of those more in tune with the times, and since he refuses
to renounce the sense of morality which distinguishes him
from them, he considers it better to surrender to brute force
rather than degrade himself by trying to fight it on its own
terms. In this respect the Siberian steppe appears almost as
a welcome refuge from the fray. In the primitive beauty of
the blue foxes he sees purity, in the all-enveloping steppe
warmth and honesty. The pine trees, aspiring upwards, contrast
favourably with the sights which meet his eyes in the so-
called 'civilised' world:

> Чтоб не видеть ни труса, ни хлипкой грязцы,
> Ни кровавых костей в колесе   (I No.227)

In 1931 little blood had as yet been shed; nevertheless there
are two references to it in the finished text and another in
the first variant. The appearance of any such image in his
poetry was for Mandelstam a sure prophecy of what was to come.
The voice, 'тот голос' (variant 4), which prompts him to
prepare for his sentence is that of the 'кто-то властный'
(variant 2). The voice, which needs no identification, causes
him to make his way in the direction of the 'топоры', another
association with blood-letting (variant 4), while even tears
of suffering freeze on the eyelashes in the relentless Enisei
night: 'И слеза на ресницах как лед' (variant 7). The eighth
variant is defiant in its assertion that, even if his own

'гордыню и труд' (synonymous in his view) are taken from him, others will take his place and fight on. According to Nadezhda Yakovlevna it was the final line of the poem which came to him last of all (N.Ya.I p.201), the scornful challenge which is made even more striking by the passive acceptance which marks the rest of the poem. There is a limit to the abuse of human dignity, and for him it lay in being hounded to death by the choicest representatives of 'век-волкодав': 'И меня только равный убьет' (I No.227).

This theme permeates the other poems in the cycle which sprang from 'Волк'. In 'Ночь на дворе. Барская лжа.' (I No. 230) the same rejection of the established poet's privileged position in society recurs. Its curt, angry lines and short, impatient phrases with, as Nadezhda Yakovlevna points out, their mass of plosives (N.Ya.I p.158), constitute a furious denunciation of the treacherous lines of Pasternak, only recently composed:

> И рифма не вторенье строк,
> А гардеробный номерок,
> Талон на место у колонн
> В загробный гул корней и лон.[1]

In this poem it was the idea of poetry seen as a ticket to comfort and special treatment which infuriated Mandelstam; this, he thought, was the precise mentality of the literary official and thus anathema to him and to any poet worthy of the name. He considered Pasternak to have sold out to the Philistines and dismisses him cursorily in his own last line: 'И да хранит тебя Бог!' (I No.230). Let him revel in the enjoyment of the good things of life; but he should also be aware of the wolf-hound age behind the illusion of the fancy-dress ball - 'Бал-маскарад. Век-волкодав.' - and of the debased values on which such an outlook on life is founded.

---

[1] Б.Л.Пастернак: *Собрание сочинений* (3 vols., Ann Arbor, 1961), vol. 1, p.341.

Apart from the ideas in these related poems there is also
a link between them in verbal repetition. The 'век-волкодав'
of 'Волк' and 'Ночь на дворе' is an obvious connection, such
as also exists between the words 'затверди' ('Ночь на дворе')
and 'твердил' ('Александр Герцович' [I No.228]). The text,
incidentally, should read 'играл' - 'твердил' apparently
kept slipping in whenever Mandelstam recited the poem, but
was always corrected at once (N.Ya.III). There are also the
'шубы' of 'Волк' and the 'вороньей шубою' of 'Александр
Герцович'. Through his introduction of a 'singing' element
into 'Волк' in the voice of one in power and in the singing
of time, Mandelstam was parodying the Soviet poets and their
tedious insistence that they were young and singing songs -
the identification of poetry with song was heresy to him
(N.Ya.I p.202). He preferred to be silent, and advises his
musical counterpart Aleksandr Gertsovich - an actual person,
their neighbour in the next flat at that time, whose practis-
ing interfered with their work - to do likewise. The cycle is
full of such peremptory injunctions - 'замолчи', 'затверди'
and here 'брось':

> Нам с музыкой-голубою
> Не страшно умереть...
>
> Брось, Александр Скерцевич,
> Чего там, все равно.   (I No.228)

The Jewish musician's love of music, shown in the care with
which he practised the jewel-like Schubert sonata, was shared
by the Jewish poet, who associated Schubert above all with
the snowy landscape of *Die Winterreise* and Goethe's 'Mignon'.
In his exile both these works came to symbolise for him the
civilised world. Music was as great a necessity as poetry,
and the two are legitimately related in the allusion to
Lermontov's 'Молитва', pointed out by Professor Struve and
Mr Filippov:

> Одну молтиву чудную
> Твержу я наизусть.   (Cf.S pp.288-9) (See I p.493)

Prayer, music and poetry act as a sort of talisman to ward
off evil, but Mandelstam in his new mood of resignation felt
that it was not only unworthy of him but also pointless to
trust in their powers. The divine music of Schubert turns
into a convict song: 'Так вот бушлатник шершавую песню поет'
(I No.229). In anticipation of his own fate he laments the
storm to come, thus perhaps forearming himself emotionally
against the time when it should strike: 'Чую без страха, что
будет и будет гроза' (I No.229). The pricking eyelids and
the tear in the first line derive from the icy tear on the
eyelids in the seventh variant of 'Волк' - 'Колют ресницы.
В груди прикипела слеза.' Mandelstam bemoans his future as a
convict, as he pictures in detail how he will rise at day-
break from the wooden labour-camp bunks at the first clang of
the iron rail. Solzhenitsyn's opening lines in *Один день
Ивана Денисовича* contain exactly this mixture of close obser-
vation of nature, splendid in its austerity, as seen from his
Karaganda camp, and the contrasting squalor of the convicts'
lives, as they rise 'дико и сонно' singing their 'шершавую
песню'. The poem is in the long tradition of Russian convict
songs (for example 'Славное море, священный Байкал') which
contrive to transform the horrific experience of prison-camp
life into beauty. Among the various forms of Russian folk
music it was these songs which Mandelstam infinitely preferred.
In his own poem the particularly close-knit sound structure,
with its emphasis on the back vowels 'o' 'a' and 'y',
together with the length and metre of the lines (dactylic
pentameters) and the repetition of the shuffling sibilant
'ш' standing out against the crisp 'п' 'к' 'т' and their
voiced equivalents illustrate the subject-matter - the long
drawn-out days of imprisonment, the harshness, the shuffling
crowds of convicts - with a curiously lyrical effect which
seems strangely appropriate here.

The question of whether such a life as the one Mandelstam

was at present leading was worth living arose the more vividly
for the fact that this life was being threatened. On the one
hand he had vehemently expressed his desire for life in the
oxymoronic 'до смерти хочется жить' (I No.229); on the other
he saw no point in continuing in his present misery: 'И не
знаю - зачем я живу' (I No.232). The need to participate in
everyday life, his natural gregariousness and his unwilling-
ness to opt out were counteracted by the realisation that he
was a nonentity in a terrible epoch: 'Я трамвайная вишенка
страшной поры' (I No.232). These words, with the exception
of the 'я', were written down beside the 'черешня московских
торцов' of the third variant of 'Волк', and are clearly
connected with the second line of the sixth variant: 'Я такой
же как ты пешеход' (I No.246). Tram rides round a spring-time
Moscow, with its flowering birdcherry, were not for him: his
was the path of the pedestrian, representing the under-
privileged in society. As in '1 января 1924' (I No.140), he
condemns Moscow for selling out to dishonour and prostituting
herself - 'курву-Москву'. Indeed the Moscow of the 'А' and
'Б' tram routes was not seen at its most advantageous. The
'А' tram took them to Aleksandr Emilevich, but the 'Б', which
they usually boarded late in the evening at 'Смоленская
площадь', was full of drunken and morose people (N.Ya.III).
However, Mandelstam saw the malaise as more deep-rooted than
alcoholic depression; Moscow's whore-like aspect embodied for
him the fundamental 'неправда' of Soviet society. 'Неправда'
is incarnated in the witch of folk-lore, 'Баба-Яга', who, in
the image of Moscow, can be seen now threatening, now vanishing by magic in every nook and cranny of the city:

A она - то сжимается как воробей,
То растет, как воздушный пирог.   (I, No.232)

Mandelstam follows her to her lair, her *izba* in the forest,
and is warmly received with traditional Russian hospitality:

A она мне соленых грибков

Предлагает† в горшке из-под нар   (I No.231)
†preferred reading (N.Ya.III)

Two things in this stanza betray the presence of evil: the
wooden bunk, the twin of the convict bunks in 'Бушлатник'
(I No.229) and the reference to the brew made from children's
entrails. Mandelstam detested all offal, without realising
that caviare, which he loved, came into this category. Nadezhda Yakovlevna relates his amazement that Joyce's Bloom
should have been so enamoured of such 'stinking food', but
came to the conclusion that Joyce himself must really have
shared his own distaste (N.Ya.III), a distaste described
earlier in *Египетская марка*:

> ... и почему-то вспомнилась страшное слово 'требуха'.
> И его слегка затошнило как бы от воспоминания о том, что
> на днях старушка в лавке спрашивала при нем 'легкие'...
>   (II p.17)

Pickled mushrooms and the 'тишь да глушь', features of the
typical dacha and its way of life, do not disguise Baba-Yaga's
true nature. He enters her cottage with a lighted splint to
guide himself through the realm of darkness; he finds himself
imprisoned, his attempts to escape are foiled, he feels
suffocated literally and metaphorically: 'Ну, а я не дышу' -
the same stifling atmosphere as the 'душно' of 'Бушлатник'.
The word 'полутюрьма' brings out into the open his constant
preoccupation with his impending incarceration and death:
'Ведь лежать мне в сосновом гробу' (I No.231). He feels
revulsion at the thought of it and of the master-mind behind
it. Stalin is an embodiment of evil equal to Baba-Yaga and is
held by Mandelstam responsible for his personal misfortune as
well as for that of others. Nadezhda Yakovlevna remembers his
amazement when one of her questions revealed that she was
unaware of the popular rumour that Stalin had six toes or
six fingers, as in the second line: 'К шестипалой неправде
в избу' (I No.231). The forest location of Baba-Yaga's
headquarters, with its repellent and oppressive contents, is

that of Stalin's labour-camps in all their horror.

Nevertheless, the ability to laugh - even to make fun of his own position - remained. In 'Я скажу тебе с последней', 'Жил Александр Герцович' and 'Я пью за военные астры' he developed a bitter humour, flippant on the surface, deadly serious beneath, which well represents his attitude. One of the most frequent terms of abuse in the campaign against him had been 'bourgeois': the poem 'Я пью за военные астры' (I No.233) gathers together the typical and archetypal in West European life and culture to hurl in his detractors' faces. Mandelstam had retained his facility for singling out the essentials, so effectively displayed in the 'Acmeist' poems of 1913 whose background is very similar to that of this one. The selection here conjurs up a lively impression of the best and the worst in Europe, much of which dates from before the First World War and his memories of his visit there. In his mock toast - where he maintains the illusion of solemnity by the spurious use of 'solemn' amphibrachs - the Rolls-Royces, the military epaulettes, the aristocratic haughtiness of the English are used to counter-attack his accusers. To the indictment of a European bourgeois outlook he obligingly adds the corresponding Russian symbols: 'За барскую шубу, за астму, за желчь петербургского дня' (I No. 233). The unhealthy climate of fashionable St Petersburg was as much *de rigeur* as the clear air of the Alps and the city smells of the Champs Elysées. Nadezhda Yakovlevna recounts the complications which invariably arose in all Mandelstam's dealings with fur coats (N.Ya.I p.203) and which resulted in the feeling expressed in one of the chapter headings of *Шум времени*, 'В не по чину барственной шубе' (II p.102). Like V.V.Gippius he had no pretensions to ownership of a fur coat, demonstrating as it did the tenacity of 'быт' in Mayakovsky's sense of the word. It belonged to a rank he felt to be far 'above' his own status of *raznochinets*. In the

sociological details of these attributes of the bourgeois
state all five senses are employed. Roses and cream, although
as symbols of luxury they form one of the metonymic elements
in the poem, none the less appeal to the reader's sight,
smell and taste, as do the wines of the last line, the
ultimate in decadent self-indulgence. Georgi Shengeli wrote
an equally amusing answer in the style of Tikhonov, this
time on the subject of colonialism, which was taken as
seriously by many as was Mandelstam's poem - although
naturally not by Mandelstam himself.

This reminder of earlier 'Acmeist' poems (in the narrow-
est and not in Mandelstam's sense of the word) may have
prompted him to write 'Рояль' (I No.234) in the way he did.
In subject and method it resembles many of the mid-*Камень*
poems; for example, it describes a particular event, here a
concert of Neuhaus, one of his less happy performances. The
piano, 'Оскорбленный и оскорбитель', fails to reveal its
Goliath-like potential. The audience fails to respond and the
pianist is seen as a faintly ridiculous little creature,
'конек-горбунок', jumping around in his concert garb. What
is peculiar to the poem is a marked sense of revulsion,
firstly in the images taken from the French Revolution, which
ever since his 'Собачья склока' (II p.465-8) had held
associations of fear and hatred for Mandelstam, and then
in the last two stanzas of the poem. Its fourth, highly
alliterative stanza was abandoned during composition, and
should not feature here, contradicting as it does the sense
of the rest of the poem - reference to 'внутренняя правота'
is quite incompatible with the context of a bad performance.
The introduction of a seemingly unrelated image, 'земная
груша', into the musical setting is explained by a conversation with Party officials on the nature of the vegetable,
which had preceded the writing of the poem: was it a sweet
potato or, as Mandelstam impatiently claimed, simply a

frozen potato? Officialdom intruding and interfering in art,
he thought, produces the same unpleasant taste in the mouth
as the thick, slimy sonata, the same repulsion as the horrific
Nuremberg spring (N.Ya.III):

> Чтоб смолою соната джина
> Проступила из позвонков,
> Нюренбергская есть пружина
> Выпрямляющая мертвецов.   (I No.234)

The images of blood and backbones from 'Век' (I No.135) were
perhaps close to the surface of his memory here. Certainly a
horrible death is envisaged in both. Very rarely does Mandelstam use such strong terms of disgust and abhorrence, but in
1931 his position had been forcibly brought home to him: 'Я
– непризнанный брат, отщепенец в народной семье' (I No.235).
In this poem, 'Сохрани мою речь навсегда за привкус несчастья
и дыма', the period of complete isolation and rejection, not
only by Evgeny Emilevich but by his friends and fellow-writers
– in his notebooks of the time he called it 'глухо-немая пора'
(II p.151) – is seen as merely a prelude to worse things. The
cruelty with which the Tatars executed rebellious princes was
still to be found: he promises bitterly to cooperate in cons-
tructing their crude equipment, knowing for whom it is intended. The inevitable reward for having written his poetry is
a life of persecution and a painful death, which he almost
goes out of his way to meet, knowing it to be inescapable:

> Я за всю жизнь прохожу хоть в железной рубахе
> И для казни петровской в лесу топорище найду. (I No.235)

The poem was not actually dedicated to any particular person,
but Mandelstam said that only Akhmatova could have found the
last word necessary to its completion, namely the epithet
'совестный' applied to 'деготь труда' (N.Ya.III). She, almost
alone among other writers, would certainly have understood
this reference to the supreme importance of the conscience in
his work, but the appeal to preserve this work is in fact
addressed to Nadezhda Yakovlevna, 'Мой друг и помощник мой

грубый':

> Сохрани мою речь навсегда за привкус несчастья и дыма,
> За смолу кругового терпенья, за совестный деготь труда.
> (I No.235)

Written, this time in all seriousness, in a 'testamentary' ternary (anapaestic) metre, the poem is a desperate appeal for the poet's voice to be heard, not least on account of the misery and unhappiness which have been his constant companions in recent years. The poem completed the 'Волк' cycle; it was the final, total acceptance of exile and death, coupled with a plea for some form of immortality.

'Канцона'

By the time 'Канцона' (I No.236) came to be written, Mandelstam's attention had turned to the writing of 'Путешествие в Армению', which initiated a new phase in his work. The poems which conclude the first half of the Moscow *Новые стихи* do not constitute a cycle, although they share many common themes. Armenia, the younger sister of the Holy Land, features together with the latter as the landscape of his 'Канцона'. The 'Край небритых гор' described there could equally well refer to the mountains of Palestine or to those of Armenia, whose colours are stark (See I No.205) and vivid, while the valleys below are green and lush:

> И свежа, как вымытая басня,
> До оскомины зеленая долина.   (I No.236)

- a clear allusion to the fable about the fox and the grapes. That both countries were intended to be borne in mind is shown by consideration of the poem's theme - that of sight, not so much physical as historical sight. This is closely linked with a passage in *Разговор о Данте*, written a year later, where Dante's powers of sight are compared to those of a bird of prey, incapable of orientating itself on a small radius, being used to too large a hunting area seen from a great height. In the same way the poet is absolutely blind to

everything but the distant future, having the gift of
historical sight (II p.381). The thought is not fully developed in the poem, but is clearly presented in connection with
the Egyptologists and numismatists - 'То зрачок профессорский,
орлиный' - who, with their ability to look back over the past,
are in some way equally gifted in foreseeing the future. The
old scholars whom the Mandelstams met in Armenia had impressed
them by their integrity, their objectivity and their refresh-
ingly 'European' approach to their work, a striking contrast
to the tendentious and chauvinistic work of their mediocre
Moscow colleagues. Mandelstam endows these scholars with
visionary powers and emphasises their provenance: 'Прозорливцу
дар от псалмопевца' and 'Дорогой подарок Царь-Давида' (I No.
236). The biblical psalmist transmits this particular gift
to the wise man in order that he might see and understand
history, past and future. Mandelstam uses the image of seeing
through binoculars to illustrate this form of sight. In
'Путешествие в Армению' he describes the view from his window
in Sukhumi as seen through military binoculars (II p.158).
How he came to acquire them is not stated, but they were of
Zeiss manufacture - 'Он глядит в бинокль прекрасный Цейса':

    Я люблю военные бинокли
    С ростовщическою силой зренья   (I No.236)

This reference to usurers, like the one to bankers in the
first stanza, strengthens the connection with Dante: in
Разговор о Данте a whole paragraph deals with usury and its
place in the Mediterranean world in Dante's time (II p.380).
In the fifth stanza all these distinct images are synthesised:

    Я покину край гипербореев,
    Чтобы зреньем напитать судьбы развязку   (I No.236)

The poet abandons the northern, Hyperborean, regions for the
South - here specifically Palestine - where his destiny and
those of others will be unfolded to him through the gift of
historical sight. He will respectfully exchange what he took,

mistakenly, to be the traditional Jewish greeting (the text
here should read 'Села') with the chief of the Jewish peoples
from whose cultural tradition this gift arose. It is important to realise that Mandelstam came to Judaism not through
his blood but through the medium of Judaeo-Christian culture,
approaching it in the same spirit as any other educated
European did. The 'малиновая ласка' in this stanza is a
reminder of this fact. Mandelstam felt oppressed not only by
the limitations of physical sight, but especially by the
physical impossibility of travel, for which this imagined
journey is both compensation and secret revenge. As far as
culture was concerned he was perfectly free to roam unimpeded
through the recesses of his memory, lighting on treasures
from his past experience. Here he has in mind a particular
example from the Hermitage, in which he had practically lived
during the previous winter, Rembrandt's *Prodigal Son* (See
N.Ya.II, pp.614-23). In this picture the father's hands and
cloak are a warm red, and the light from this floods the whole
picture. Mandelstam felt himself to be something of a prodigal
son, cut off from his cultural homeland and only too willing
to crave the indulgence promised by the 'малиновая ласка' of
the Jewish elder's hands. The golden hands of the artist-
craftsman, capable of the most intricate work, are red like
this, stained by the mahogany - 'Золотыми пальцами красно-
деревца'. The colouring of the historical land provides a
vivid contrast with the colourless modern world, with all its
unpleasantness:

> Две лишь краски в мире не поблекли:
> В желтой - зависть, в красной - нетерпенье.   (I No.236)

The Moscow poems

The 'real' world is treated with scorn and derision in the
satirical poem 'Полночь в Москве' (I No.260) which Mandelstam
wrote at the end of May and beginning of June 1931 (*not* 1932,

as given in I). As regards its relationship with 'Канцона',
the significant phrase comes in its first line: 'Полночь в
Москве. Роскошно буддийское лето' (I No.260). 'Buddhist'
Moscow is the antithesis of Armenia and Palestine, distinguished from them by its apathy, inertia and lack of historical
movement - Chaadaev's strictures loom large in the background
here. This is Mandelstam's fiercest attack on the Asiatic
element in Russia's make-up, the passivity which he holds
responsible for the state of society which made the imminent
Terror apparently unavoidable, as history repeated itself.
The example of cinema-goers emerging numb and dazed into the
fresh air is typical of his view of the Muscovites: 'Убитые,
как после хлороформа' and 'до чего им нужен кислород' (I No.
260). It is not so much they as the epoch which produced them
which stands in need of movement and air; the epoch is said
to have a hempen soul, coarse, unrefined, totally lacking in
sensitivity. There is no point in trying to establish contact
with it, since it is itself alien and uncomfortable in its
new surroundings: 'Как сморщенный зверек в тибетском храме'
(I No.260). Its sub-human character is underlined in the
antics of the arrested bear, nature's eternal loser, and in
the monkey being cajoled to play the fool for the benefit of
others - 'Изобрази еще нам, Марь Иванна!' (I No.260). The
time he lives in resembles these creatures, innocent of human
intelligence, as it does the mechanical movements of a kitchen
cuckoo-clock. He enjoys pulling its tail and producing an
automatic response from it; its stupidity prevents it from
understanding that it is being mocked. In this context
Mandelstam's avowed determination to assert himself as a full
citizen and contemporary man rings very hollow. The mood here
contrasts strikingly with that of resignation which pervades
the 'Волк' cycle:

> Пора вам знать, я тоже современник,
> Я человек эпохи Москвошвея   (I No.260)

In proof of this he cites one of the greater achievements of
contemporary society - the elimination of good tailoring in
favour of shoddy materials and workmanship. He was fond of
pointing out how, on modern statues, the subject's jacket
always rode up, as in modern life. But the claim that he was
indissolubly bound to his age is undermined by his reference
a few lines earlier to the tartan rug:

Ты меня им укроешь, как флагом военным, когда я умру.
Выпьем, дружок, за наше ячменное горе   (I No.260)

Nadezhda Yakovlevna, to whom this instruction is addressed,
still preserves the rag which is all that remains of the rug,
but was denied the opportunity of performing these bizarre
final rites over him. She did, however, drink with him to
their hopeless situation: the epithet refers to the coffee
in which the toast was drunk, whose composition often included
ingredients considerably less palatable than barley.

The ferocious humour of the poem is shown not least in
its sudden changes and irregularities of metre; a dactylic
stanza introduces the mainly iambic poem, but with great
variation in line lengths and in the number of lines in a
given stanza, ranging from two to eight lines. Paradoxically,
perhaps, the stanza which displays the greatest diversity of
of form is the most serious in content:

Чур! Не просить, не жаловаться! Цыц!
Не хныкать! Для того ли разночинцы
Рассохлые топтали сапоги, чтоб я теперь их предал?
Мы умрем как пехотинцы,
Но не прославим ни хищи, ни поденщины, ни лжи!(I No.260)

In its broken lines, its violent interjections and its
categorical statements there is an obvious similarity to the
rhetoric of much of Mayakovsky which is most untypical of
Mandelstam, even at his most virulent. It testifies to the
strength of feeling about the responsibility of present-day
raznochintsy, himself among the first, to continue their
traditional fight for human rights. There could be no

contemplating a compromise with the exigencies of the moment, an adjustment to inferior values, an acceptance of lies, rapaciousness and venality - still the code of conduct for the majority. 'Поденщина', the hiring out of oneself indiscriminately, is the exact opposite of 'труд' - 'Есть блуд труда' - that is genuine work, authorised by the conscience.

Yet there is a love for Moscow the city, with its bird-cherry trees, which transcends what was happening in it. Raphael, Rembrandt and Mozart would have loved it for its character and self-assurance, the cockiness in the eyes of noisy town sparrows: 'За карий глаз, за воробьиный хмель' (I No.260) and, as in the last stanza, for its fresh, cold draughts, blasting the much-needed oxygen through the city: 'Как майские студенты-шелапуты' (I No.260). Perhaps this is a reminder of the hooligan wind of Esenin ('Я такой же как ты хулиган'), whose influence could also have operated in the sixth variant of 'Волк' (I No.246 [X]) where Mandelstam had proclaimed 'Я такой же как ты пешеход': Mandelstam's position outside respectable society was very much that of the hooligan and the untameable wind.

The same invigorating chill, this time as of cold shampoo being poured over his head, revitalises him in the poem 'Довольно кукситься! Бумаги в стол засунем' (I No.247). He seems to have been fired by a new determination to make his presence felt - 'что я еще могу набедокурить' - and to be possessed by a 'славный бес' to create havoc and thus assert his effectiveness in a world which considered him as good as dead. In this respect the variant versions of the poem, which clearly could not have been published in the *Новый мир* version of 1932, are much more explicit with regard to the attempts made to suppress him. The beginning of the fourth stanza here is decidedly less innocuous than the published version:

Меня хотели, как пылинку, сдунуть -

> Уж я теперь не юноша, не вьюн,
> Держу пари, меня не переплюнут   (Cf.S p.289)(N.Ya.III)

It is a protest of the most vigorous sort. Human dignity has
reached the limits of its tolerance of abuse. In the lyrical
third stanza the variant second half gives the stanza a quite
different complexion:

> И что еще не народилась стерва,
> Которая его перешибет.   (Cf.S p.289)(N.Ya.III)

The predatory imagery introduced in 'Полночь в Москве' and
used, with a different significance, in 'Канцона' is further
developed here: the new year begins to blossom out, the agent
of its destruction as yet unborn. There is never any doubt
that beauty will inevitably be destroyed, for an air of
stifling corruption hangs over Moscow, symbolised in the
figure of the gipsy girl and the antics of the two clowns in
'Полночь в Москве'. Both poems share the imagery of horse-
racing and betting - in the first 'Когда покой бежит из-под
копыт'/'Ведь в беге собственном' (I No.260), in the second
'Держу пари'/'И, как жокей'/'На рысистой дорожке беговой'
(I No.247). Mandelstam is backing himself against all odds to
keep pace in the frenzied race for survival. He entertains no
hope of winning, with all the power and glory which accrues t
the successful contestant, and the most he can hope for is to
wreak havoc among the rest of the field. But he insists on
running, and protests at being thought of as a non-starter.

The collection of five fragments from uncompleted poems
of this period (I Nos.237-41) demonstrates how certain themes
in the post-'Волк' poems arose, and indicates the direction
in which they might have turned. The first two of these (I
Nos.237 & 238) were perhaps too direct and unsubtle to be
more than a first draft of his thoughts, but it is worth not-
icing several points about them, firstly their use of the
word 'насильно':

> Я возвратился, нет - читай: насильно
> Был возвращен в будийскую Москву.   (I No.237)

Mandelstam made several attempts to establish himself in Armenia during his stay there and it was only their failure and the need for money which forced him to return to Moscow. His association of Armenia with Palestine brought about the line 'Библейской скатертью богатый Арарат', a clear identification of the two countries, a more oblique allusion being his description of the water from the spring of Arzni as 'самая правдивая вода' (I No.237). Also illustrated here is one aspect of his ambivalent attitude to Moscow, for in a variant version of the last four lines of the first fragment it is not the cold, tart water of Armenia which flows through the city, but:

> Из раковин кухонных хлещет кровь
> И пальцы женщин пахнут керосином.   (N.Ya.III)

This duality is equally obvious in the second fragment. Moscow has its birdcherry, always his great favourite, and its telephones with their promise of converse and friendship, but in the unpublished last line (where I No.238 has a row of dots) it is also seen to have other features: 'И казнями там имяниты дни' (N.Ya.III).

In the third such fragment an assortment of Moscow scenes provides a curious picture of the city, its sky, milky white with patches of lazy, motionless blue, the infidel drum beating after a secular funeral, while the hearse returns at an undignified gallop, a cart with its strange load of cushions. A further paragraph follows this one:

> Не разбирайся, щелкай, милый кодак,
> Покуда глаз - хрусталик кравчей птицы,
> А не стекляшка. Больше светотени -
> Еще, еще!
> - Сетчатка голодна...   (N.Ya.III)

His need for colours, expressed in 'Канцона' (I No.236) and here in the image of the hungry retina, is partially satisfied by the passing scenes, although he makes a plea for more chiaroscuro to relieve the pictorial monotony of life. But

it is Mandelstam's exploration of the nature of sight which
is of particular interest. The human eye is not merely a
piece of glass, but resembles more the lens of the eye in a
live bird of prey, whose piercing glance is above all cognitive. An attempt to compare it with the inability to understand or analyse of a camera lens, presumably in order to
make this distinction between animate and inanimate vision,
did not achieve full expression in a poem - in his notebooks
there are similar references to the eye of a fly, in all its
complexity (III p.151). Neither did Mandelstam's reference
to the grave in the fourth fragment proceed further:

Ты, могила,

Не смей учить горбатого - молчи!
Я назову тебя† с такою силой...   (I No.240)
  † textual correction from N.Ya.III

There is an implicit contrast here between the curved back
of a living man and the corpse straightened out by the Nuremberg spring. Death hovers around and in the poems of this
period - the poet even takes a bet that he is not dead - and
it seems that by naming it with such force he finds that some
of its power to terrorise him is diminished.

Another incompletely developed image occurs in the play
on 'небо/нёбо' and its reference to the act of poetic composition. The palate broadens out to merge with the sky (perhaps
suggested by the third fragment), taking in the whole of life
which goes on about it, and the lips quiver as they begin to
express this life in poetry:

Чтоб нёбо стало небом, чтобы губы
Растрескались,† как розовая глина.   (I No.240)
  † textual correction from N.Ya.III

This is precisely the pink clay of Armenia. The idea of the
speech organs expanding to cosmic proportions is repeated in
the fifth fragment:

Язык-медведь ворочается глухо
В пещере рта.   (I No.241)

The mouth is as large and all-embracing as a cave, and the

language moves restlessly about in it, wild and clumsy like
a bear - the bear here probably being suggested by the Moscow
street scene from 'Полночь в Москве' (I No.260). Mandelstam
traces the tradition from the psalmist of 'Канцона' (I No.
236) down to Lenin, most recent of rhetoricians but, perhaps
because the analogy left much to be desired, leaves it at
that. In a passage from his 1931 notebook Mandelstam summarises his purpose in going to Armenia, part of which had been
the enjoyment of its wild language:

> ...чтобы пощупать глазами ее города и могилы, набраться
> звуков ее речи и подышать ее труднейшим и благороднейшим
> историческим воздухом.   (III p.149)

It was a purpose completely fulfilled, and the return to
Moscow was the more disillusioning in the knowledge of what
he had left behind.

Reminiscences of the Armenian journey return in the poem
'Фаэтонщик' (I No.248) which follows immediately on the fragments discussed above; the whole of this first section of
Moscow poetry might equally well have been called an Armenian
notebook, so strongly does the country's atmosphere pervade
the poems, if not directly then by contrast.

'Фаэтонщик' (I No.248) concerns a particular episode, the
Mandelstams' last excursion from Yerevan to Nagorny Karabakh,
in autumn 1930, the end of their travels in Armenia. Nadezhda
Yakovlevna recounts (N.Ya.III) that at dawn they left by bus
to go from Gyandzhi to Shusha. A bleak scene greeted their
arrival there, beginning with an endless cemetery, then a
diminutive bazaar square, where the streets of the ruined
town descended and met. Before this they had seen abandoned
and half-ruined villages, but never had they witnessed the
aftermath of catastrophe on quite such a scale - roofless,
doorless, windowless houses, empty rooms with the tattered
remains of wallpaper on the walls, broken stoves, sometimes

broken furniture, and the sky always visible through the
skeletal frame of the house. These were the horrifying effect
of the Armenian massacre of the autumn of 1920, when, they
heard, the wells were said to be blocked with corpses. The
town was deserted apart from a small knot of people in the
bazaar, not Armenians but Muslims of some sort, whom Mandelstam hysterically took for the murderers of the local inhabitants and so refused to buy the maize flour and flat cakes
which they were offering for sale. There was nothing in the
way of a hotel or hostel to sleep in, and they both feared
native hospitality, Mandelstam because of his idea of the
inhabitants' murderous nature and Nadezhda Yakovlevna because
of the risk of disease. They decided to press on to Stepanokert, the biggest town in the province, and hired a carriage
and its driver, the subject of the eponymous poem. Shusha,
the object of Mandelstam's initial fear, is depicted here:

> Сорок тысяч мертвых окон
> Там глядят со всех сторон,
> И труда бездушный кокон
> На горе похоронен.   (I No.248)

The houses made of Armenian pink tufa 'розовеют' although
shamelessly exposed to the sky. Mandelstam sees the sky as
symbolising the plague which had afflicted Shusha - ubiquitou
and unavoidable. The driver, who was indeed noseless as a
result of some disease -'безносой канителю' - and wore a
leather mask over his face as described, seems in some way t
be in control, presiding over their fate, directing them as
did Pushkin's director of the feast during the plague:

> Это чумный председатель
> Заблудился с лошадьми.   (I No.248)

In the circumstances in which the poem was being written lif
seemed to Mandelstam very like this nightmare journey; his
present career was a senseless, frenzied, apparently endless
carousel - 'До последней хрипоты' - in which it was not he,
but a figure very similar to the driver on whom his fate

depended:

> Пропеченный, как изюм,
> Словно дьявола поденщик,
> Односложен и угрюм.   (I No.248)

The appearance of Stalin's skin, marked by smallpox, was well
known, in spite of efforts to conceal it. Salvation came to
the Mandelstams on their journey only when they finally
managed to 'слезть...с горы' and descend to Stepanokert. It
was the sight of a herd of people - 'многоярусное стадо'
(I No.249, not a separate poem but part of I No.248) - moving
slowly along like a floating armada in all its variety of
calves, heifers, bullocks and 'священники-быки' - stately
and slow, but alive and normal, which delivered them from
their fearful adventure and its sinister guide.

This was the last poem to be written on Starosadsky, in
Aleksandr Emilevich's flat. The background changed on his
return home from leave to Zamoskvoreche, where Margulis had
arranged temporary accommodation for the Mandelstams in a
flat belonging to a Rostov lawyer. In 'Путешествие в Армению'
Mandelstam wrote a full description of the area and of the
type of 'обыватель' who inhabited it. Thankful that he was
only a chance guest here, he added: 'Нигде и никогда я не
чувствовал с такой силой арбузную пустоту России' (II p.146).
One compensation, however, came in the form of Leonov, a
young biologist from Tashkent University, with whom Mandelstam became friendly at this time. He, together with Boris
Kuzin, was to influence Mandelstam's wider reading in the
natural sciences and, by a strange quirk of fate, to determ-
ine indirectly the place of his exile. His father was a
prison doctor in Voronezh, where Leonov was born, and it was
his father's bizarre profession which attracted the Mandelstams to the town after the alarming episode in Cherdyn.
Apart from these young biologists they lived in complete

isolation in Moscow. 'Сегодня можно снять декалькомани'
(I No.265, whose last stanza is I No.250) was written during
this summer (again, not in 1932 as in I), and expresses more
deeply than any other poem his affection for the city of
Moscow: the charm of the Kremlin churches, the transparent
waters of the Moskva river, the four chimneys on its bank,
belonging to factories which seemed to be bathing in the
water, its parks - Moscow spread out in all its diversity and
complexity, like the inside of a piano when the rosewood lid
is removed:

> Не так ли,
> Откинув палисандровую крышку
> Огромного концертного рояля,
> Мы проникаем в звучное нутро?   (I No.265)

Nadezhda Yakovlevna thinks this attempt to reconcile himself
with the realities of life was bound to fail(N.Ya.III). The
present, he thought, was justified by the noise and bustle
of life itself, by what he called the 'piano of Moscow'; yet
his attitude to the future, as shown in the rest of the poem,
belies this reconciliation. There is some belief in a future,
towards which he is moving like a small boy following adults
into the water. Yet he was certain that he would not be seeing
this future himself:

> Я, кажется, в грядущее вхожу
> И, кажется, его я не увижу.   (I No.265)

The new world of the future appeared to him like some sort of
sports meeting (he used to go to football games from time to
time), organised, crowded, tense, or else, more ominously,
like the Crystal Palace of Dostoevsky's *Записки из подполья*
- huge, impersonal and anti-human, the product of a wholly
rational mind:

> Уж я не выйду в ногу с молодежью
> На разлинованные стадионы...
>
> В стеклянные дворцы на курьих ножках
> Я даже тенью легкой не войду.   (I No.265)

He could not bear the thought of a highly organised society

in which no deviation or expression of individuality could
be tolerated. He saw it taking shape before his eyes, as
houses designed after Le Corbusier rose on Myasnitskaya, an
affront to all his notions of architecture and a sinister
portent of the future. He told Nadezhda Yakovlevna that the
felling of trees described in 'Путешествие в Армению' (II p.
147), also the work of the rising generation, was connected
in his mind with the felling of 'trees of freedom', planted
in France at the time of the Revolution, of whose demise he
had just recently heard (N.Ya.III). He put the new construct-
ions in the same category as Baba-Yaga's *izba*, standing on
chicken legs, inimical to humanity from their foundations
upwards. He could in no way participate in such a future;
his shade, through his poetry, would mean nothing to the
rational man of action stepping out from Dostoevsky's pages,
perfectly at home in the Moscow of the early thirties.
Physically his health was failing - in the fifth stanza he
complains of the increasing difficulty he finds in breathing
and again, as in 'Канцона', refers to his heart, wearing out
in the race to keep abreast of life. But instead of fading
decently from the scene he writes of the proverbial devil in
a man of his age: 'В январе мне стукнуло 40 лет. Я вступил в
возраст ребра и беса.' (III p.151):

А Фауста бес – сухой и моложавый –
Вновь старику кидается в ребро.   (I No.265)

His new lease of life causes him to follow his whims and
simply to live - to go boating, walking on the Sparrow (Lenin)
Hills, to take a tram round Moscow, to enjoy and, like
Tyutchev, to exclaim at the marvellous summer: 'Какое лето!'
(I No.250). Watching the young workers' slavishly bent backs
he hails one of the chief symbols of life in his poetry,
'Могучий некрещенный позвоночник' (I No.250).

The will to live is at its most fierce in the defiant
poem 'Еще далеко мне до патриарха' (I No.251), written

written between 21 August and 19 September, which closes the
collection on a note of resolution (the eighth stanza given
in I and S should be deleted - it was abandoned by Mandelstam). Its themes are essentially those of the poems immediately preceding it, but in comparison it is considerably
less opaque, though no less poignant. He again protests at
being considered a back number - he has many years to go
before reaching patriarchal age, a point underlined by the
intentional resemblance of his first line with that of
Baratynsky: 'Еще, как патриарх, не древен я' (See S p.289).
His circumstances are dire:

> Одна сумятица да безработица
> Пожалуйста, прикуривай у них!   (I No.251)

His isolation is increased by the failure of the telephone
to provide the hoped-for friendship; instead of reassurance
and assistance only Polish greetings overheard, gentle reproaches from crossed lines, or unfulfilled promises reward
his puppy-like dash to the telephone. He can laugh bitterly,
try to look dignified, and go for walks with his white-
handled cane for support - an accurate detail of his life -
but this is not life as he had known it: 'И не живу, но все-
таки живу' (I No.251). Only these walks, via street photo-
graphers (they were snapped in the street with Aleksandr
Emilevich's wife) and via the endearing sparrows, whom
Mandelstam thought of as the true citizens of Moscow, to the
Chinese laundry (theirs was on what is now Ploshchad Nogina),
but especially to museums for the solace of their art treasures, restored his faith in life, however poor its quality.
The last stanza to be written at the Polyanka house in
Zamoskvoreche, before their move to the more central
Pokrovka where 'Путешествие в Армению' was to be completed,
summarises with immense pathos the isolation, the need for
human warmth, for integrity and a very little pleasure,
which had dominated all the 1931 poetry:

И до чего хочу я разыграться,
Разговориться, выговорить правду...

Взять за руку кого-нибудь: — будь ласков, —
Сказать ему, — нам по пути с тобой...   (I No.251)

2. *НОВЫЕ СТИХИ:*
ВТОРАЯ МОСКОВСКАЯ ТЕТРАДЬ

May 1932 - February 1934

Housing difficulties in the winter of 1931-2 brought about
an unsettled period for the Mandelstams which coincided with,
and doubtless contributed to, the break in his poetry. Lack
of stimulus from the outside world can practically always be
traced as the cause of such a break in his work. It was the
stimulus from meeting people, learning from their conversatio
and discussions of new books and ideas which he lacked at
this time. When the second *Тетрадь* poetry appeared it was as
a direct response to meeting new friends and discovering or
rediscovering new books. The friends and the books were many
and varied, but the poems which resulted from them divide
into distinct groups: one deals with 'biological' and 'evolutionary' friendships and reading, one with Russian poetry,
the single group entitled 'Восьмистишия' with the composition
of poetry in general, and the Stary Krym poetry with Bely
and with death.

The opening poems

The first two poems of the collection, written in May 1932
(not April, as in I), illustrate another characteristic of
Mandelstam's poetry, namely that at the beginning of a new
stage in his work he reverts briefly to the preoccupations
and usually to the style of the poems with which the last
stage had concluded. It is as though he feels a need to
demonstrate the difference between the period just beginning
and its predecessor, while at the same time furnishing a link

between them in a prologue to the main body of the collection.
Here the opening poems continue two themes which had featured
extensively in the first *Тетрадь* - Moscow and his own isolation in it. 'Там, где купальни-бумагопрядильни' (I No.252)
bears a marked similarity to 'Сегодня можно снять декалькомани' (I No.265) in its affection for the city and its
realistic description of tiny details in Moscow life. The
river scenery, for example - 'Купальщики-заводы и сады' (I
No.265) is the same in the new poem, where the factories
stand practically in the water, like bathers. The poem
originated in Mandelstam's walks and rides round the city in
the spring of 1932, in particular in the Neskuchny Sad by the
river - 'Скучные-нескучные, как халва, холмы' (I No.252),
which had been renamed, like many others, a park of culture
and rest - 'С гребешками отдыха, культуры и воды'. The landscape is seen as though depicted on a picture-postcard, so
consciously scenic does he feel his view from the river to
be:

    Эти судоходные марки и открытки
    На которых носимся и несемся мы.   (I No.252)

This even leads him to identify the smell on the river as
that of post-office glue - 'На Москве-реке почтовым пахнет
клеем' (I No.252). From his vantage point on the river boats
the Lenin Hills (as they were dubbed instead of Sparrow Hills)
displayed the colouring and consistency of halva, while the
park on the flat bank of the river seemed to extend for miles
in a mass of luxuriant greenery - 'широчайшие зеленые сады'.
Mandelstam's perception of light was always acute, but particularly so at this period, as the poems on painting demonstrate. Here not only the contrasting green, brown and blue, but
also the interplay of light and shade create a small riot of
vivid light effects - 'светоговорильня'. Similarly the sun-
light glinting on water sprayed by a water-cart circulating
in the park becomes 'вода на булавках', little pinpoints of

spray in the air. The faintly humorous nature of Mandelstam's
affection for the city is reflected in his characterisation
of the river Moskva - 'Эта слабогрудая речная волокита';
unlike the powerful Volga, the mighty Don or the great
Siberian rivers, the Moskva is a puny, dandified creature,
flowing languidly through the picture-postcard. Like a
'ladies' man' it is beguiling and alluring, but lacks verve
and strength. This jocular tone extends to the Oka's other
tributary, the Klyazma and to the Yauza (tributary of the
Moskva), the 'удельные речки', as Mandelstam called them,
provincial in comparison with Moscow, and all inextricably
linked together geographically, even politically, if the pun
on 'волокита' (red tape) is to be understood here:

У реки Оки вывернуто веко
Оттого-то и на Москве ветерок   (I No.252)

There is so much sound-play here that it seems certain that
the origin of 'веко' and later 'ресница' lay in a light-hearted pun on the semantic potential of the name 'Ока'. In his
typically irreverent description the rivers appear faintly
comic, very much a part of the pleasure-garden atmosphere,
where Schubert blared from every loudspeaker and absurd
balloons floated in the gentle spring air:

...и воздух нежнее
Лягушиной кожи воздушных шаров.   (I No.252)

Purely descriptive poems are rare in the work of this period.
Nearly always Mandelstam relates external events or his
surroundings to his own preoccupations. Even here there is a
serious undertone not apparent from its superficial subject-
matter. When visiting the Neskuchny Sad Mandelstam always
remembered, and reminded Nadezhda Yakovlevna, that it was
here that Herzen and Ogarev exchanged vows to remain faithful
to their ideals. He saw some relevance to himself in these
vows: the historical parallel encouraged him in his attempt
to steer the same course as they. His ever-increasing sense

of isolation is plainly stated in the poem where old themes
are linked with new, 'О, как мы любим лицемерить' (I No.253):

> А мне уж не на кого дуться,
> И я один на всех путях.   (I No.253)

Mandelstam's concern with death in the 'Волк' cycle had not
diminished in the intervening year. A slight hint of shame
at such constant reference to it may account for his argument
- intended to console, but totally lacking in conviction:

> (мы) ... в детстве ближе к смерти,
> Чем в наши зрелые года.   (I No.253)

Anna Akhmatova remembers that in Mandelstam's youthful verse
there had been something very similar to this first stanza
(N.Ya.III). It is quite conceivable that he should revive
'бродячие строки' even at this distance in time: indeed, were
it not for the firm dating, it would be easy to assign the
first two stanzas to the poetry of his Symbolist phase, with
its self-pity, its abstract ratiocination, its egocentricity
and its love of categorical statement. However, in 1932 there
was no question of affectation or posturing; his complaint
of loneliness was nothing less than the unvarnished truth.
He continually attempted to remove the last stanza, and it
was without it that the poem appeared, together with the one
preceding it and 'Ламарк' (I No.254) in *Новый мир*, perhaps
because he felt that it had more in common with the 'Lamarck'
group (Cf.S p.290). It does differ markedly from the first
two in its reflection of his new interest in the natural
sciences and evolutionary theory in particular, which had
sprung up as a result of his friendship with Kuzin, Leonov
and their young fellow biologists.

'Ламарк', 'Импрессионизм', 'Новеллино'
As usual, Mandelstam's prose of this period provides a substratum to the poetry, clarifying and supplementing many of
its ideas. In the article 'Вокруг натуралистов' (1932) and

his first rough drafts of it (1931-2) he makes plain the
connection between Lamarck, Dante - his other great preoccupation - and his present situation:

> На место неподвижной системы природы пришла живая цепь
> органических существ, подвижная лестница, стремящаяся к
> совершенству.   'Вокруг натуралистов'   (III p.136)

> Ламарк выплакал глаза в лупу. Его слепота равна глухоте
> Бетховена.   'Записные книжки'   (III p.161)

Two distinct subjects figure here: classification of species
(Lamarck) and their evolution (Darwin), which here includes
the possibility of its reverse process. Hierarchical structures appealed to Mandelstam's love of order and rightness.
They represented a certainty in the social order which he
felt to be necessary to the proper functioning of society.
As early as 1910, in his essay on Villon, and in the article
of 1912 'Утро акмеизма', he had praised the medieval version
of hierarchy in the feudal system:

> Средневековье, определяя по-своему удельный вес человека,
> чувствовало и признавало его за каждым, совершенно
> независимо от его заслуг.   'Утро акмеизма'   (II p.323)

> Средневековый человек считал себя в мировом здании столь
> же необходимым и связанным, как любой камень в готической
> постройке, с достоинством выносящий давление соседей и
> входящий неизбежной ставкой в общую игру сил.
>   'Франсуа Виллон'   (II p.308)

Lamarck's rigid classification of animal species satisfied
Mandelstam's desire for definition within the social structure
a desire naturally alien to his own society's accepted ideology. Man's position at the top of the ladder he found equally
fitting, since this gave man the central position in the whole
of creation. In an age of dehumanisation, when efforts on
behalf of humanity in the abstract had replaced concern for
the individual, Lamarck's work gave Mandelstam timely support
for his own social views. The theory of natural selection,
however, held more sinister implications in his opinion,
since it coincided with one of his most hated ideas, that of
inevitable progress. He greatly loathed determinism in any

form - for example as shown in the passivity of Islam - and
the thought that the evolutionary process would continue its
course, with no chance of its being hindered or deflected,
was abhorrent to him. In a short, but revealing fragment from
his notebooks, which can probably be dated to the same year,
1932, he denounces 'progress' for its lack of historical
events:

> Прообразом исторического события – в природе служит гроза.
> Прообразом же отсутствия событий можно считать движение
> часовой стрелки по циферблату. Было пять минут шестого,
> стало двадцать минут... Схема изменения как будто есть,
> на самом деле ничего не произошло. Как история родилась,
> так может она и умереть; и, действительно, что такое, как
> не умирание истории, при котором улетучивается дух
> события, – прогресс, детище девятнадцатого века? Прогресс
> – это движение часовой стрелки, и при всей своей бессод-
> ержательности это общее место представляет огромную
> опасность для самого существования истории.   (III p.191)

The same contempt for relentless mechanical progress reappears
in Mandelstam's comparison of the modern cinema with a tape-
worm in *Разговор о Данте*. The frames replace each other
automatically; there is no tension or conflict (II p.364).
Evolution exactly resembles this mechanical progress. In the
poem 'Ламарк' (I No.254) he renounces it:

> Если все живое лишь помарка
> За короткий выморочный день,
> На подвижной лестнице Ламарка
> Я займу последнюю ступень.   (I No.254)

If everything is seen in retrospect to have had no intrinsic
value whatsoever, but to have been merely the next stage on
the ladder upwards, then he refuses to be a party to the
whole charade. He will join the lower forms of life, which
constitute a living hell for man. As he envisages the reverse
of the evolutionary process, he sees man gradually losing
his distinguishing features, firstly his warm blood, and
acquiring the characteristics of lower beings:

> Роговую мантию надену,
> От горячей крови откажусь,
> Обрасту присосками и в пену

Океана завитком вопьюсь.   (I No.254)

It is as though nature had dissociated herself from man -
'Так, как будто мы ей не нужны' - and has sheathed the sharp
sword of the human brain, no longer necessary. She has, as
he says in the last stanza, forgotten to lower the connecting bridges between man and the more primitive forms of life,
and has left on the wrong side those whose breathing, laughter and land-bound existence - and their death - differenti-
ated them from the molluscs:

> У кого зеленая могила,
> Красное дыханье, гибкий смех...   (I No.254)

A variant version underlines nature's sudden disappearance,
the withdrawal of support which undermines the whole vertebrate world:

> И подъемный мост она забыла
> Опоздала (Не успела) опустить на миг,
> Позвоночных рвами окружила
> И сейчас же отреклась от них.   (Cf.S p.290) (N.Ya.III)

Lamarck had been particularly sensitive to the gaps between
the evolutionary classes: 'Ламарк чувствует *провалы* между
классами./ Это интервалы эволюционного ряда. Пустоты зияют.'
(III p.161). Nature's sudden abandonment of her favourite
children creates one of Lamarck's 'провалы' - the void in
which all of life sinks to the lowest level. In this case
Mandelstam feels there to be insuperable obstacles to his
return to civilisation:

> Он сказал: довольно полнозвучья, -
> Ты напрасно Моцарта любил:
> Наступает глухота паучья,
> Здесь провал сильнее наших сил.
>   (I No.254)

Brains, sight (stanza five), hearing were all vanishing. The
terrible encroaching deafness - 'глухота паучья' - is as
great a catastrophe as it had once been for Beethoven: man's
finest expression of himself in the creative artist's work,
here epitomised in Mozart, has all been in vain. Primeval
chaos is destined to gain the upper hand, as in the poetic

world of Tyutchev. Mandelstam was indeed reading and thinking of Tyutchev at this time, as subsequent poems confirm,
and with him in mind formed an association of related ideas,
linked by their common impulse towards harmony and the ordering of chaos. In this respect the figures of Mozart, Dante,
Beethoven, Tyutchev and the natural scientists are as one,
symbolising the high points in human culture:

> Паллас насвистывает из Моцарта, мурлычет из Глюка. Кто
> не любит Генделя, Глюка и Моцарта, тот ни черта не поймет
> в Палласе... Телесную круглость и любезность немецкой
> музыки он перенес на русские равнины.   (III p.163)

The loss of the higher faculties and the descent into hell
are no abstract, hypothetical speculation, but an oblique
reference to Mandelstam's own situation, another way of
representing the same position as had featured in the first
Тетрадь. Soviet ideology required a constant upward movement
on the path to an inevitable socialist utopia, precisely the
deterministic, dehumanising outlook which he so detested. He
prefers instead to revert to primeval chaos, where at least
spontaneity has not vanished, in his rebellion against the
Dostoevskian Crystal Palace of the future.

'Разбойничать' defines exactly Mandelstam's irreverent
response to pressure to conform and exhortations to strive
for a world whose very ideals, let alone their implementation,
he considered misguided if not pernicious. In 'Когда в
далекую Корею' (I No.255) he reviews various stages of his
own development towards maturity, and comes to the conclusion
that, however much he may have changed since his youth, this
fooling around and refusing to behave in the manner approved
by society is still of importance:

> Иные сны, другие гнезда,
> Но не разбойничать нельзя.   (I No.255)

This last stanza was finished in Voronezh, when the possibil-
ities for such activity had become somewhat fewer, yet the
defiance implicit in the lines was nevertheless as great in

1932 as then. The poem was another by-product of Mandelstam's voracious reading at this time, the connection between them once again being furnished by his prose - in this case by jottings in his notes from the section devoted mainly to Pallas:

> Мы читаем книгу, чтобы запомнить, но в том-то и беда,
> что прочесть книгу можно только припоминая.
> Будучи *всецело* охвачены деятельностью чтения, мы больше
> всего любуемся своими *родовыми* свойствами. Испытываем
> как бы восторг классификации своих возрастов. (III p.166)

The activity of reading necessarily involves remembering one's own experiences and development, and Mandelstam conducts a review of his own in the poem. In fact it deals with a particular age, that of the adolescent between eleven and fourteen years. At eleven there were the idolisation of Taras Bulba, the capturing of his imagination by the Iliad, the fighting and war games in the playground of the Tenishev School:

> Была пора смешливой бульбы
> И щитовидной железы,...
>
> Самоуправство, своевольство,
> Поход Троянского коня,
> А над поленницей посольство
> Эфира, солнца и огня. (I No.255)

It was still in the school playground that he felt the impact of 1905, the 'подступающей грозы':

> И Петропавловску, Цусиме
> Ура на дровяной горе. (I No.255)

His schoolboy imagination was fired by tales of all and any heroes, and of their prowess, rather to the shame of the grown man looking back at them:

> К царевичу младому Хлору
> И - Господи благослови! -
> Как мы в высоких голенищах
> За хлороформом в гору шли... (I No.255)

Derzhavin's work had figured prominently in his reading of Russian late-eighteenth and nineteenth-century poets during May 1932, and this had obviously included either or both of

'Фелица' and 'К царевичу Хлору'.[1] In both these Derzhavin
makes humorous reference to the little 'Сказка о царевиче
Хлоре' written by Catherine for her grandson, Aleksandr
Pavlovich, in 1781, and printed in a very limited edition.
It related the tale of Khlor, son of the Prince of Kiev, who
was seized and abducted by a Kirghiz khan in his father's
absence. The khan, wishing to test the truth of the boy's
rumoured prowess, required him to obtain a rose without thorns.
After many trials and a great deal of temptation he found
such a rose tree on a steep stony mountain ('гора') and
brought it back to the khan, who allowed him to return to
Kiev. 'Фелица' was the name of the khan's daughter whom Khlor
encountered on his travels, which explains why the 'Сказка'
should have been in Derzhavin's mind when he was writing his
famous ode of 1782. Mandelstam saw his equivalent of the
thornless rose as being a palliative, merely a sop for his
youthful enthusiasm; his own allusion to Khlor, both by name
and in the pun on it, 'хлороформом', is considerably less
playful than Derzhavin's. In this poem the method of his
Шум времени is resurrected in Mandelstam's choice of what
were for him the significant details of the period, the background which formed a counterpoint to the figures of the
Sinani family and Yuli Matveich, even down to the most personal, irrelevant details of his own actions:

> Я убегал в оранжерею,
> Держа ириску за щекой.   (I No.255)

The first version of the opening line of the last stanza
originally read: 'Я пережил болезни роста' (N.Ya.III).
Mandelstam saw the mistakes and enthusiasms of his youth as
being his own particular folly, and only later came to
realise that his experience had not been unique. This was

---

[1] Г.Р.Державин, *Сочинения*, 2nd edn. (7 vols., St Petersburg,
1868-78), vol. 1, p.90 and vol. 2, p.259 respectively.

simply the nature of adolescence, when enthusiasm for war
and for socialist revolution were a perfectly natural and
normal development - hence the correction of the first line
to 'Я пережил того подростка'. He had come through the
'illness' unscathed and could evaluate it objectively, even
learning from it the value of playing the bandit in adult
life.

'Путешествие в Армению', amazingly heterogeneous as it is,
succeeds quite happily in moving from discussion of the
Zamoskvoreche *moeurs* through nineteenth-century French
painters and through natural scientists on the way to its
main subject, Armenia. A related progression can be seen in
Mandelstam's poetry, from Armenia to Moscow to natural science
to French painting. In the section of 'Путешествие в Армению'
entitled 'Французы' Mandelstam's visits to Moscow museums to
view the work of the French artists, chiefly the Impression-
ists, whom he found of especial interest at this period, are
described with some brilliance. Passages in the section itself and in the rough notes for it suggest that the artists
whose work forms the subject of the poem 'Импрессионизм'
are probably Pissaro and particularly Monet, to whom he
returns constantly in his viewing:

> ..серо-малиновые бульвары Писсарро, текущие как колеса
> огромной лотереи с коробочками кэбов, вскинувших удочки
> бичей, и лоскутьями разбрызганного мозга на киосках и
> каштанах.   (Cf.S p.291)(II pp.160-1)

> В комнате Клода Монэ... воздух речной./ Входишь в
> картину по скользким подводным ступенькам дачной
> купальни...   (III p.159)

> Роскошные плотные сирени Иль-де-Франс, сплющенные из
> звездочек в пористую, как бы известковую губку, сложив-
> шиеся в грозную лепестковую массу; дивные пчелиные сирени
> исключившие... все на свете, кроме дремучих восприятий
> шмеля -...   (Cf.S p.292) (III p.160)

The paintings which he most likely had in mind were Monet's
Lilas au soleil and Pissarro's *Boulevard Montmartre* and

Place du Théâtre Français, Printemps. Many points of resemblance in the poem enhance the reader's picture of how these paintings struck Mandelstam (Cf.also S pp.291-2). Bright, fresh colours and astonishing lilac shade characterise both, Monet in particular:

> Художник нам изобразил
> Глубокий обморок сирени,
> И красок звучные ступени
> На холст, как струпья, положил...
>
> Его запекшееся лето
> Лиловым мозгом разогрето,...
>
> Угадывается качель,
> Недомалеваны вуали,
> И в этом солнечном развале
> Уже хозяйничает шмель.   (I No.258)

Together with his own appreciation Mandelstam conveys the important features of Monet's and of Pisarro's painting: the colour and texture of the paint, the method of application and the general effect of understatement. Monet's swing, the veils, the bumble-bees in the lilac are at one remove from the observer, who notices first the opulent lilacs and the clarity of the brilliant colouring, and receives an immediate impression of cold spring water when he first looks at the painting, without as yet defining the cause for the drop in temperature. The play of light and shade, forming the basic contrast here, is supported by the poem's structure: the first half deals with strong summer colours in bright light, the second with the delicate, lilac-coloured shadow, and the expansive 'o' -sounds which dominate the first half are muted into the vaguer 'a', 'и' and 'e' of the second half. But it is clearly the magnificent lilacs of the Île-de-France on which all attention focuses; the marvellous account of them in the prose passage contains not only the essence of the lilac flowers, but also the impressionist method of making them seem three-dimensional, with their own specific texture - 'сплющенные из звездочек в пористую, как бы известковую

губку'. In 'Канцона' (I No.236) Mandelstam had lamented the
absence of colour in Russian life. It was hardly surprising
that, when he emerged into the May sunshine of Moscow from
the museums, he should react to it in the same way as after
his imaginary Palestinian journey in the poem:

> Сразу после французов солнечный свет показался мне фазой
> убывающего затмения, а солнце – завернутым в серебряную
> бумагу.   'Путешествие в Армению'   (II p.162)

Palestine, France and then Italy, compensated for the drab-
ness around Mandelstam by supplying his inner vision with a
riot of uninhibited colour, reflected in, for example,
'Новеллино' (I No.256) (Cf.S pp.290-1). He is elaborating on
Dante's description of the participants in the spring games
held outside Verona:

> По темнобархатным лугам
> В сафьяновых сапожках
> Они пестрели по холмам
> Как маки на дорожках.   (I No.256)

This poem is otherwise simply a joke at the expense of the
Florentines, whose character and exploits - as outlined here
- were such as to land them in Dante's Inferno. Although
Разговор о Данте was not written until the summer of 1933,
Mandelstam had already begun rereading the *Divine Comedy* in
earnest, learning Italian the while, in 1932. For the moment,
however, humorous appreciation preceded the serious study of
Dante's masterpiece. Both the rascally youths and the ladies
of easy virtue awoke in Mandelstam a yearning for the frivolity and irresponsible fun of an easy life, probably bound up
with memories of his youth - the ladies here are at only one
remove from the captivating 'нежные европеянки' of his
twenties. In Voronezh he decided to replace the first two
stanzas of the poem with what now appears as an independent
poem, the two sharing a common first line - 'Вы помните, как
бегуны' (I No.257) (Cf.S p.291), and to abandon all but the

last two stanzas from the rest of the original poem. Nadezhda
Yakovlevna found the 'молодчики каленые' more interesting
than the ladies, and wanted him to reprieve them. The result-
ing compromise involved preserving the *status quo* of both
versions.

In the second version Mandelstam describes Brunetto
Latini's position in relation to the youth of his day. Later,
in *Разговор о Данте*, he quoted the passage concerning Dante's
former teacher from the fifteenth canto of the *Inferno* (in
Russian translation):

> В дантовском понимании учитель моложе ученика, потому
> что 'бегает быстрее'.
> 'Он отвернулся и показался мне одним из тех, которые
> бегают взапуски по зеленым лугам в окрестностях Вероны,
> и всей своей статью он напоминал о своей принадлежности
> к числу победителей, а не побежденных...'
> Омолаживающая сила метафоры возвращает нам образованного
> старика Брунетто Латини в виде юноши – победителя на
> спортивном пробеге в Вероне.   (II p.367)

This could well have seemed to Mandelstam to have some relevance to his own position. He would dearly have loved to be
able to demonstrate publicly his superior abilities in the
poetic field, but naturally no opportunity to do so would be
given him.

The Russian poetry cycle

'Новеллино', its variant, and the two poems which prefigure
the 'Стихи о русской поэзии' (I Nos.262-4) provide a rare
example of a return to the 'Acmeist' style of Mandelstam's
1912-13 poetry. The nineteenth-century poets in 'Дайте
Тютчеву стрекозу' (I No.259) are treated with a familiarity
and jocularity which gives the poem, otherwise unspectacular,
a certain charm and attraction. It merits attention as a
sharp little study of the poets concerned, also serving as
an indication of what Mandelstam was reading at the time
(See N.Ya.I pp.257-8, where his reading among the Russian

eighteenth- and nineteenth-century poets, Latin, Italian
and German writers is described). They are both amusing and
idiosyncratic - even Nadezhda Yakovlevna could not guess and
still has no idea why Tyutchev should be presented with a
dragon-fly; it occurs only once in Tyutchev's entire poetic
oeuvre:

В душном воздуха молчанье,
Как предчувствие грозы,
Жарче роз благоуханье,
Звонче голос стрекозы...[1]

(Cf.S p.292)

Possibly the insistent voice of the insect before the storm
breaks found an echo in Mandelstam's own; earlier references
to storms and the return to primeval chaos in his own work,
by no means infrequent, may have made him select this apparently incongruous image, not least because, in the next
stanza of Tyutchev's poem, the storm does break:

Чу! За белой дымной тучей
Глухо прокатился гром;
Небо молнией летучей
Опоясалось кругом...[2]

The Mandelstam poem is not without serious observations; he
forbids the awarding of the seal-ring of authority to any
poet, presumably a concealed reference to Pushkin, the ultimate authority for Mandelstam, since Pushkin's property cannot
belong to another. There is also a sober assessment of
Batyushkov's achievement in the poem which bears his name
(I No.261), and which lacks the jocose flavour of the other
verses on Russian poetry:

Наше мученье и наше богатство,
Косноязычный, с собой он принес -
Шум стихотворства и колокол братства
И гармонический проливень слез.

(I No.261)

Mandelstam's assertion, in the second stanza, that it is

---

[1] Ф.И.Тютчев, *Полное собрание сочинений*, 2nd edn. (Leningrad, 1957), p.138.
[2] *ibid.*

impossible to believe that he and Batyushkov have ever been
separated by time epitomises his views on the extra-temporal
personal relationships between poets of different centuries.
Poetic friendship has nothing to do with chronological time
- a feeling expressed emphatically in the poems on Russian
poetry and in *Разговор о Данте*.

The first part of 'Стихи о русской поэзии' (I No.262)
begins in the same way as the poems which form a prelude to
it, in that the slightly teasing tone continues together with
the same four-footed trochaics. The jaunty, almost sing-song,
impression they produce helps to imagine the poet making
himself comfortable in the company of his august predecessors,
while inviting them to relax and be similarly sociable. This
involves no lack of respect for Derzhavin and Yazykov on his
part, but is simply the natural social relationship between
poets of which his own with Batyushkov had been but one
example. He fully appreciates not only their poetry but their
personalities - Yazykov's exuberance, Derzhavin's acid wit,
not quite as sour as *кумыс*, but obviously of the same order:

И татарского кумыса
Твой початок не прокис.   (I No.262)

Nadezhda Yakovlevna derives the word 'початок' - here the
first thread in Derzhavin's weaving of poetic fabric - from
the Ukrainian 'початы', obsolete or found only in dialects
in Russian, and she remarks that 'кат' in the second of these
three poems is also a native Ukrainian word ('executioner')
(N.Ya.III). Mandelstam felt very distinctly the Old Church
Slavonic and Old Russian nature of many Ukrainianisms,
according to her testimony (N.Ya.III), and their inclusion
here may be a reminder that Derzhavin and Yazykov were writing
much nearer to the time when these were current usage, either
in everyday speech or the written word or the liturgy. The
earlier poets would have been more aware of this linguistic
substratum in their own poetic language.

The second poem, 'Гром живет своим накатом' (I No.263),
mirrors the poetic world of the early nineteenth century, from
Derzhavin to Tyutchev, in the image of a thunderstorm, so
familiar in the work of both. For Derzhavin the storm was
mainly a rhetorical aid, lending grandeur and cosmic scale
to comparatively mundane subjects; but there are instances
in his work where nature's intrinsic fascination moves him.
One of these is 'Водопад', two lines of which provided the
source of inspiration for Mandelstam's use of the storm
images in 'Гром живет своим накатом':

> Грохочет эхо по горам,
> Как гром гремящий по горам.[1]

Whereas Derzhavin's descriptions are somewhat academic, even
when he is enthralled by the spectacle, Mandelstam enters
into the spirit of the storm much more like Tyutchev does in
his 'Весенняя гроза':

> Когда весенний первый гром,
> Как бы резвяся и играя
> Грохочет в небе голубом.
>
> Гремят раскаты молодые...
>
> С горы бежит поток проворный...[2]

Mandelstam's approach appeals wholly to the senses: the storm
itself revels in the sounds, the light and the smells it
produces:

> И глотками по раскатам
> Наслаждается мускатом
> На язык, на вкус, на цвет...   (I No.263)

The poet takes an equal sensual pleasure in its effects. The
poem is one of the very few in which any coincidence of style
or theme with the work of Pasternak can be discerned:

> Пахнет городом, потопом,
> Нет - жасмином, нет - укропом,
> Нет - дубовою корой.   (I No.263)

Through Mandelstam's apparent indecision over determining the

[1] Державин, *Сочинения*, vol. 1, p.322.
[2] Тютчев, *Полное собр. соч.*, p.89.

exact aroma he achieves a cumulative effect, in which all
those smells suggested mingle to form a composite aroma in
the reader's imagination. The sound of the storm is already
in his ears, assaulted by a battery of consonants based on
those of 'гром' 'накатом' and 'потопом' - a few examples
being 'глотками' 'раскатом' 'галопом' 'рабским потом' 'конским
топом'. The energy and speed of the storm are those of something elemental and uncontrollable:

> Капли прыгают галопом,
> Скачут градины гурьбой...   (I No.263)

The whole of Moscow and its inhabitants tremble and quail
before its lashing torrents, while it remains indifferent to
human tribulation - 'Что ему до наших бед?'. Mandelstam's
use of metaphor in this poem indicates a more serious consideration of the subject, Russian poetry, than had been the
case in its prelude. The storm, metaphorically speaking
Russian poetry, leads an independent self-sufficient life,
and the boldness of the images indicates how elemental and
uncontrollable in its vigour it is:

> Катит гром свою тележку
> По торцовой мостовой   (I No.263)

- an exact detail of the Moscow scene (N.Ya.III). The grandeur
of the storm transcends petty human cares: correspondingly
the lofty, magnificent poetry of the nineteenth century
dwarfs the petty cares of twentieth-century humanity.
Perhaps this is the sort of storm prefaced by the voice of
the Tyutchevan dragon-fly; but perhaps not, for in the third
poem of the 'Стихи' (I No.264) it is these cares which return
to dominate the subject-matter. Against the forest background
of traditional Russian folklore a dramatic conflict is about
to be enacted. Mandelstam perceives nature's deceptive,
illusory character and presents her as fickle and unreal as
a pack of cards painted with symbols:

> Полюбил я лес прекрасный,
> Смешанный, где козырь – дуб.   (I No.264)

The 'фисташковые... голоса' of poetry fall silent in the
forest, and any attempt the poet makes to compose rings false:

> И когда захочешь щелкнуть,
> Правды нет на языке. (I No.264)

The forest is affected by the evil influence of the forces
of 'Неправда', echoing Mandelstam's poem of 1931 where he
was preparing to go 'К шестипалой неправде в избу' (I No.231).
He returns to this setting in the 1932 poem, with its 'народец
мелкий' in acorn caps, its unclean spirits, its repulsive
squirrels:

> И белок кровавый белки
> Крутят в страшном колесе. (I No.264)

However, a difference in his earlier and present attitudes to
the sinister forest is discernible: fear and terror are no
longér present here, although the grounds for such feelings
are all too much in evidence:

> На углях читают книги
> С самоваром палачи. (I No.264)

- the same executioner figure as in the preceding poem: 'И
в сапожках мягких ката' (I No.263), perhaps a joke at the
expense of the reader who might be expecting to find 'вата'
here. Mandelstam's acceptance of the situation is so complete
that he is able to make fun of it, thereby reducing it to
the diminutive proportions used in the poem. The forest is
peopled with small folk, small animals, small plants (sorrel
and mushrooms), mostly rather repellent. It is interesting
that Mandelstam gives so much detail about these flora and
fauna; no doubt this particularisation owes much to his
reading of Linnaeus, Pallas, Lamarck, Buffon and Darwin (See
N.Ya.I p.259), which gave him a greater awareness of the
natural world. This may explain why Sergei Klychkov particularly liked the poem and asked that it should be dedicated
to him - a request which was granted. A measure of Klychkov's
understanding is his remark to Mandelstam that it was the
two of them and many such as they who were the subject of

the penultimate stanza:

> Там без выгоды уроды
> Режутся в девятый вал   (I No.264)

While the forest seethes with menace freaks such as they
continue to play frivolously and recklessly up to the moment
of the final catastrophe. Mandelstam was shocked by the inter-
necine nature of this confrontation between the two groups,
as he had been by the 'literary spite' of the tribe of
writers who had tried to eliminate him through the Eulenspiegel affair. In singling this out as the most frightening
aspect of the campaign he had pointed with remarkable fore-
sight to the chief condition of Stalin's success in imposing
wholesale terror on the country. Without the horrifying
numbers of people who were willing and even eager to denounce
and betray their fellows Stalin's career might have been
different. In Mandelstam's reference to one of Lenin's by-
words, 'Кто кого', which came to be used by Lenin's enemies
as a description of his ruthless and unscrupulous elimination
of all rival political groups, the brutality of Stalin can
be seen in embryo. The point is made yet more explicitly in
the last stanza:

> И деревья - брат на брата -
> Восстают: понять спеши:
> До чего аляповаты,
> До чего как хороши...   (I No.264)

Notwithstanding the baseness of actions committed in the name
of humanity, Mandelstam still retains a love of life as seen
in his fellows. However, the 'Стихи' do end on this note of
pessimism. The downward progression from the exhilarating
merriment of the beginning is completed in this picture of
poetry and the poet surrounded by hostility and under threat
of extinction. It is unlikely that he ever doubted the ability
of poetry to survive in the way that Nadezhda Yakovlevna did
(See N.Ya.I pp.287-95), but he did recognise that its future
looked bleak.

The poetry of Germany

This would perhaps account for Mandelstam's urgent desire to
immerse himself in the languages of others - at this time
they were German and Italian - which tormented him because
of the feeling of guilt, almost a sense of treachery, which
accompanied his excursions into foreign literatures. Enjoyment of an alien speech and poetry seemed like a betrayal of
his own, yet, as he acknowledges in 'К немецкой речи' (I No.
266), he was drawn involuntarily to them:

> Себя губя, себе противореча,
> Как моль летит на огонек полночный   (I No.266)

Russian contemporary literature offered no stimulus comparable with that of nineteenth-century poetry or with the excitement he felt at rereading the classics of foreign literature.
Setting aside the idea of betrayal was difficult, but when he
managed to do so he was able to evaluate the true relationship
between himself and his foreign counterparts as one of sincere
mutual admiration, genuine friendship and, on his part,
indebtedness:

> Поучимся ж серьезности и чести
> На западе у чуждого семейства.   (I No.266)

This last phrase demonstrates the curious ambivalence of his
heart-searching. The West and western culture appear here as
a family, its members held together by their common upbring-
ing and interests, close-knit, interdependent and exhibiting
a mutual loyalty in confrontation with the outside world.
The family unity of western Europe differentiates it from the
family of Russian culture, since the two are not related by
ties of birth. None the less, a rough draft of the poem
(cited in I as a variant) includes personal reminiscences
from the time of the Seven Years' War, a picture of himself
standing somewhere on the Rhine:

> Воспоминаний сумрак шоколадный,
> Плющем войны завешен старый Рейн.

И я стою в беседке виноградной :
Так высоко, весь будущим пророян. (Cf.S p.294)(I p.506)

It is as though from this time and place he sees himself
projected into the future, and from the future he looks back
to here, remembering his blood ties with the land from which
he assumed his ancestors to have come to Russia. Interestingly
this is not the medieval Germany which had endeared itself to
him during his youthful stay in Heidelberg, but eighteenth-
century Germany, in literature the period of the Romantic
poets and of Goethe. Awareness of his German-Jewish origin
was a deeply hidden feeling in Mandelstam, and came to the
surface only rarely. Another such manifestation of it was his
interest in the fact that Goethe, in his pre-Strasbourg days,
had visited the Jewish quarter of Frankfurt in order to talk
with and learn from the Jewish elders renowned for their
wisdom. This episode would have been included in the radio
broadcast of 1935, 'Юность Гете', had it not been censored -
not on account of the Jewish element, but because the subject
of Goethe's discussions was frequently a biblical one (N.Ya.
III). Both examples illustrate his paradoxical attitude to
Germany and in particular to its lyric poets, treated at once
as a race apart and as one with whom he has a strong blood
relationship. When he spoke in 'К немецкой речи' of being
stunned by his 'meeting', this was not only with Kuzin, but
also with German poetry in general (Cf.S pp.294-5):

Когда я спал без облика и склада,
Я дружбой был, как выстрелом, разбужен.   (I No.266)

Kuzin loved Goethe and was the prime mover in Mandelstam's
renewed enthusiasm for him. Kuzin, however, greatly disliked
this poem of Mandelstam's and spent the whole of one evening
grumbling about it. Its dedication to him is partly in
recognition of the service he had rendered its author, but
more because of Mandelstam's amusement at Kuzin's grousing.

The effect of the poet's meeting with his German poetic

precursors was the more startling for the overwhelming sensa-
tion of familiarity and foreknowledge which accompanied it.
Mandelstam knows that there is nothing new in his creative
friendship with the German poets and that their influence on
him has been of inestimable value, but precisely where or
when this had come about remains a source of mystery:

> Скажите мне, друзья, в какой Валгалле
> Мы вместе с вами щелкали орехи,
> Какой свободой мы располагали,
> Какие вы поставили мне вехи.　　　　　(I No.266)

In the seventh stanza he casts his mind back to his own pre-
history, portraying himself as poetry in embryo - a letter
of the alphabet, a 'виноградной строчкой' (typically an image
for poetry in his work, as in the 'стихов виноградное мясо'
of 'Батюшков'), and ultimately a book, of which the German
poets can only dream. His meeting with Kuzin was very much a
thing of the present, whereas the meeting with them took place
when Mandelstam was as yet formless and faceless; as yet he
was merely poetic material without shape or individual identity. Thus he gives a conspect of the past, present and
future of his relationship with them - as to the future, he
can only appeal for assistance to the nightingale of Romantic
poetry, the generalised concept of German poetic inspiration:

> Бог-Нахтигаль, дай мне судьбу Пилада
> Иль вырви мне язык - он мне не нужен.　　　(I No.266)

The fate of Pylades was an enviable one in comparison with
that of Orestes, but Mandelstam was prepared for either.
Ideally he would imitate the exemplary conduct of Pylades,
a byword for friendship and loyalty, however adverse the
circumstances. He would maintain fidelity to poetic song for
its own sake - as symbolised in the nightingale - but if this
fate were to be denied him, by implication through his own
weakness or cowardice, then he asks for more dramatic steps
to be taken. Should he not live up to the demands on his
courage and integrity, then better that his tongue should be

torn out, in the manner of Orestes' eyes, since his poetry
would have lost its foundation of 'rightness' and therefore
would be valueless. In the last stanza he makes clear the
threat which is being posed to his moral stand, and laments
that poetry is becoming ever less tractable:

> Бог-Нахтигаль, меня еще вербуют
> Для новых чум, для семилетних боен,
> Звук сузился, слова шипят, бунтуют   (I No.266)

The reference here to the Seven Years' War is all that remains
from his earlier identification with the epoch; he does,
however, cite a second historical precedent for fidelity.
The strange fate of Christian Kleist, the uncle of Heinrich,
struck Mandelstam as curious: wounded in the fighting round
Berlin in October 1760, he lay helpless until rescued by
Russian soldiers in Chernyshev's advancing line, who happened
to recognise him and carried him on a stretcher to a medical
post. Mandelstam, in a rough draft, speaks of the seriousness and sense of honour of Kleist's example, as also in the
poem itself:

> Я вспоминаю немца-офицера,
> И за эфес его цеплялись розы,
> И на губах его была Церера.   (I No.266)

> И прямо со страницы альманаха
> Он в бой сошел и умер так же складно,
> Как пел рябину с кружкой мозельвейна.   (S p.294)

In the allusion to Ceres Mandelstam synthesises the two distinctive features of Christian Kleist's work, his love of
nature and his fondness for classical allusions; in his poems
mention of the earth, flowers, streams, nightingales occurs
together with Zephyr, Diana, Endymion, Chloris and other
pastoral deities or figures. It was Kleist's particular
achievement to have produced poetry of such an idyllic kind
in such dire straits. Perhaps this partly explains the first
line in the Kleist stanza: 'Поэзия, тебе полезны грозы'.
Periodic upheavals may be positively beneficial to poetry,
giving it a sense of challenge and excitement which keep it

on its mettle and prevent it from sinking into apathy and
subsequent mediocrity. If its existence is threatened, the
best in it will fight for survival, the worst will quite
properly go under. When Mandelstam had written of storms as
nature's equivalent of an historical event (III p.191), as
opposed to mechanical progress, the same underlying idea was
intended. If the automatic progress of poetry is taken for
granted, the effect is bound to be a harmful one. It was in
this spirit that Mandelstam faced the prospect of new plagues,
new Seven Years' Wars. At the end of the winter of 1932-3 he
was given two 'вечера' in Leningrad and one in Moscow, at
which he read this poem, prefaced by an assurance that it was
written before the final seizure of power by the Nazis in
1933. So not only in Russia but in the family of western
culture new plagues and new wars loomed ominously on the
horizon.

Stary Krym and the Italian poetry
'К немецкой речи' was finished in August 1932 and the next
poem in the collection, 'Холодная весна. Голодный Старый
Крым' (I No.271), did not come until nearly a year later,
in May 1933. This gap hides no particular calamity, as had
previous silences. He tended to write in bursts with long
periods in between, periods of recharging and accumulating
poetic material; he was continually amazed that Pasternak
sat down and 'wrote' every morning without fail. During the
silent phases he read, chatted, tried to travel, absorbed new
ideas and impressions, all of which was of equal importance
with the moments when these impressions crystallised into
their poetic form. Nadezhda Yakovlevna recounts (N.Ya.III)
that he told Anna Akhmatova that for the lines building up
in his head to crystallise some event - it transpired that
this was usually a journey or a move to another flat - was
necessary, whether this event was good or bad being of no

moment. Only when the poems arrived could he see whether a
new stage in his work had begun, or whether they were a cont-
inuation of the previous one. In the case of the break between
1932 and 1933 no radical new developments are apparent, either
in the themes or in their presentation, in spite of the length
of the interval between them.

When the Mandelstams returned from their Leningrad trip
they found out that Kuzin had been arrested. Although he was
released shortly afterwards, it seemed prudent to leave Moscow
and take Kuzin with them to the Crimea. They stayed in Stary
Krym with Nina Grin, the novelist's widow, who had earlier
been staying with them during the winter after her husband's
death. They revisited Feodosiya and Sevastopol in the spring
and found the whole of the Crimea, with its almond trees in
full blossom, as lovely and as tragic as in the days of the
Civil War:

> Холодная весна. Голодный Старый Крым,
> Как был при Врангеле...
>   ...и вызывает жалость
> Вчерашней глупостью украшенный миндаль.   (I No.271)

Acute famine conditions gripped the whole region, and they
were appalled by the spectacle of fields made unrecognisable
by the absence of crops and cattle, the result of the destruction which followed enforced collectivisation and of the
inefficiency of the first Five-Year Plan. Most of all they
were appalled by the emaciated inhabitants of the Ukraine
and the Kuban, who were guarding the gates to their store-
houses with the help of dogs, so that vagrants should not
break the windows and steal the last supplies of flour:

> Природа своего не узнает лица,
> А тени страшные – Украины, Кубани...
> Как в туфлях войлочных голодные крестьяне
> Калитку стерегут, не трогая кольца.   (I No.271)

They viewed cynically shops of the 'closed' type, where Party
officials could still obtain adequate food, while the peasan-
try starved (N.Ya.III). Dangerous though much of the poem

was, there had been even more overt reference to the callous
and brutal treatment of the peasants in the words which in
the final form of the line read 'Все так же хороша рассеянная
даль', but had first appeared as 'расстрелянная даль'. The
agony of the South impressed Mandelstam deeply, especially
by comparison with the country as he had known it:

> Овчарки на дворе, на рубищах заплаты,
> Такой же серенький, кусающийся дым.   (I No.271)

In his 1915 poem 'Обиженно уходят на холмы' (I No.79), where
he describes Rome and the Mediterranean world in general,
sheepdogs and smoke from camp fires or small houses are two
of the most characteristic details in the landscape, and help
to link it in his mind with that of the Russian South, here
the Crimea, of which they were similarly characteristic. It
was thus entirely natural that he should have spent his time
in Stary Krym avidly reading Italian poetry against the background he had always associated with Italy. *Разговор о Данте*
was also conceived there, although nothing of substance was
actually written until they reached Koktebel.

Mandelstam's Italianate surroundings were conducive both to
intensive study of his favourite Italians and, as a by-product
of this, the composition of his own poetry inspired by their
work. The two poems on Ariosto resulted directly from this,
but were followed immediately by two in which the ethics of
reading in another language were again questioned. Nadezhda
Yakovlevna is slightly puzzled as to why Ariosto in particular was so necessary to Mandelstam at this juncture. The
answer may lie partly in the words 'посольская лиса' (I No.
268) addressed to Ariosto, who indeed undertook diplomatic
missions to Rome and other Italian cities on behalf of the
rulers of Ferrara. Mandelstam clearly thought of him as
another Villon, in that he was frequently at odds with
conventional society, in the persons of the dukes d'Este,

but contrived not only to survive but even to flourish by
coming to terms with it - something of which Mandelstam
would himself have liked to have been capable. Ariosto is
the unrepentant son of 'черствая' Ferrara, 'город ящериц, в
котором нет души' (I Nos. 267 & 268). The political situation
is one of tyranny, an obvious analogy with modern times:

В Европе холодно, в Италии темно.
Власть отвратительна, как руки брадобрея.   (I No.267)

In the second version of 'Ариост' (I No.268) - Mandelstam's
attempt to remember the poem in Voronezh, where all manuscr-
ipts of this period were assumed lost - these two lines open
the poem, but the remaining half of the quatrain gives them
a rather different complexion:

О, если б распахнуть, да как нельзя скорее,
На Адриатику широкое окно.   (I No.268)

However dark and cold Europe might have been in 1933 and 1935,
just as in Ariosto's time, it was nevertheless better than
Mandelstam's circumstances of exile in provincial Russia.
Throughout both versions runs the constant theme of physical
and spiritual longing for Italy and Europe, the desire for
an impossible merging of the two with their Crimean surrogate:

В одно широкое и братское лазорье
Сольем твою лазурь и наше черноморье.
И мы бывали там. И мы там пили мед.   (I No.267)

Only in the South would he have ever indulged in such delightful fantasies: perhaps only in the South would Ariosto, with
his 'Запутанный рассказ о рыцарских скандалах' (I No.267),
have charmed him as he did. A revealing aspect of some
interest is the role of intermediary between him and Ariosto
played by no less a personage than Pushkin. In the first
written notes for *Разговор о Данте*, which preceded these
poems by some months, there is evidence to suggest that it
may have been during Mandelstam's recent perusal of Russian
poetry that he observed the Italian influence on Pushkin,
perhaps giving him his initial enthusiasm for the Italians:

> Незнакомство русских читателей с итальянскими поэтами –
> я разумею Данта, Ариоста и Тасса – тем более поразительно,
> что не кто иной, как Пушкин воспринял от итальянцев
> взрывчатость и неожиданность гармонии...
> Славные белые зубы Пушкина – мужской жемчуг поэзии русской.
> Что же роднит Пушкина с итальянцами? Уста работают, улыбка
> движет стих, умно и весело алеют губы, язык доверчиво
> прижимается к небу.   (III p.179)

In Mandelstam's poems the essence of the Italian language,
the 'language of the cicadas', is described as a:

>   ...пленительная смесь
> Из грусти пушкинской и средиземной спеси.   (I No.267)
>   & I No.268)

Mandelstam even illustrates this with a near-quotation from
Pushkin's poem 'Буря' in his line 'И деве на скале: – Лежи
без покрывала...':

> Ты видел деву на скале
> В одежде белой над волнами...
> И ветер бился и летал
> С ее летучим покрывалом?[1]   (Cf.S p.296)

The standard Russian folk-tale ending in Mandelstam's poem,
slightly modified, may have derived as much from Pushkin's
Руслан и Людмила as from more primary sources. The plural
subject - 'И мы бывали там. И мы там пили мед.' (I No.267)
can be seen as including both the Russian poets as having
supped the honey of Italian verse. Concerning the sounds
themselves, Mandelstam uses the image of the pearl previously
applied to Pushkin:

> Язык бессмысленный, язык солено-сладкий
> И звуков стакнутых прелестные двойчатки,
> Боюсь раскрыть ножом двухстворчатый жемчуг.   (I No.267)

He likens the dual character of the Italian language to the
two halves of a pearl, frighteningly delicate and intense,
to the extent that he fears breaking it by forcing it to
reveal its riches. In the single quatrain whose last three
lines are identical with these - 'Друг Ариоста, друг Петрарка

---

[1] Пушкин, vol. 2, p.51.

Tacco друг' (I No.269), this meaning has changed somewhat by
means of a shifting of emphasis in the poem which intervenes
between it and the Ariosto poems in Mandelstam's own ordering
of them, 'Не искушай чужих наречий, но постарайся их забыть'
(I No.270). Written in a stern, moralising tone, it contains
a reprimand and a warning for those who indulge themselves
in the illicit pleasures of other languages, a fuller and
more severe restatement of the theme than in 'К немецкой
речи' (I No.266). In making any sort of pronouncement Mandelstam's instinct was to use a longer line than usual, generally
the hexameter, composed of ternary metres and making up a
four-line stanza. However, 'Воронеж, авг.1935', which should
appear below the poem, suggests that, whatever the original
of May 1933 may have been, its final couplet form of 1935
may have been influenced by that of 'Нет, не мигрень, но
подай карандашик ментоловый' (I No.317), written in July 1935.
As before, he rejects alien tongues, whose seductive influence
has no power to save him from the fate awaiting him or to
make his struggle against his hostile surroundings an effective one. The glass here may be a reminder of Dostoevsky's
Crystal Palace of earlier poems, for example 'Сегодня можно
снять декалькомани' (I No.265):

> Ведь все равно ты не сумеешь стекла зубами укусить!
> Ведь умирающее тело и мыслящий бессмертный рот
> В последний раз перед разлукой чужое имя не спасет.
>
> (I No.270)

This points to a return to the fatalism of 'Волк' days. It
is interesting to speculate on a possible connection between
this poem and one of 1920, 'В Петербурге мы сойдемся снова'
(I No.118), where poetry is spoken of as 'бессмысленное слово'
and the word 'бессмертный' also features. The circumstances
are similar - imminent separation from a beloved world,
but there is little hope in the later poem for a future
reunion. In contrast with his rejection of the alien tongues,
the terms in which their impact on him is described -

'восторги' 'обворожающие' (I No.270)- leave no doubt as to
their fascination for him, the 'неисправимый звуколюб' of the
last couplet. As in the prose fragment about Pushkin and the
Italians, so in the poem Mandelstam emphasises the aspect of
speech production - the teeth, lips, the mouth, even the
facial expression are of paramount importance, whereas the
visual aspect of the 'чужого клекота' is totally neglected.
In *Разговор о Данте* (for instance on II p.365) this approach
to the work under consideration predominates throughout the
essay.

Mandelstam tries to stir up feelings of aversion in himself by imagining Ariosto and Tasso as 'Чудовища с лазурным
мозгом и чешуей из влажных глаз' (I No.270), familiar enough
images when he is expressing the loathing produced in him by
reptiles. The attempts lack conviction, and in order to
chastise himself for his treachery to the Russian language
he resorts to outright threats of the most definitive punishment of all: 'Получишь уксусную губку ты для изменнических
губ' (I No.270). When, therefore, the isolated quatrain
addressed to '.язык бессмысленный' as the friend of the Italian
poets (I No.269) was written, its meaning had altered considerably and the key word of the poem had become 'боюсь'. He
had tried to regard the 'друг Ариоста' as inimical to a
Russian of integrity because of the implicit disloyalty to
his own tongue, and now he feared the inevitable penalties
which his inability to suppress this love would bring.

Разговор о Данте

Разговор о Данте (II pp.363-413) is the final proof of Mandelstam's failure to stay away from the Italians. Any feeling
of dishonesty or hypocrisy in connection with his poetry
always stifled the poetic impulse in him and this case was no
exception. He turned to prose as he had done in 1923-30, in
order to say what could not 'honourably' be said in poetry.

He wrote *Разговор о Данте* in Koktebel in the summer of 1933
when he was in constant consultation with Andrei Bely, who
had made his home there. Although Bely's poetry and philosophy of life differed radically from Mandelstam's at most
points, he was nevertheless a fellow poet, and as such able
to provide a stimulus and criticism which Mandelstam found
invaluable, for his young biologist friends were unable to
do this. Nadezhda Yakovlevna describes the immediate warmth
of the two poets' relations, marred only by the disapproval
of Bely's wife. At the same time as Mandelstam was writing
on Dante Bely was finishing his own critical work on another
illustrious author, *Мастерство Гоголя*, a common factor which
helped them both (N.Ya.I p.162).

The importance of *Разговор о Данте* in the context of
Mandelstam's poetry lies in the application to his own work
of its theoretical utterances about the nature of poetic
material and poetic speech. A résumé of his thoughts, mostly
in his own words, must serve as a substitute for a full
study, although the short summary and commentary by L.E.Pinsky
in his postcript to the essay in its Moscow edition of 1967
(quoted at length in II pp.653-62) provides an admirable
starting point.

Mandelstam declares the study of 'порывы' (variously
translated as 'impulses' or 'élans') to be the basis of a
true appreciation of Dante. Existing Dante scholarship has
been of a purely conventional nature and thus concerned
exclusively with the finished text. This scholarship comprises
such exercises as a systematic analysis of the work, the
mechanical collation of passages from it, the correlation
of the *Divine Comedy* with his earlier works - all beyond
question worthy and, from the limited point of view of the
textual critic, self-justifying pursuits. However, what
should be merely the tools of scholarship have become ends
in themselves. Full appreciation of the poetry is presumed

to result from the determination of the schema of the *Divine Comedy*, or the enumeration of its Virgilian similes. Without condemning too harshly this type of pedantry, Mandelstam indicates its inadequacy:

> Здесь все вывернуто: существительное является целью, а не подлежащим фразы. (II p.413)

> В поэзии, в пластике и вообще в искусстве нет готовых вещей.
> Здесь нам мешает привычка к грамматическому мышленью – ставить понятие искусства в именительном падеже. Самый процесс творчества мы подчиняем целевому предложному падежу и мыслим так, как если бы болванчик со свинцовым сердечком, покачавшись как следует в разные стороны, претерпев различные колебания по опросному листку: о чем? о ком? кем и чем? – под конец утверждался в буддийском, гимназическом покое именительного падежа. (II p.384)

It is not so much the text *per se* with which we should be concerned as the dynamics of the text, its evolution and the movement towards its final form. It is syntax which is mis-leading us: 'Все именительные падежи следует заменить указующими направление дательными.' (II p.413). What emerges after this evolutionary process by no means represents the sum of the poet's creative effort; on the contrary, the finished work is but a lifeless relict, the sum only of the paper and ink of which it consists. Only in its performance can it be brought back to life:

> Поэтическая материя не имеет голоса. Она не пишет красками и не изъясняется словами. Она не имеет формы точно так же, как лишена содержания, по той простой причине, что она существует лишь в исполнении. Готовая вещь есть не что иное, как каллиграфический продукт, неизбежно остающийся в результате исполнительского порыва. Если перо обмакивается в чернильницу, то ставшая, остановленная вещь есть не что иное, как буквенница, вполне соизмеримая с чернильницей. (II pp.412-3)

Informed by its original creative process, as this is re-enacted, the dead opus is transmuted into living poetic material:

> Вообразите нечто понятое, схваченное, вырванное из мрака, на языке, добровольно и охотно забытом тотчас после того,

как совершился проясняющий акт понимания-исполнения...
В поэзии важно только исполняющее понимание - отнюдь не
пассивное, воспроизводящее и не пересказывающее. Семант-
ическая удовлетворенность равна чувству исполненного
приказа.   (II p.364)

Access to the mind of the poet, which is of such supreme
importance, is greatly facilitated in the presence of any of
three supplementary sources - marginalia, rough drafts and
articles. Their absence can lead to the sort of misinterpret-
ation to which Dante has always been subject:

Уже который век о Данте пишут и говорят так, как будто
он изъяснялся непосредственно на гербовой бумаге.
Лаборатория Данте? Нас это не касается! Какое до нее
дело невежественному пиетету? Рассуждают так, как если
бы Дант имел перед глазами еще до начала работы соверш-
енно готовое целое и занимался техникой муляжа...
                                         (II pp.383-4)

Any medium in which the thoughts of the poet at work are
recorded is necessarily invaluable and should be preserved at
all costs. The preservation of something of such moment takes
on the form of an ineluctable physical law: 'Итак, сохранность
черновика - закон сохранения энергетики произведения.' (II p.
385). Given the existence of drafts or articles, plus the use
of imagination or intuition, an immensely more rewarding
approach to the work becomes possible.

Abandoning the limitations of nominalism - that is, an
exclusive concern with the end product - the reader is now
able to advance from a 'dative', directional angle. The idea
consequent on this approach - 'порывообразование' - is central
not only to the study of Dante but also to Mandelstam himself
and his poetry.

He explains the sense of the word 'порыв': it is both
the general principle behind the poetry and at the same time
the impetus which drives it on. In other words, the key lies
in the motivation, literal and figurative, of a literary
work. These impulses are both the cause of the 'narrative'
and its driving force, responsible for its inception as for

its perpetuation. In terms of physics they generate kinetic
energy - the exact opposite of the stasis which the finished
text represents. By way of illustration, the rough draft of
Разговор о Данте cites the relationship of Florence to the
writing of the *Inferno*:

> Inferno - высший предел урбанистических мечтаний средне-
> векового человека. Это в полном смысле слова мировой
> город. Что перед ним маленькая Флоренция с ее 'bella
> cittadinanza' поставленной на голову новыми порядками,
> ненавистными Данту. Если на место inferno мы выдвинем
> Рим, то получится не такая уж большая разница. Таким
> образом, пропорция Рим-Флоренция могла служить порыво-
> образующим толчком, в результате которого появился
> 'Inferno'.   (III p.190)

Everything proceeds from Dante's concept of his mother
city as the centre of the action: her history, her great men,
her internal politics form a magnetic field which never
relaxes its hold on her sons, even in hell, 'с ее толкотней
назойливых флорнетийских душ, требующих - во-первых, сплетен,
во-вторых, заступничетсва, и в-третьих, снова сплетен...'
(II p.412):

> Городолюбие, городострастие, городоненавистничество -
> вот материя inferno... Мне хочется сказать, что inferno
> окружен Флоренцией.   (II p.402)

The narrative circles round within this orbit, as in the
seventeenth canto, always attracted back to its pole. This
attraction to the central point of reference is embodied in
the physical yearning of the damned:

> Нет синтаксиса - есть намагниченный порыв, тоска по
> корабельной корме, тоска по червячному корму, тоска по
> неизданному закону, тоска по Флоренции.   (II p.408)

The role of Florence as the creative focus of the work does
not preclude the independent existence of other, ancillary
impulses which figure prominently:

> Говоря о Данте, правильнее иметь в виду порывообразование
> а не формообразование - текстильные, парусные, школярские
> метеорологические, инженерийные, муниципальные, кустарно-
> ремесленные и прочие порывы, список которых можно
> продолжить до бесконечности.   (II p.413)

All engender image clusters in accordance with the law of
the transformability of poetic material. This he defines as
the ability of an image, while in full flight, to beget
another perfect and autonomous image, which in turn begets
an image no less perfect or autonomous than those which have
preceded or will follow it. This continuous act of spontane-
ous generation is far beyond all the associative processes
of modern European poetry, according to Mandelstam, since
each image is an essential and integral part of those which
surround it, not merely a stepping-stone in the pattern of
what is traditionally known as image development. The
necessarily linear nature of a train of images whose progression is easily traceable bears no comparison with Dantean
imagery:

> Надо перебежать через всю ширину реки, загроможденной
> подвижными и разноустремленными китайскими джонками, –
> так создается смысл поэтической речи. Его, как маршрут,
> нельзя восстановить при помощи опроса лодочников: они не
> расскажут, как и почему мы перепрыгивали с джонки на
> джонку.   (II pp.364-5)

External, explanatory imagery of the paraphrasable kind
favoured by scholars could hardly be more irrelevant here
since, if it is amenable to paraphrase, 'там простыни не
смяты, там поэзия, так сказать, не новевала.' (II p.364). To
relive the author's poetic experience one must undertake a
second time the inspired leaps from junk to junk, for this
is the law of reversible and convertible poetic material,
which exists only in the performing impulse. Only with such
awareness of the play of interwoven 'порывы', not least of
these the impulse towards the creation of a final form, does
the prospect of a full appreciation in Mandelstam's sense
become a significant one. Mutual relations of the contribut-
ing impulses and their relation to the text are the true
sphere of the literary scholar's research: 'изучение сопод-
чиненности порыва и текста.' (II p.413)

The Furmanov pereulok poems; the epigram on Stalin

On returning from Koktebel to Moscow the Mandelstams settled
into a new flat, this time on the old Nashchokinsky pereulok,
by then Furmanovy pereulok, close to the home of Furmanov's
family. Although Mandelstam placed the poem about Stalin
which led to his exile after his arrest, 'Мы живем, под собою
не чуя страны' (I No.286), after the other three poems of
November 1933, its composition in fact preceded theirs. The
impressions of famine and suffering under forced collectivisation and the elimination of the kulak class were still
fresh in his mind. In the towns few people realised the
extent of the brutality with which the programme was being
implemented, since they were all too preoccupied with the
dangers they were themselves facing. Mandelstam had seen the
situation in the country and then in the towns in quick
succession and finally he could restrain himself no longer.
Nadezhda Yakovlevna speaks of the first impulse in the writing of the poem as 'не могу молчать' (N.Ya.I p.165). In the
first version of the second couplet explicit reference is
made to the role of Stalin in the countryside:

> Только слышно кремлевского горца –
> Душегубца и мужикоборца.   (I p.511)

The poem itself is too well-known and frequently-quoted for
any detailed elucidation of its meaning to be necessary. Like
the other three poems (I Nos.272, 273, 274) it was intended
as an example of 'гражданские стихи' which he felt it his
duty, perhaps not unmixed with pleasure, to write. His use
of the anapaest alone would testify that Mandelstam thought
of the poem as historical documentation, a putting on record
of the miseries of his time. There are no hidden meanings,
no subtlety of nuance or complexity of imagery in the Stalin
poem. There is a brilliant, vicious caricature of the man,
his cronies and his actions. Mandelstam again has recourse
to imagery taken from the most primitive, and therefore to

him the most odious, forms of life:

> Его толстые пальцы, как черви, жирны...
> Тараканьи смеются усища   (I No.286)

As he looked at the leaders' portraits in a shop-window, he
remarked to Nadezhda Yakovlevna that he feared only the hands
in a man (N.Ya.I p.167); with hands as fat, pallid and slimy
in appearance as Stalin's such fears would be multiplied.
Around the central figure clusters a mob of half-people,
like the denizens of the forest, whose lack of physical
resemblance to real human beings is appropriate to the lack
of any trace of humanity remaining in them: 'А вокруг его
сброд тонкошеих вождей' (I No.286). 'Тонкошеий', as Nadezhda
Yakovlevna explains (N.Ya.I p.167), appealed to Kuzin by its
bizarre neuter singular ending with three 'e's, and since
Mandelstam had described Molotov's head in his portrait as
having a thin neck sticking out of his collar and making him
look like a cat, the adjective became associated with animal
rather than human life. The snivelling, whining noises made
by Stalin and his colleagues echo this subhuman quality:

> Кто свистит, кто мяучит, кто хнычет,
> Он один лишь бабачит и тычет.   (I No.286)

Stalin's actions are those of a grotesque Vulcan, whose unli-
mited power is abused without the slightest scruple:

> Как подковы кует за указом указ -
> Кому в пах, кому в лоб, кому в бровь, кому в глаз.
>   (I No.286)

Like the onomatopoeic animal noises, the sound effects here
contribute greatly to the impact: the staccato 'к', the
vindictive spitting of 'пах' and 'лоб', the brilliant use of
the anaphoric 'кому' in such a way that the whole stress in
each foot lands, like a violent blow, on its last syllable -
on those vulnerable parts of the body where the blow of each
iron 'указ' indeed falls.

Both Mandelstam and Nadezhda Yakovlevna lived in constant
expectation of such a blow:

Я не помню ничего страшнее зимы 33/34 года в новой и
единственной в моей жизни квартире. За стеной - гавайская
гитара Кирсанова, по вентиляционным трубам запахи писат-
ельских обедов и клопомора, денег нет, есть нечего, а
вечером - толпа гостей, из которых половина подослана.
(N.Ya.I p.166)

The first (in the final order) of Mandelstam's November poems
came to be written in direct response to a remark made by
Pasternak, one of the few guests who had not been sent to
them for a purpose: 'Ну, вот, теперь и квартира есть - можно
писать стихи' (N.Ya.I p.157). Nadezhda Yakovlevna writes with
some contempt of Pasternak's inability to work other than at
a desk with a sheet of paper in front of him and reiterates
Mandelstam's conviction that nothing could prevent an artist
from doing what he had to do, least of all lack of money or
an unsettled, insecure way of life. Pasternak's unfortunate
remarks spurred him to write an aggressive denunciation of
their new flat and all that the allocation of such a flat
normally implied in the way of lip-service and more tangible
signs of servility to the regime on the part of the other
writers there. In 'Квартира тиха, как бумага' (I No.272) he
firstly outlines his unenviable life as an occupant of the
wrong type, a life which consists of a permanent feeling of
silence and emptiness - 'Лягушкой застыл телефон' - so oppressive that even his belongings are begging to leave. His own
position was that of a clown or puppet, unable to escape from
his torture and forced to act out the remainder of the farce
for the sadistic delight of his torturers:

А стены проклятые тонки,
И некуда больше бежать -
А я как дурак на гребенке
Обязан кому-то играть... (I No.272)

The following stanza also merits quotation in full for its
depth of feeling, equal in anguish to the preceding one. So
seldom did Mandelstam lash out in uncontrollable fury at the
aspects of Stalinism which he had always quietly loathed,

that an outright attack such as this shocks by its very
malice and vehemence:

> Наглей комсомольской ячейки
> И вузовской песни наглей,
> Присевших на школьной скамейке
> Учить щебетать палачей.   (I No.272)

If Mandelstam could no longer depend on the integrity of the
majority of his coevals in distinguishing between good and
the evil of Stalinism, the prospect of a future in the hands
of an indoctrinated youth, with its self-righteous complac-
ency and crippled moral sense, must have sickened him. In the
expression 'пеньковые речи' all his contempt for the cant,
hypocrisy and deliberate falsification of the Stalinist state
is concentrated. When it was directed against himself he was
by now completely unmoved by it (N.Ya.I p.172), but its all-
pervasive quality, one of the main reasons for its effectiveness, angered and distressed him. In the new flat he felt its
presence especially acutely, almost as though by his residence
there he had allied himself with its apologists in the
neighbouring flats.

In the first closely related, but separate, octet he
shows the flower of the Soviet 'святой молодежи' singing
songs:

> На баюшки-баю похожи,
> И баю борьбу объяви.   (I No.274)

He imitates them sarcastically, for his own good reasons,
and sings a gruesome lullaby to the children of the disposs-
essed kulaks, lulling to sleep the collectivised landowners
at the same time:

> И я за собой примечаю
> И что-то такое пою:
> Колхозного бая качаю,
> Кулацкого пая пою.   (I No.274)

> И грозное баюшки-баю
> Кулацкому паю пою.   (I No.272)

Later he laughed at his use of the words 'бай' (a Central

Asian landowner) and 'пай', since he could never remember
which was which, but there was no difficulty in understanding what he meant in the poems. His mental image of a kolkhoz
is closely associated with the former word, perhaps because
of the connotations of stagnation and oriental despotism in
Asia. In the second octet (I No.273) this Asiatic element
recurs in the identity of the races mentioned:

> Татары, узбеки и ненцы...

> Меня на турецкий язык
> Японец какой переводит   (I No.273)

Despair at the lack of understanding in his own country
forces him to turn elsewhere in the hope of reaching the
reader who will appreciate him, but the interesting fact is
that western Europe now seemed to him like a forbidden
territory and he was resorting to races he had never before
associated with poetry or even with culture in general, but
had dismissed as eastern and therefore philistine. Yet the
whole tendency of the Russian political system was towards
oriental despotism, and it was perhaps involuntarily that
his thoughts turned in the same geographical direction.
However, this hypothetical empathy with the barbarians
'abroad' and the simulated empathy in the poems about the flat
full of the agents of barbarianism at home were short-lived.
He dropped sarcastic pretence in favour of full-blooded
denunciation by disowning and rejecting his Moscow flat and
all it stood for in the second half of 'Квартира тиха, как
бумага'. His placing of its exact address at the foot of the
poem is unique and far from accidental: Furmanov pereulok
really belonged to another sort of person, and it was to
this species of humanity that he was proposing to return it
- to the 'изобразитель' of the kolkhoz, 'Чернила и крови
смеситель', and to the honest traitor:

> Какой-нибудь честный предатель,
> Проваренный в чистках, как соль,
> Жены и детей содержатель   (I No.272)

The extent of his bitterness can be judged only in the light
of his previous use of words like 'честный' and 'соль' in
his 1921 poems about duty and conscience (I Nos.126 & 127),
where their meaning had been entirely positive, and his
longstanding hatred for the 'семьянин' of his 1923 translations of Barbier's *Iambes*. In 'La curée', which he translated
as 'Собачья склока', the recognised morality was 'закон
собачьей чести' (already a negative quality), obedience to
the law of family loyalty. The good 'семьянин' drags home to
its mate:

> Дымящуюся кость в зубах
> И крикнул:'Это власть!'- бросая мертвечину -
> 'Вот наша часть в великих днях...'   (II No.491a)

Mandelstam in any case knew perfectly well that he himself was already condemned - 'как на плахе' - but he could
still make his gesture of renunciation by walking out:

> Тебе, старику и неряхе,
> Пора сапогами стучать.   (I No.272)

Instead of his poetry, 'ключа Ипокрены', a new stream would
flow into the hated flat, as the hacks, traitors to their
art and to its principles, once theirs, moved in again:

> Давнившего страха струя
> Ворвется в халтурные стены
> Московского злого жилья.   (I No.272)

'Восьмистишия'

Mandelstam had written a whole series of eight-line poems
in November 1933, but was unwilling to have them written
down or collected together at the time, trying to convince
Nadezhda Yakovlevna that they were simply an unsuccessful
attempt at a large-scale poem. Nevertheless she gradually
noticed that he never read them to anyone (N.Ya.III). They
were first written down in January 1934 as 'Восьмистишия'
(I Nos.276, 277, 280, 281, 282, 283). In February he added
eight lines which had split off from the poems on the death

of Bely (I No.279) and immediately remembered another eight
which had remained unrecorded, dating from the 'Lamarck'
period of 1932 (I No.278). Only in Voronezh did he resurrect
the last two 'восьмистишия' which had been allowed to lapse
(I Nos.284 & 285), and it was then that he wrote the variant
version of 'Люблю появление ткани' (I No.275) which now opens
the group. Like 'Армения' it is not so much a cycle as a
'подборка'. Mandelstam never stipulated a definitive order
for the majority of the verses, but it was certainly not
intended to be a chronological one. There are definite,
authorised placings only for the first three 'восьмистишия'
(I Nos.275, 276, 280). Then follows a group comprising Nos.
277, 281, 283 and 282, but he was not absolutely certain of
their final order. The other four form two distinct pairs
(I Nos.278 & 279, Nos.284 & 285), but he was unable to decide
which pair should conclude the selection (N.Ya.III)[1].

The 'Восьмистишия' are all concerned with various aspects
of one theme - cognition, the different ways in which man
discovers and apprehends the world about him. In particular
they deal with poetic cognition and the actual composition
of poetry. It may well be that the impulse to treat this
subject was a reaction against the 'гражданские стихи'
which he was writing simultaneously in November 1933. Encirc-
led by hacks and bureaucrats masquerading as poets, he no
doubt felt, as he perceived Count Ugolino to have done in
hell (II p.397), that it was his last chance to be heard on
the subject closest to his heart. Here he defines and describes cognition as he understood it. With regard to this,
Nadezhda Yakovlevna's account of how he composed and what
each stage of composition signified for him is invaluable.
In 'Ариост' he had spoken of the noise ringing in his ears,

---

[1] Cf.Clarence Brown, 'Mandelstam's Notes towards a Supreme
Fiction', *Delos*, 1 (1968), 32-48 for a different order.

which signalled the imminent arrival of poetry - 'в ушах покуда шум'(I No.267) - and she takes up the story here:

> В какой-то момент через музыкальную фразу вдруг проступали слова и тогда начинали шевелиться губы...
> У меня создалось ощущение, что стихи существуют до того, как они сочинены... Весь процесс сочинения состоит в напряженном улавливании и проявлении уже существующего и неизвестно откуда транслирующегося гармонического и смыслового единства, постепенно воплощающегося в слова. Последний этап работы — изъятие из стихов случайных слов, которых нет в том гармоническом целом, что существует до их возникновения...
> В работе над стихами я замечала не один, а два 'выпрямительных вздоха' - один, когда появляются в строке или в строфе первые слова, второй, когда последнее точное слово изгоняет случайно внедрившихся пришельцев. (N.Ya.I pp. 74-5)

The first two 'восьмистишия' with a common first half (I Nos. 275 & 276) depict exactly this process whereby a 'выпрямительный вздох' appears in what were previously incoherent mutterings - 'в бормотаньях моих'. In the first, chronologically the second, poem it is the stanzaic outline which appears, rather than the actual words. He compares it to the sweep of sails, as the boats describe an arc when turning round in a sailing race:

> И дугами парусных гонок
> Открытые формы чертя   (I No.275)

In *Разговор о Данте* both sailing and textile impulses are examined in detail, where sailing includes the delight of flying down through the air on Geryon's back as well as Odysseus' voyaging over the ocean (II pp. 381 & 387), while the study of material is chiefly from the point of view of its colouring (II p.379). But the connection between them and poetry, once made, outlived the work in which they were first associated. In addition, the unexpected rhythm which suddenly materialises in the poet's laboured breathing echoes a phrase on exactly the same subject from a poem of over twenty years earlier:

И мгновенный ритм – только случай,
Неожиданный Аквилон?   (I No.25)

Thus through the association of breathing with the wind,
which is made again later in the selection, and hence with
sailing, a further link between breathing, sailing and poetry
is established. The general outline of the poem, before the
rhythmic line appears, is like free movement in space -
something felt by both Dante and Odysseus - which is given
an extra dimension by Mandelstam's experience in Voronezh.
In the line ' – Нет, не мигрень, но холод пространства бесполого' (I No.317), which was written at the same time as
the first 'восьмистишие' in July 1935, Mandelstam is overwhelmed by the vast, empty sky and air stretching out over
the *chernozem*, and in the new version of the earlier poem he
united his new apprehension of space with his metaphorical
description of poetic cognition:

Играет пространство спросонок –
Не знавшее люльки дитя.   (I No.275)

This somnolent, unconstricted flight through the air is as
free, playful and unselfconscious as a child; the absence of
artifice or restriction is what matters here.

The second 'восьмистишие' produces another stage in the
process, the rhythmic line - 'дуговая растяжка', as the
'ткань' of the poem is stretched into shape. The third is
devoted to the crowning moment of poetic composition, the
moment when the 'период' appears, that is, all the fundament-
als necessary for the poem in coherent form. The process is
again an auditory one. The poem can certainly still change
during the transfer to paper, but it is already a self-
sufficient architectural unit:

И он лишь на собственной тяге,
Зажмурившись, держится сам –
Он так же отнесся к бумаге,
Как купол к пустым небесам.   (I No.280)

Mandelstam is again referring back to an image whose age in

no way diminishes its truth or force for him, the Gothic
arrow of 'Утро акмеизма' (1912) piercing the heavens in a
reproach for their emptiness, in conjunction with the image
of the cupola of Hagia Sophia, 'Как на цепи подвешен к
небесам' (I No.38 [1912]). Correspondingly the cupola and
the nearly-fashioned poem reproach the paper for its emptiness – the quiet of the Mandelstams' Moscow flat had been
compared to that of paper (I No.272). The emptiness has to
be combated, filled with life and harmony by the artist,
whether architect or poet. The 'space' of the two previous
poems is the underlying reality which has to be filled with
human consciousness.

The fourth 'восьмистишие' (I No.277) gives an example of
failure in making a firm and lasting impression on the void.
Butterflies belonged in any case to the insect world and,
with it, symbolised the transience of life, a short flight,
a moment of beauty and then death. The feelings evoked in
Mandelstam by a close inspection of a butterfly, described
in 'Путешествие в Армению', were still operative three years
later:

> Длинные седые усы этой бабочки имели остистое строение и
> в точности напоминали ветки на воротнике французского
> академика или серебряные пальмы, возлагаемые на гроб.
> Грудь сильная, развитая в лодочку. Головка незначитель-
> ная, кошачья.
> Ее глазастые крылья были из прекрасного старого, адмир-
> альского шелка...
> И вдруг я поймал себя на диком желании взглянуть на
> природу нарисованными глазами этого чудовища. (II p.164)

Decay and death are still the vital characteristics in 'О,
бабочка, о, мусульманка' (I No.277), where he remembers this
experience. The butterfly is Moslem not so much because of
its gaudy attire but because of the lack of movement and the
lifelessness Mandelstam associated with Islam and the orient,
the inertia of the grave:

> В разрезанном саване вся –
> Жизняночка и умиранка,

Такая большая, сия!   (I No.277)

Its wings, slit in the middle by the body, reminded him of a
shroud, and in comparison with them the size of the body, 'с
большими усами', seemed gross and offended him by its size.
Overriding the distaste, however, was the fear of death which
was the negation of all creative work, the undoing of all
human achievement:

О, флагом развернутый саван, –
Сложи свои крылья – боюсь!   (I No.277)

Within this group of four 'восьмистишия' the most closely
related to the butterfly one is the seventh in the present
order, 'И клена зубчатая лапа' (I No.282). Their obvious
common factor is the butterfly, but on a deeper level the
link lies in the theme of cognition. Mandelstam had felt a
curious desire to see the world through the 'painted' eyes
on the butterfly's wings: another method of apprehension,
another viewpoint. While looking at the pattern of etched
maple leaves and speculating as to whether something similar
might be achieved by using butterflies' wings against a wall,
it occurred to him that this would at least be a living
temple rather than a dead insect - again it is the Islamic
'мечети' as opposed to Hagia Sophia which come to mind:

Бывают мечети живые,
И я догадался сейчас:
Быть может, мы – Айя-София
С бесчисленным множеством глаз.   (I No.282)

Through the idea of temples and monuments to humanity,
through the cupola of the third poem he returns to Hagia
Sophia. The key word is of course 'живые'; in the eponymous
1912 poem Mandelstam had seen the cathedral as a living
thing and its windows - 'сорок окон – света торжество' (I No.
38) - as eyes through which the world can be discovered, in
the same way as through the 'eyes' of a butterfly wing. The
subject, however, is no longer the poet alone but 'мы', no
longer individual but collective. These 'eyes' of Hagia

Sophia represent the innumerable millions of human eyes,
their common weapon being cognition: 'Глаз как орудие мысли'
(III p.170) is but one instance of the many occasions on
which Mandelstam emphasised this function of the eye. In
relating individual to communal experience he reiterates
another of his firmest principles, namely that the artist
should not be aloof and isolated in the sense of his own
superiority, but one of the crowd, drawing his material from
the crowd and from his interaction with it. In the fifth
'восьмистишие' he states this unequivocally:

> И Шуберт на воде, и Моцарт в птичьем гаме,
> И Гете, свищущий на вьющейся тропе,
> И Гамлет, мысливший пугливыми шагами,
> Считали пульс толпы и верили толпе.   (I No.281)

He considers that none of these - the poet, the thinker, the
composers - would have achieved what they did had they
divorced themselves from everyday life and human concerns.
As Nadezhda Yakovlevna suggests, poetry is all around the
poet and exists before its moment of apparent creation:

> Быть может, прежде губ уже родился шопот
> И в бездревесности кружилися листы,
> И те, кому мы посвящаем опыт,
> До опыта приобрели черты.   (I No.281)

The poet's task is to employ his more acute awareness in
ordering the 'шопот', the same noise as he heard in his ears
in 'Ариост'. Schubert, Mozart and Goethe apprehended and
understood the noise of water, birdsong, whistling sounds
and twisting movements, Hamlet the rhythm of his steps - like
the gait of Dante (II p.367) - and each knew how to create
from the noise and movement about him. Even those less
illustrious, the potential audience for Mandelstam's 'опыт',
will have had previous experience of some part of it by their
participation in everyday noise and movement. In the sixth
'восьмистишие' (I No.283), where he addresses the wind as a
fellow-artist, 'чертежник' was perhaps the phonetic predecessor of 'черты', and the idea of leaves of paper (a play

on words) turning in the wind when there was no tree from which they could have fallen represents a further development of the wind's scope of action.

The value of 'чертежник', as of 'геометр', lies in the connotations of precision and craftsmanship on which Mandelstam insisted that every artist should pride himself. The wind carefully outlines the shifting (in a variant, Arabian) sands of the desert into crescent-shaped dunes, in order to combat the formlessness of the open space, the 'пустыня'. He questions the wind as to whether the instability of these geometrically exact shapes which it has moulded out of sand, the 'безудержность линий', is not stronger than the force of the wind keeping them in place. The wind, in its self-confident reply, dismisses with contempt such a trivial and obvious enquiry:

> — Меня не касается трепет
> Его иудейских забот —
> Он опыт из лепета лепит
> И лепет из опыта пьет.   (I No.283)

The Jewish poet is made to sound querulous and pernickety; the scale of their work differs. The wind sweeps freely without let or hindrance over limitless space, whereas Mandelstam's work appears minute and limited in comparison. But the wind has no quarrel with the poet's work, the synthesising of senseless noises into the final 'опыт', the enjoyment in drinking in these sounds once marshalled into order. Only in the phonetics does the sense of the poet's work emerge as charming child's play, compared with the wind's grandiose gestures.

This downward progression from the wind to the poet is continued in the 'Lamarck' period poem (I No.278), which forms a pair with that of the 'Bely' period (I No.279). Mandelstam does not exclude the possibility that the lowest forms of life may have their own specific approach to cognition, a pitiful sixth sense unknown by man, but quite adequate for their own requirements of cognition and communication:

Шестого чувства крохотный придаток
Иль ящерицы теменной глазок,
Монастыри улиток и створчаток,
Мерцающих ресничек говорок. (I No.278)

Dissatisfied by the possibility of such a phenomenon which he is incapable of comprehending - 'Ни развязать нельзя, ни посмотреть' - he compares it to a letter for which an immediate answer is expected. The letter is hastily and insufficiently scanned, not properly analysed, and no satisfactory account of it can be given. In total opposition to this is human understanding as expounded in the 'Bely' poem, where the 'голуботвердый глаз' (I No.279) - an obvious relation of the 'голубые глаза' of No.288 and the 'голуботвердой...рекой' of No.289 - is primarily that of man in general in his capacity of observer, rather than of Bely or other poets as a separate group. Having mechanically learnt off the dry facts about nature, the possessor of an observant eye can conquer this disadvantage and penetrate into the very laws of its existence:

В земной коре юродствуют породы,
И как руда из груди рвется стон. (I No.279)

Inanimate nature, apparently still and silent on the surface, is making an agonised effort to break out of its confinement into the articulate world, thus producing the tension and conflict necessary for any advance, even of the despised evolutionary sort. Like a deformed foetus it turns in on itself in its desperate attempt to escape into a life of full human consciousness:

Понять пространства внутренний избыток
И лепестка и купола залог. (I No.279)

The perfect form of a petal or a cupola are familiar images of artistic perfection such as the rocks like a misshapen foetus who 'юродствуют', tearing out ore from beneath the earth's crust, are trying frantically to attain.

In the final pair of 'восьмистишия' deceptive causality,
the 'наважденье причин' of the tenth poem (I No.284), is the
object of a fierce attack. Causality is said here to be drunk
in 'игольчатых, чумных бокалах' because it is only a small
part of the whole, one aspect of cognition which is taken
wrongly by man for the complete answer and thus taints all
his thinking. Cognition is conveyed in a new metaphor, the
game of spillikins. Man has chanced to hook out of the pile
of spillikins only 'small magnitudes', a limited capacity
for thinking in mathematical powers, and the summit of his
imaginative endeavour in explaining his environment is
conformity with the laws of cause and inevitable effect.
This is what Mandelstam had been railing against not only
earlier in the selection but in his anti-determinism in
respect of evolutionary theory, in his tirade against the
mechanical action of frames on the cinema screen, in his
polemic against the soulless progress of the hand around the
clock face. This one spillikin, causality, has been hooked
out of a whole heap which, when coupled together, defy any
such breaking down into artificial and distorted component
parts:

> И там, где сцепились бирюльки,
> Ребенок молчанье хранит   (I No.284)

The child wisely keeps his counsel and makes no effort to
explain what he alone has understood. In the first poem of
the group, written two years later, the child and the open
space merge into one; but here it is the entire universe
which has taken on child-like characteristics:

> Большая вселенная в люльке
> У маленькой вечности спит.   (I No.284)

When Mandelstam announces, in the eleventh and last
'восьмистишие', his intention of leaving the spatial world,
it is not by abandoning the world of 'опыт' but by trying to

achieve those mathematical leaps into greater magnitudes,
that is into eternity, which will make causality irrelevant
and inapplicable:

> И я выхожу из пространства
> В запущенный сад величин,
> И мнимое рву постоянство
> И самосознанье причин.   (I No.285)

He does this by tearing to bits the illusion under which the
temporal and spatial world labours, to wit the certainty of
constant laws of cause and effect. It is a flight of poetic
cognition into the most fundamental and, as the imagery -
'сад' 'лечебник' 'корней' - shows, natural element, from
which he learns the undistorted truth and is healed from
deception:

> Безлиственный, дикий лечебник, -
> Задачник огромных корней.   (I No.285)

Eternity is the setter of problems like the discovery of
mathematical roots: conversely, the roots are the foundation
of the tree of eternity. The man adept in poetic cognition
is able to master the process of taking imaginative leaps
of a purely mathematical quality, ending in eternity.

The four Petrarchan sonnets

'Восьмистишия' was written mainly during November 1933 and
January 1934. In December 1933 and early January 1934 Mandelstam was translating the cycle of four Petrarchan sonnets
(I Nos.487-90) which he intended as poems in their own right
and not as the usual type of translation written for the sake
of expediency. 'Or che 'l ciel et la terra e 'l vento tace'
('Когда уснет земля и жар отпышет', I No.489) is No.CLXIV in
the first half of Petrarch's *Canzoniere*, 'In vita di Madonna
Laura', while the other three, 'Valle che de'lamenti miei se'
piena', No.CCCI ('Река, разбухшая от слез соленых' [in the
manuscript 'распухшая' although Mandelstam actually read
'разбухшая'], I No.488), 'Quel rosignuol, che si soave piagne'

No.CCCXI ('Как соловей, сиротствующий, славит', I No.487),
'I di miei piu leggier' che nesun cervo', No.CCCXIX ('Промчались дни мои — как бы оленей', I No.490), are taken from
the second half, 'In morte di Madonna Laura'. In her splendid
article on these sonnets and Mandelstam's translation of
them,[1] to which nothing of value can be added here, I.M.
Semenko describes the changes through which the work passed,
summarised briefly in the following paragraph.

In *Разговор о Данте* Mandelstam had fought hardest against
the 'academic' image of Dante as producer of allegory, theology and symbolism. When he came to translate Petrarch he no
doubt felt the desirability of doing away with the cool,
sophisticated figure to which traditional scholarship had
reduced the poet. In his versions of Petrarch's work he
strengthened the emotional force and removed a great deal of
the 'dolce' element. Another source of change lay in Mandelstam's dislike of concentration on self, particularly when,
as in the case of Petrarch, this was a divided self, torn
between love of life and hatred of life. There is considerably less of self-examination and soul-searching in his
Petrarch; for example, in 'Valle che de'lamenti miei se'
piena' Petrarch is partially consoled for the death of Laura
by her becoming immortal, but still mourns the loss of her
beauty and some part of the earth's beauty which was bound
up in it and was thus also mourned by nature. Mandelstam
concentrates on the beauty of the earth rather than on the
feeling of loss.

Yet it is the feeling of loss which links these translations with the cycle of poems which Mandelstam wrote immediately afterwards about the death of Bely and which he called
a 'requiem to Bely and to myself' (N.Ya.III). There are

---

[1] И.М.Семенко, 'Мандельштам — переводчик Петрарки',
Вопросы литературы, 10 (1970), 153-69.

external links: in 'Голубые глаза и горящая лобная кость'
(I No.288) an echo of 'Промчались дни мои, как бы оленей'
(I No.490) can be discovered, since I.M.Semenko has deciph-
ered the line 'И, клянусь, от тебя в каждой косточке весточка
есть' in one of the rough drafts to it.[1] In the opposite
direction, the first half of a line in the variant version of
its second stanza, which reads 'Печаль жирна и умиранье
наго' (I No.491), found its way into the poem to Bely '10
января 1934' (I No.289) as 'печаль моя жирна', both lines
deriving directly from the *Слово о полку Игореве*: 'Печаль
жирна тече средь земли Руской', with perhaps a diversion via
Pushkin's famous 'печаль моя светла'. But the connection
between the two poems is basically an inner one, the feeling
of a life lost beyond recall and the disintegration of the
physical body in death:

> Промчались дни мои, как бы оленей
> Косящий бег. Срок счастья был короче,
> Чем взмах ресницы. Из последней мочи
> Я в горсть зажал лишь пепел наслаждений...
>
> Ночует сердце в склепе темной ночи,
> К земле бескостной жмется   (I No.490)

In the last poem of the Petrarch group, 'Как из одной высокогорной щели' (I No.287), which Mandelstam thought the most
important, he took the last two tercets of 'Когда уснет земля
и жар отпышет' (I No.489) and altered their meaning completely while preserving their imagery. Petrarch had likened his
beloved Laura, tormenting in her physical closeness to him
(this sonnet is concerned with her in life), to the water of
a mountain spring, beautiful yet severe and intentionally
unattainable:

> Хоть ключ один — вода разноречива —
> Полужестка, полусладка... Ужели
> Одна и та же милая двулична?   (I No.489)

---

[1] Семенко, *Вопросы литературы*, 10 (1970), 167.

The miracle for Petrarch is that, although he should die
from this torture a thousand times a day, 'воскресаю так же
сверхобычно'. In 'Как из одной высокогорной щели' (I No.287)
Mandelstam uses Petrarch's simile for Laura to describe
poetry in his first tercet; but the second is radically
different:

> Так, чтобы умереть на самом деле,
> Тысячу раз на дню лишусь обычной
> Свободы вздоха и сознанья цели.   (I No.287)

No possibility of resurrection is envisaged here; for him
and his poetry to die only his freedom to breathe the poetry-
laden air and his sense of purpose need to be eliminated. He
does this to himself in the consciousness that death is
liable to strike him down at any moment. This was not a
passing mood, but that of the whole winter and, to a great
extent, that of the whole *Тетрадь*. A variant version of its
very first poem, 'Там, где купальни-бумагопрядильни' (I No.
252) included the line 'Сам себя по улицам за руку водил',
paraphrasing a remark made to him by Markish at a *vecher* of
Mandelstam's in winter 1932-3, 'Вы сами себя берете за руку
и ведете на казнь' (N.Ya.I p.165). Anna Akhmatova confirms
this:

> Несмотря на то, что время было сравнительно вегетариан-
> ское, тень неблагополучия и обреченности лежала на этом
> доме... (Февраль 1934 г.) ... Осип сказал: 'Я к смерти
> готов'.[1]

The requiem to Bely

It was not only the shadow of doom hanging over the Moscow
flat but more especially the death of Andrei Bely, who had
been, in the absence of Akhmatova, the closest of his poet
friends in 1933, which convinced Mandelstam that his turn
was soon to come. The requiem to Bely was finished only in

---

[1] Ахматова, vol. 2, p.179.

Voronezh, being reconstructed around a selection which
included the first two poems, 'Голубые глаза и горящая лобная
кость' (I No.288) and '10 января 1934' (I No.289), and
entitled, even in 1933, 'мой реквием'. Another, more oblique,
indication of their relevance to himself lies in their
similarity to his translation of a passage from 'La vie de
Saint Alexis' of 1922; the resemblance lies chiefly in the
theme, but with distinct verbal echoes in addition:

> О, как жалко мне твоей юности благородной –
> Что она теперь гниет в земле сырой и холодной!
> О, нежный рот! Лицо, походка и улыбка!
> Что сталось, что стряслось с вашей прелестью гибкой?
>
> (I No.462)

In 1922 these lines had seemed prophetic to Mandelstam in
respect of his own fate. Bely's death made him visualise the
possibility that he would be thrown unceremoniously into a
hole in the ground, with none of the last respects or funeral
rites then being accorded to Bely. He therefore treated the
poems in memory of him as a substitute for the requiem he
himself could never hope to be given.

'Голубые глаза и горящая лобная кость' (I No.288) was
written, according to Ehrenburg (I p.514), the day after
Bely's death and is concerned with the man himself. Nadezhda
Yakovlevna describes the electrifying effect which Bely's
presence produced on those with whom he came into contact
and his ability to arouse new and exciting ideas in them
(N.Ya.I pp.162-3). A recognised *maître* in the poetic world,
an original thinker among the Symbolists, he was treated by
the new authorities as an eccentric and was as restless
and unhappy as Mandelstam:

> На тебе надевали тиару – юрода колпак,
> Бирюзовый учитель, мучитель, властитель, дурак.
>
> (I No.288)

In the notes to the Soviet edition the origin of the phrase
'юрода колпак' is given as the final poem in Bely's cycle of
1903, 'Вечный зов':

Полный радостных мук,
утихает дурак.
Тихо падает на пол из рук
сумасшедший колпак. (S p.297)

At the end of his life Bely was depressed and finally broken
not only by the repeated arrests and deportations of his wife
and friends but also by the knowledge that thought of any
type was no longer free to develop naturally, but would be
controlled and channelled in predetermined directions. This
became clear to him only in Kamenev's preface to his book on
Gogol (N.Ya.I p.163). Mandelstam's play on words, 'Не Гоголь,
так себе, писатель... гоголек' (I No.294), is based partly
on this, partly on the fact that Vyacheslav Ivanov used to
call Bely a 'гоголек' (S p.297). More seriously, one of the
rough drafts for the selection opposes the flowing 'лазурь'
(the azure of 'Ариост') to 'official' literature, whose
practitioners he calls by the unambiguous name of fratricide:

Из горячего черепа льется и льется лазурь,
И тревожит она литератора-каина хмурь. (S p.297)

Bely's brilliance and lightness emerge very clearly in Mandelstam's account of him, with his sparkling, bird-like,
youthful, active mind, reflected in his manner and in his
movements: 'бирюзовый' 'как снежок' 'легок' 'птенец'
'бубенец' 'щегленок'. Mandelstam even reproduces the way in
which Bely had once used a sequence of nouns to characterise
himself, 'Я - ребенок, отрок, студент, писатель, мировоз-
зритель', in his line 'Сочинитель, щегленок, студентик,
студент, бубенец' (I No.288) (Cf.S p.297). In this poem and
in '10 января 1934' (I No.289) he sees Bely as the human
incarnation of one of his most constant symbols - the dragonflies of death:

О Боже, как черны и синеглазы
Стрекозы смерти, как лазурь черна! (I No.289)

The brilliant insect, with its dark-blue eyes, lives for a
fleeting day before the blackness of night closes in on it,

as on the azure sky, turning it to dark blue as blackness -
the darkness of death - begins to cover the heavens. All
shades of the colour blue meet in Bely, from the azure of
sky, sea and poetry through turquoise (a favourite epithet
of his) to dark blue, merging into black. In another series
of metaphors flame and iron meet ice and frost:

> У конькобежца в пламень голубой -
> Железный пух в морозной крутят тяге,
> С голуботвердой чокаясь рекой   (I No.289)

The pale-blue flame and the ice-hard river over which Bely
seems to pass with a skater's speed and dexterity convey to
perfection Nadezhda Yakovelvna's impression of Bely as a
cold, penetrating and at the same time fiery intelligence.
The loss of this mind and spirit and of their fusion in his
poetry cause Mandelstam to mourn his friend and value what
united them:

> Где прямизна речей,
> Запутанных, как честные зигзаги?   (I No.289)

> Прямизна нашей речи не только пугач для детей:
> Не бумажные дести, а вести спасают людей.
>   (I No.288 amended N.Ya.III)

Even if systematic lying and deceit were the order of the day
the honesty and directness - not necessarily a question of
simplicity, rather one of complexity - of what Bely and his
like had to say could not be dismissed as the roaring of
paper tigers. Speech is again contrasted with the written
word, to the detriment of the latter, which is indeed a form
of death in comparison with the sound of the living language.
This predictable opposition reflects a more general one
between the living body and the lifeless corpse, brought home
forcibly to Mandelstam at the funeral. Around Bely's coffin
all was life and bustle, affecting even the mourners' fur
coats:

> Дышали шуб меха. Плечо к плечу теснилось,
> Кипела киноварь здоровья - кровь и пот   (I No.289)

By contrast with this intense physical awareness of their

rude health and activity, the figure for whom the funeral
violins were weeping lay silent and inert:

> И вдруг открылась музыка в засаде..
> Лиясь для мышц и бьющихся висков,
>
> Лиясь для ласковой, только что снятой маски,
> Для пальцев гипсовых, не держащих пера,
> Для укрупненных губ, для укрепленной ласки
> Крупнозернистого покоя и добра.   (I No.289)

The music lamented the stilling of motion in Bely's muscles,
heart and lips with the sympathy felt by both the creators
of music and poetry, for only a fellow poet, a 'собиратель
пространства' (I No.288), could truly appreciate the role
of what Mandelstam called 'divine physiology' in creative
composition; only he would have the sense of a double loss
in death. In the midst of the overwhelming grief he still
needed to define Bely's intellectual and poetic stature in
life, commensurate with the grand scale attributed to him
here in retrospect:

> Ему кавказские кричали горы
> И нежных Альп стесненная толпа   (I No.292)

Bely's position in the world of culture, or what remained of
it, was at least equal to that of those who influenced him,
the German idealistic philosophers and their Russian success-
ors among the 'mystical' thinkers. The allusion to Solovev's
works in Mandelstam's line 'Толпы умов, событий, впечатлений'
(I No.293) (N.Ya.I p.248) indicates Bely's place in the
succession:

> И мудрецов германских голоса,
> И русских первенцев блистательные споры   (I No.289)

The second *Тетрадь* of Moscow poems closes with Mandelstam's
delightful love poem to Maria Sergeevna Petrovykh, 'Мастерица
виноватых взоров' (I No.295), which is justly well-known and
too transparent to need any comment; its charm and simplicity
are so far removed from the subject and tone of those preceding it that its impact is strengthened by the contrast.

It is certainly among the most beautiful of Mandelstam's
poems and possibly among the great love poems of the world.

The manuscript of another poem which might have taken
the final place in the collection disappeared in the search
following Mandelstam's arrest. It was written in March 1934
and only these lines remain out of the original twenty:

В оцинкованном влажном Батуме,
По холерным базарам Ростова,
И в фисташковом хитром Тифлисе...

Над Курою в ущелье балконном
Шили платье у тихой портнихи.   (N.Ya.III)

These lines arose from memories of his frantic journeying
in the South of Russia after the Revolution, when they were
on the return trip to Moscow with all its adventures and
upsets. The last two lines refer to some material which
Mandelstam 'earned' by a lecture he gave on Blok in Batum and
which was being sewn into a suit for him and two dresses for
Nadezhda Yakovlevna (N.Ya.II p.87). In Voronezh he wanted to
finish the poem under the tentative title 'Наши ночлеги',
but circumstances did not allow this.

However, from this fragment it is evident that Mandelstam's southern journey in 1933 had affected him more deeply
than might have been thought. The memories of it which still
haunted him might explain why he persisted in reading his
epigram on Stalin to his guests, frightening many and earning
the disapproval of all who heard this, including the more
fearless such as Pasternak and Ehrenburg (N.Ya.I pp.165-70).
The circumstances of Mandelstam's arrest and deportation as
a result of this epigram are recounted in minute detail by
Nadezhda Yakovlevna (N.Ya.I, pp.7-107). But the steps leading
to his arrest had been taken considerably earlier, as far
back as 1930 and 'Четвертая проза', when he had taken a
conscious decision to stand up for what he thought worth
defending and to admit no compromise, although even then the
consequences were perfectly clear to him.

3. *НОВЫЕ СТИХИ:*
ПЕРВАЯ ВОРОНЕЖСКАЯ ТЕТРАДЬ
April - July 1935

After nearly a year of silence - 'после удушья' as Mandelstam
himself described his arrest and exile in 'Стансы' (I No.312)
- the poems he produced in spring 1935 astound the reader by
their energy and their joy in life. The first *Тетрадь* written
in Voronezh was begun in early April and embodies four main
cycles of poems, in which Mandelstam came to terms with life
in exile, although never unmindful of the prospect of death.

The opening poem
The opening poem stands on its own, isolated in theme as in
mood,with no link between it and the cycle which succeeds it.
Work on 'Твоим узким плечам' (I No.296) had already started
in summer 1934 and the poem was finished in the early spring
of 1935. During this summer of 1934 Nadezhda Yakovlevna
contracted typhus and then dysentery (N.Ya.I p.130) and had
to spend two periods in an isolation hospital. Mandelstam
was terrified for her and had so firmly convinced himself
that she was dying that he insisted on her coming to stand at
the hospital window to reassure him, gravely ill though she
was (N.Ya.III). As is obvious from his letters (e.g.Letter
No.71, III p.277) physical separation from her actually
brought on his own illness, but while she was alive nothing
could really frighten him. The possibility of her outliving
him seems not to have occurred to him; on the contrary, it
was the prospect of her illness and death which tormented
him above all else. He never doubted the prophetic quality
of his poetry, and for this reason was mortally afraid of the

poem 'Твоим узким плечам' inasmuch as her death is foreseen
in it. He never showed it to her and she knew only odd lines
from it until N.I.Khardzhiev, the editor of the Soviet edition, found the text in letters of Sergei Borisovich Rudakov
to his (Rudakov's) wife (Cf.N.Ya.I pp.290-2). Indications
that it was the fate of Nadezhda Yakovlevna to which the poem
relates abound. For instance, poems addressed to her were
frequently portraits:

> Куда как страшно нам с тобой,
> Товарищ большеротый мой!   (I No.202)

> И холодком повеяло высоким
> От выпукло-девического лба   (I No.105)

Mandelstam was given to teasing her about the largeness of
her mouth and her broad forehead. However, adjectives applied
to her usually reflect the quality of Mandelstam's love for
her rather than an objective observer's description of her
physical features. While it can be argued that 'Твоим узким
плечам' could refer to many of the women with whom he was
associated during his life, like Maria Sergeevna Petrovykh
- the 'Маленьких держательница плеч' of I No.295, conclusive
evidence of the intended addressee's identity is given in
the emotional content of the epithets in 'детским рукам' and
'нежным ногам'. Countless examples of the way in which Mandelstam habitually wrote to her as would a nanny to a small
child can be found:

> Не плачь, ребенок мой, не плачь дочурка.
>   (Letter No.19, III p.213)

> Надик, доченька моя, здравствуй, младшенький! Няня с
> тобой говорит.   (Letter No.25, III p.222)

This fiercely protective love of Mandelstam for his wife and
his idea of her as a delicate, helpless child were frequently
expressed in the endearment 'нежный'. In 'Европа' (I No.128),
the poem about her written after their marriage, he speaks of
the 'нежные руки Европы' and the epithet recurs throughout
his letters to her: 'Родная моя нежняночка!' (Letter No.14,

III p.206) or 'Пташенька, беляночка нежная' (Letter No.16,
III p.210). Practical details from their life together confirm
that it was she who inspired this lament. Ironing was one of
her least favourite occupations, yet in an unpublished letter
to Benedikt Livshits Mandelstam wrote, asking for money or
linen, that his wife was especially skilful at ironing shirts
(N.Ya.III); a far cry from the luxury of his express laundry
days as depicted in *Египетская марка* (II p.16). In the same
line another activity with which she was particularly associated is mentioned: 'Утюги поднимать да веревки вязать', her
basket-weaving made necessary by their peripatetic life.
Another internal clue lies in the metre, whose four anapaests
are identical with the metre of the triptych 'Кама' (I Nos.
308-10), also written in couplets, in which the memory of
their journey to Cherdyn and exile is evoked. The last
couplet of the first of these poems is most significant:

И со мною жена – пять ночей не спала,
Пять ночей не спала – трех конвойных везла.   (I No.308)

Since Mandelstam's illness prevented him from taking part in
any strenuous activity it fell to Nadezhda Yakovlevna to
cope with their luggage, consisting of these battered
'корзинки',although on this occasion their escorts did assist
her - 'трех конвойных везла'. Looking at the journey, whose
horrors she had fully shared, in retrospect, Mandelstam saw
in it a portent of her fate whose details he had already
begun to imagine in the previous year. He attached such
importance to 'Твоим узким плечам' that he insisted on its
being placed at the very beginning of the first Voronezh
Тетрадь (N.Ya.III). It serves both as an epigraph to the
collection and as a premonition of the Terror to come.

    The poem's imagery is horrific in its harshness and
violence and in this respect it is outstanding, almost unique
in his work. Cruelty is everywhere - in the scourging whips,
the heavy irons and biting frosts. With his acute awareness

of the physical senses Mandelstam must have found this
contemplation of his delicate wife being subjected to torture
'под бичами' agonising. Stark images of sheet ice and cold
metal vie with their exact opposites in temperature, the
bloody sand and the burning redness of beaten, exposed
shoulders, in frightfulness. The picture presented is of a
sort of hell on earth; indeed, in the phrase 'По стеклу
босиком да кровавым песком' Mandelstam may have had in mind
Dante's seventh circle of Hell, consisting of a plain of dry,
burning sand traversed by a streamlet of blood, and even the
eternal ice of the lowest depths. Perhaps the most terrible
is the last couplet:

Ну а мне за тебя черной свечкой гореть,
Черной свечкой гореть да молиться не сметь.   (I No.296)

Repetition of the infinitive - 'краснеть' 'гореть' 'поднимать'
'вязать' - produces an atmosphere of despairing fatalism,
with even a certain imperative quality, as though Mandelstam
wished the whole experience to have taken place rather than
living in expectation of it, inevitable as it seemed. The
word 'гореть' with its *double entendre* - 'rope' also sounds
in it - epitomises his agony in its mingling of sorrow with
ritual mourning. Like the black sun of his poetry in the
tragic revolutionary years, the black candle is the negation
of hope and serenity, such as the burning of candles in
memory of the dead would normally signify. The poet himself
burns with love, grief and anguish, yet does not dare to
utter a prayer which would in any case be futile; here his
faith has deserted him completely.

This utter misery was exacerbated, if not partially
caused, by his failure to produce a single line of poetry
since the day of his arrest. With the two most important
elements in his life, his poetry and his wife, 'suppressed',
at least in his imagination, there remained nothing in life
for him. At this time he had been making several fruitless

attempts to fulfil the social decrees laid down by the
official arbiters of literature, and produced poems all of
which he classified as 'собачья чушь'. Although he sent these
efforts to the Writers' Union and to Fadeev, he emphatically
wished them to be destroyed, and his wishes have been
respected (N.Ya.III).

The 'Чернозем' cycle

After so apocalyptic an opening the first Voronezh *Тетрадь*
is suddenly transformed into a joyful hymn to the new earth
emerging with the thaw. The arrival of spring to the Voronezh
steppe excited a spirit of defiance in Mandelstam. It provided the impulse for the 'Чернозем' cycle of April-May 1935,
in which the poet affirms his faith both in himself and in
his poetic voice.

In this cycle the master poem, round which all the rest
are grouped, is the eponymous 'Чернозем' (I No.299). Not only
do all the poems share a common theme, but the phonetic
composition of each one has close links with the key poem,
from which its originates, and with others in the cycle.
Whole lines are identical or near-identical:

> Как на лемех приятен жирный пласт,
> Как степь молчит в апрельском провороте
>
> (I Nos.299 & 305)

None the less it is rather the recurrence of certain syllables which demonstrates the interdependence of formally
separate poems. The 'вор' of 'Воронеж' is one of these:
'Пусти меня, отдай меня, Воронеж' (I No.301) is the opening
line of a haunting quatrain in which Mandelstam's obsessive
play with the component parts of the word is at its most
inspired, as in 'Уронишь ты меня иль проворонишь'. The last
word shares its 'вор' element, suggesting the theft of all
he valued by the town, with 'проворот' in 'Чернозем': 'Как
степь молчит в апрельском провороте' (I No.299). The parallel

ideas of upheaval - in the case of the black earth by the
plough, in his own case by exile in Voronezh - become
inseparable. Throughout the whole cycle (I Nos.299-307)
echoes of 'Воронеж' and 'Чернозем' can be detected:

 Комочки влажные моей земли и воли!   (I No.299)

 И в полночь с Красной площади гудочки   (I No.300)

The words 'комочки' and 'гудочки' have the same close relationship. In the poem 'Наушники, наушнички мои' (I No.300) the
line 'Не спрашивай, как набухают почки' appeared at first as
a result of 'почки' being used to rhyme with 'комочки' from
'Чернозем' (N.Ya.I p.204). When 'комочки' shifted back to
the beginning of the line - 'Комочки влажные...' - a whole
new poem was already growing up around another line:
'...воронежские ночки: ...сжатого до точки', as image begat
image. Red Square, mentioned incidentally in this poem - 'И
в полночь с Красной площади гудочки' - is expanded to form
the basis of the school-child's geography lessons in the poem
'Да, я лежу в земле, губами шевеля' (I No.306): 'На Красной
площади всего круглей земля'. In the same way, Mandelstam's
understanding of his own death, first mooted in this collection in 'Я живу на важных огородах' (I No.304): 'И своя-то
жизнь мне не близка', is confirmed by repetition in more
categoric terms in the next poem, 'Я должен жить, хотя я
дважды умер' (I No.305). The subjects of his own death and
burial supply the next link in the cycle: 'Да, я лежу в
земле, губами шевеля' (I No.306). And the 'шевелящиеся губы',
the symbol of poetry which was his foremost weapon of
defiance, reappear in the final poem: 'Губ шевелящихся отнять
вы не могли' (I No.307).

 The common origin of all these images lies in the feeling
of sheer amazement at the sight of the black earth, which he
characterised as the last weapon in the poet's arsenal, thus
equating it with his verse. As frequently happened, this

concomitant idea of poetry as a weapon appeared in his work
involuntarily and it was not until the following cycle of
poems that he was able to rationalise and evaluate it:

> И в голосе моем после удушья
> Звучит земля - последнее оружье -
> Сухая влажность черноземных га. (I No.312.8)

The *chernozem* is both instrument and inspiration in Mandelstam's reassertion of his human dignity and his right as a
poet to create. In the heavy clods of earth, saturated with
rain and melt-water, he sees his freedom: 'Комочки влажные
моей земли и воли!' (I No.299). Seldom has the left-wing
slogan of the Populist movement 'Земля и воля' been used
with such bitterness and disillusionment. Yet the earth was
the only source of freedom in the context of exile and he
delighted in its richness, with the promise of abundance to
come: 'Переуважена, перечерна, вся в холе'. The satisfying
blackness and fatness of the steppe earth are a particular
source of pleasure:

> В дни ранней пахоты - черна до синевы...
> Как на лемех приятен жирный пласт (I No.299)

This transformation from the images of sterility and cruelty
in 'Твоим узким плечам' (I No.296) to the fruitfulness and
geniality of the steppe could scarcely offer a greater
contrast: 'Как он хорош, как весел, как скуласт' (I No.305).
Mandelstam is clearly overwhelmed by the *chernozem*'s assault
on the senses, by its weight, its colour, its dampness and
its silence. In a seemingly paradoxical line this silent work
is shown to be the key to the whole spring cycle:

> Ну, здравствуй, чернозем, будь мужествен, глазаст -
> Черноречивое молчание в работе. (I No.299)

The analogy between the silent work of the ploughed soil and
the work of the silenced poet is revealed as Mandelstam iden-
tifies his poetic freedom with the *chernozem*. Both are defence
less in the face of brute force - 'И безоружна в ней зиждится
работа', but both offer sturdy resistance to bullying:

И все-таки земля - проруха и обух -
Не умолить ее, как в ноги ей ни бухай   (I No.299)

From the beginning he thinks of the earth in musical terms;
for he is also listening to silence, the silence preceding
composition when the poet's hearing is sharpened and he has
to strain to catch each embryonic word before it sinks back
into oblivion, into Lethe's underground waters - 'беспамят-
ствует слово' (I No.113). Here his poetic ear is alerted by
the music of the black earth:

Гниющей флейтою настраживает слух,
Кларнетом утренним зазябливает ухо.   (I No.299)

One of the many affinities of the poet with the flautist lies
in their lip movements. Both try to seize and trap the sounds
in the air, audible to them alone. A detailed description of
the process of poetic composition had been given by Mandelstam in his 'Восьмистишия' of 1932-5; the muttering of the
poet's lips there - 'в бормотаньях моих' (I No.276) - is
paralleled in a 1937 poem by the whispering of the flautist's
lips in his efforts to recall what his inner ear has caught
and can so easily lose:

Звонким шопотом честолюбивым,
Вспоминающим топотом губ
Он торопится быть бережливым,
Емлет звуки, опрятен и скуп.   (I No.387)

This is the reason behind the phrases 'молчание в работе'
and 'степь молчит'; the silence conceals an inward turbulence,
a creative turmoil which is given outward expression only by
the musical 'топот и шопот' (N.Ya.I p.192). The apparent
oxymoron of 'черноречивое молчание' contains no contradiction.
Whatever is fermenting is merely below the surface. An interesting detail shows the extent to which Mandelstam had
recouped his strength and independence. Not only did he feel
able to fight back against the forces working against him; he
exhorted himself to be 'мужествен, глазаст' like the earth
and, in the line 'Черноречивое молчание в работе', returned

to the offensive. The line, in its way scarcely less barbed than his Stalin epigram, replaces the 'красно-' element in the common adjective 'красноречивый' with 'черно-', thus stressing his link with the black earth and the dark obscurity into which he has been hurled while cunningly implying his repudiation of everything connected with the word 'красный' - a word more emotionally loaded for the Soviet citizen than most. Mandelstam's silence is pointedly contrasted with the 'fine speech' of state orators, among them, no doubt, those responsible for his present position. His silence springs from the underground, the unexpected fertility of the black earth, than which his work is no less well-tended and no less abundant.

The same linguistic parrying reappears in 'Наушники, наушнички мои' (I No.300), but the *double entendre* here is of an almost skittish nature. 'Наушники', meaning both 'informers' and 'earphones', is fully exploited as Mandelstam reproaches his betrayers with his exile from Moscow. This poem naturally aroused fury in the Union of Writers, to whom he rather foolishly sent it by way of Nadezhda Yakovlevna, then on one of her visits to Moscow (N.Ya.III). In his letters he asks her to find out what reaction the 'Чернозем' cycle has provoked, though he is adamant in his refusal to humiliate either himself or her:

> Надюша: никого ни о чем не проси. Никого. Но постарайся узнать, как отвечает Союз, то есть Ц.К. партии, на мои стихи, на письмо.   (Letter No.60, III p.266)

It transpired that the poem had been either misunderstood or only too well understood. He writes, as though perplexed: 'я против наушников' (Letter No.64, III p.272).

In exile it seemed to be the small rituals of life at home which excited the most nostalgia. In Mandelstam's case it was the supposedly stirring, albeit sentimental, practice of playing the midnight chimes of the Kremlin bells, followed

by the national anthem, on Moscow Radio just before close-
down every night which brings back the city to him:

И в полночь с Красной площади гудочки...

А вы, часов кремлевские бои   (I No.300)

As in so many of his poems real objects and actual events
are introduced - the radio earphones here did enable him to
listen to Moscow Radio (N.Ya.III). In a figurative sense
there is a hidden sting even in the apparently harmless
'часов кремлевские бои' (I No.300). Certainly the bells are
striking midnight from the 'Спасская Башня'; but deadly
political battles still raged in and around the Kremlin and
he felt far from secure, although protected by distance from
the main carnage. In the chimes he sensed the concentrated
threat of a danger which was by no means localised and by no
means neutralised by the comparative immunity of exile:
'Язык пространства, сжатого до точки'. In 'Чернозем' the
spaciousness of the steppe, spreading vast and limitless
away from the town, had partly compensated for his own very
circumscribed existence: 'Знать, безокружное в окружности
есть что-то!' (I No.299). Anna Akhmatova remarked of his work
at this time:

Поразительно, что простор, широта, глубокое дыхание
появились в стихах Мандельштама именно в Воронеже, когда
он был совсем не свободен.[1]

However, as he demonstrates in 'Наушники', even space can be
subjugated, compressed to a point and forced into service
for nefarious ends.

Red Square symbolises the rotten core of the system and
from it radiate waves of evil and corruption. Nevertheless,
in an *exegi monumentum* spirit, Mandelstam prophesies that
the fruits of his experience, even in exile, will not be lost

---

[1] Ахматова, vol. 2, p.185.

to future generations: 'Но то, что я скажу, заучит каждый
школьник' (I No.306). These are bitter fruits in comparison
with the poetic harvest extolled by Horace, Derzhavin and
Pushkin. For Mandelstam tells of the stranglehold of the
Kremlin over the whole land, his message to posterity being
clearly delineated in politico-geographical terms. Red Square
as the centre of tyranny runs down to the Moskva River and
this curve runs on further carrying with it despotism and
suffering:

> И скат ее нечаянно раздольный,
>
> Откидываясь вниз до рисовых полей,
> Покуда на земле последний жив невольник.   (I No.306)

It is the Stalinist Terror, not space, which knows no limits.
While the so-called 'volunteer' is engaged in heavy labour
to repair its uncertain structure, slave labour is simultaneously toiling for the same end across the Soviet Union,
right up to the Chinese border lands, with their paddy fields.
Mandelstam obviously considered using the Siberian mines to
illustrate the extent of Stalin's power: 'Каменноугольный –
добровольный – сохранить' (Letter No.55, III p.263). He may
have decided that the curve of the enslaved earth formed a
more effective contrast to the curve of the cupola-like sky,
free and unfettered: 'А небо, небо – твой Буонаротти!' (I No.
305) - a reference to the grandiose sweeping movements of
Michelangelo's sculpture.

Mandelstam had begun to accept exile. By the end of April
he had realised that from now on he could no longer actively
participate in the everyday life of his own country. Useless,
then, to ask after the bustle and animation of the Moscow
metro, the warmth of contact with crowds of people so necessary to him: 'Ну, как метро? Молчи, в себе таи' (I No.300) he
adjures himself with the words made famous by Tyutchev a century before. He had learnt to keep his counsel, contenting
himself with the creative miracle of his own poetry which had

at last returned to him. He must refrain from eager enquiries
about the progress of another miracle, that of the Moscow
spring, as life returned to the capital: 'Не спрашивай, как
набухают почки' (I No.300). After a final, anguished appeal
for release, addressed to Voronezh - 'Пусти меня, отдай меня,
Воронеж' (I No.301) - he had given in and was adapting to
life in the provinces. Details of this mundane life begin to
feature in his work: the melt-water flooding and intoxicating
the town - 'И город от воды ополоумел' (I No.305); the unco-
operative landlord, an agronomist who feared the consequences
of renting his room to a political exile (N.Ya.I, pp.135-8)
- 'обиженный хозяин Ходит, бродит в русских сапогах' (I No.
304); the floorboard warped by the damp in a house so inundated as to resemble a ship afloat:

И богато искривилась половица –
Этой палубы гробовая доска   (I No.304)

At this point, however, a note more sinister than discordant
creeps in. For the first time Mandelstam mentions by name the
paraphernalia connected with normal, civilian burial; the
floorboard appears to him as a coffin lid - his own. He saw
his own life as from a distance - 'И своя-то жизнь мне не
близка' - whereas death was much more real and much closer,
as close as the bench outside the window, on which he would
often sit: 'Только смерть да лавочка видна/близка' (Variants,
N.Ya.III & S p.300). These are the poems of a man condemned
to life, of a sort, although he has already suffered two
experiences as traumatic for him as death, his arrest and
his journey to exile: 'Я должен жить, хотя я дважды умер'
(I No.305). He even writes lines in which he jokes about his
posthumous fame:

Эта какая улица?
Улица Мандельштама.   (I No.303)

The third line of this poem was to have been 'Жил он на улице
Ленина' (N.Ya.III) - the name of the street on the outskirts

of town in which they were then living. But the temerity of
juxtaposing so illustrious a name with his own caused Mandelstam to 'forget' this line. He writes of himself in obituary
style:

> Мало в нем был линейного,
> Нрава он не был лилейного   (I No.303)

- an apt description in every way. Nothing of the straight,
undeviating, party-line mentality could be found either in
him or in his poetry. Never did he attempt to solve problems
by specious argument, as did the conformist, neither would
he submit and surrender his own viewpoint.

In his letters Mandelstam mentions the poem 'Чернозем'
as concluding the cycle: 'Готовую рукопись... кончил черно-
земом' (Letter No.55, III p.263), but ultimately the momentum
of the *chernozem* impulse came to a standstill in the poem
which summarises the theme and the mood of the cycle and
leads on to the next group:

> Лишив меня морей, разбега и разлета
> И дав стопе упор насильственной земли,
> Чего добились вы? Блестящего расчета   (I No.307)

More than many Russians he felt the deprivation of freedom to
travel around acutely, since from early childhood he had been
accustomed to travelling at home and abroad. The sea, for him
usually the Black Sea, with all that it represented for him
'culturally', was an equally great loss, which he was to
mourn in more detail shortly after this. Freedom to travel,
the sea, his poetry - all were being systematically denied
him, but in the case of poetry he could afford to be triumph-
antly sarcastic, exclaiming gleefully: 'Блестящего расчета'.
For he had turned the earth which was intended to crush him
into a support for himself, 'стопа' in the physical sense,
and for his poetry, 'стопа' in the sense of a poetic foot,
and no one could deprive him of his inspiration - 'Губ
шевелящихся отнять вы не могли' (I No.307).

The 'Стрижка детей' and 'Урал' group

At the end of April the Mandelstams moved into the centre of
Voronezh from the suburbs (N.Ya.I p.138). Living in the town
itself made life much easier since the endless journeys to
the centre were no longer necessary. Spring facilitated
movement around Voronezh and the warmer weather eased the
financial burdens of heating and adequate food for the cold
weather. In addition Mandelstam was commissioned to write
for Voronezh Radio and the local theatre periodically gave
them both work. It was a particularly exciting time, for
Nadezhda Yakovlevna had returned from Moscow with the manusc-
ripts of poems they had thought irretrievably lost; when
the 1930-4 poetry disappeared during the house search on the
night of his arrest prudent friends would have had little
inclination to retain their own copies. Notwithstanding,
Nadezhda Yakovlevna discovered caches of these poems in the
keeping of loyal friends and Mandelstam's father had kept
his copies. During this period the poems were resurrected
and a definitive typescript version of these *Новые стихи*
was authorised by Mandelstam; they called it the 'Ватиканский
список' with this definitive quality in mind (N.Ya.III).
Meanwhile the 'Урал' or 'Кама' cycle was taking shape.

Recovering from his joy and amazement at the sight of the
black earth, Mandelstam made a sober assessment of his position. Once he had come to terms with the condition of exile he
found himself able to write with conviction on the theme
'life goes on'. And indeed the routine of normal life
continues uninterrupted, no matter what upheavals break up
the lives of individuals: 'Еще мы жизнью полны в высшей мере'
(I No.302). The poem 'Стрижка детей' (I No.302) was written
in May (not in April, as in I) and opens the new cycle. It
owes its existence to a long wait for the hairdresser who
was engaged in shearing school-children like sheep, for the

first of May celebrations (N.Ya.III). In spite of the dramatic events in his own life, Mandelstam observed with interest
how the hairclippers carried on with their work, exacting
their tribute of chestnut locks:

> Еще машинка номер первый едко
> Каштановые собирает взятки   (I No.302)

It was spring and spring brought with it migrant visitors;
the birdsong mingles with twittering sounds from the bird-
like children:

> Еще стрижей довольно и касаток,
> Еще комета нас не очумила
> И пишут звездоносно и хвостато
> Толковые лиловые чернила.   (I No.302)

Natural phenomena, like the appearance of a comet - his
arrest must have hit him rather like a comet - fail to drive
him mad; its poetic equivalent, trailing stars in its tail,
is the lilac-coloured ink of the writer. In the same way as
the comet has broken away from its parent body and rushes
through the sky, so the poet's ink is the relict of the
whole trajectory of composition, the only trace visible to
the observer. The comet scatters stars over its path through
the sky: the ink leaves words and lines in its path across
the paper.

In general the poem would seem to breathe optimism. Yet,
perhaps unconsciously, a phrase with associations from quite
another sphere finds its way into the text: 'Еще мы жизнью
полны в высшей мере'. Mandelstam insisted that the use of
'в высшей мере' was involuntary and unintentional (N.Ya.III).
But the connection of one of the Russian expressions for
capital punishment with hair-cutting suggests, not unnaturall
the cutting-off of heads. The language of prison life had
entered so insidiously into common speech that such phrases
simply formed part of day-to-day conversation. In 'Чернозем'
(I No.299) the word 'обух' may have been suggested by 'под
обух идти', while the words 'наушники' (I No.300), 'собирает

взятки' (I No.302), 'невольник' (I No.300), 'насильственной'
(I No.307) and the unpronounced word 'тюрьма' implied in the
rhyme 'кутерьма/тьма' (No.312.4) all testify to the existence
of a linguistic substratum of convict language just below the
surface. In *Разговор о Данте* Mandelstam had pointed out how
prison had played an organic role in the life of Dante's
Florence. The diffusion between inmates and the outside
world had led to an acceptance of imprisonment as an essential part of contemporary life (II p.398). Such a diffusion
now existed in twentieth-century Russia.

Having established his position in Voronezh, Mandelstam
felt strong enough to cast his memory over the journey which
had eventually landed him in the town. Deported in the first
instance to Cherdyn, on the upper Kama River in the virgin
forests of Perm, he passed through the administrative centre
of the NKVD for this area, Ivdel; this lies to the east of
the Urals, where the Tobol flows into the Ob. By this stage
he was extremely ill and in addition the imprisonment and
interrogation which followed his arrest had driven him half-
crazy with terror:

Там я плыл по реке с занавеской в окне,
С занавеской в окне, с головою в огне. (I No.308)

The first, and basic, version of 'Кама', which includes these
lines, was followed in the triptych by a second version
censored by Mandelstam himself (I No.309), who was still
hopeful of publication in the near future. In the second
version he omits reference to the circumstances surrounding
his trip on the Kama. No mention is made of the fact that he
was accompanied only by his wife and by three guards, or that
he was denied even a view of the passing forests by a strateg-
ically placed curtain. So distraught was he that Nadezhda
Yakovlevna had to cope with their escorts and supervise all
the practical details of luggage on the five-day journey,
while his obsession with the guards reached alarming levels:

'Где вы, трое славных ребят из железных ворот ГПУ?' (I No.
313). During the journey Nadezhda Yakovlevna had been reading
Pushkin's 'Цыганы' to him and, perforce, to them (N.Ya.I p.
55). Hence the sardonic reference to young innocents educat-
ing themselves in order that wastrels like himself should no
longer monopolise a knowledge of which the new generation of
officially approved 'пушкиноведы' could make far better
practical use:

> Чтобы Пушкина чудный товар не пошел по рукам дармоедов,
> Грамотеет в шинелях с наганами племя пушкиноведов –
> Молодые любители белозубых стишков   (I No.313)

This second poem on the subject of the journey, 'День стоял о
пяти головах' (I No.313), was written between April and June
(not only in June, as in I), but its first draft, dated April
-May, makes the connection between the lovers of Pushkin and
the guards in Mandelstam's convoy more explicit:

> Трое славных ребят из железных ворот ГПУ
> Слушали Пушкина.
> Грамотеет в шинелях с наганами племя пушкиноведов.
> Как хорошо!   (N.Ya.III)

On being asked to explain what exactly could be said to be
at all 'хорошо' about this, Mandelstam replied, somewhat
enigmatically, 'Все хорошо, что жизнь' (N.Ya.III). He does
not begrudge a living poet to the living.

Over the folk element in Pushkin's tale he exclaims:
'Сухомятная русская сказка! Деревянная ложка – ау!' (I No.
313). The wooden spoon symbolises the simplicity and wisdom
of folk tales, with their dry asperity, akin to the taste of
peppermint, salutary enough reading for the glorious children
of the GPU. The passage running through Mandelstam's brain
as he recalled this journey seems to have been the folk-style
digression in 'Цыганы' with its simile of God's little bird
flying off to the South; while 'Людям скучно, людям горе'
the bird flies off to warm, distant lands 'за сине море'
to await the spring. Whether there was any hope of such a

spring for Mandelstam or not, his cry of anguish for the sea now lost to him is made more poignant by its inclusion of the biblical phrase through which he demonstrates how modest and how impossible his demand is:

> На вершок бы мне синего моря, на игольное только ушко!
> Чтобы двойка конвойного времени парусами неслась хорошо.

(I No.313)

Apropos of his yearning for the sea, Anna Akhmatova wrote, quoting these two lines: 'Юг и море были ему почти так же необходимы, как Надя.'[1] Frequently referred to in literature and oral tradition as 'синее море', the sea in Mandelstam's case is once again the Black Sea. Meanwhile he was surrounded by impenetrable pine forests, whose grisly effect on him he summarises in the striking line: 'Глаз превращался в хвойное мясо'. This reflects the landscape of the narrow-gauge Sverdlovsk-Solikamsk railway; along both sides of the track stretched continuous, unexplored forest (N.Ya.I pp.57-8). Again the link in Mandelstam's mind between the sea and the forest is explained in a draft version:

> День стоял о пяти головах. Горой пообедав,
> Поезд ужинал лесом. Лез ниткой в сплошное ушко (N.Ya.III)

The railway track is compared to a thread passing through the eye of a needle, the 'сплошной' forest, against which the poet shrinks into insignificance, 'сжимаясь'. Later on, he transferred the phrase 'игольное ушко' to his craving for the sea, possibly because of the associative link between the sea, the Mediterranean and the Christian culture of Europe, whereas 'сплошной' was applied to the continuous, unbroken five-day journey: 'День стоял о пяти головах. Сплошные пять суток'. He apprehends the day as a five-headed monster, one head growing out of the other in a never-ending nightmare of confusion in which his sense of time has vanished

---

[1] Ахматова, vol. 2, p.178.

completely: 'Сон был старше, чем слух, слух был старше, чем сон - слитен, чуток'. He could no longer distinguish between the reality of his sensitive poetic hearing and the unreality of his nightmare journey - or *vice versa*. In his mind chaos closed in.

Towards evening on the first day the Mandelstams glimpsed a high mountain from the train, which produced a great impression on Mandelstam but was quickly swallowed up by the ubiquitous forest in the interval between dinner and supper, as the draft cited above describes. In this area there is a peak of 2500 feet not far north-west of Sverdlovsk, which would have been visible as they passed through Nizhny Tagil with its famous metallurgic factory and its mines - and its labour force, recollected in the 'Чернозем' cycle. On this stage of the journey only hard wooden benches were provided, as on all narrow-gauge trains: they had to sit up on these all night, there being nowhere to lie down, and Mandelstam's confusion and exhaustion increased by the hour.

In spite of his condition some impressions of the second stage of the journey up the Kama - 'двойка конвойного времени' - remained, including a characteristic description of the river banks in terms of human physiology: 'На дубовых коленях стоят города' (I No.308). These 'oaken knees' were the jetties or quays of riverside towns which made the towns appear to be wading up to their knees in the river. Bearded spruce trees are reflected in the water; their images, clearer and brighter, seemed younger than the originals:

В паутину рядясь, борода к бороде –
Жгучий ельник бежит, молодея, в воде.   (I No.309)

Mandelstam wanted both variants of this poem to be published, since their different endings made them into independent poems.

The third poem of the trio complements the others by revealing his personal attitude to the Urals scenery, which

had previously been described quite neutrally, in an outburst
of nostalgia:

> И хотелось бы тут же вселиться - пойми -
> В долговечный Урал, населенный людьми   (I No.310)

How comparatively settled and satisfied with life in Voronezh
he was may be judged from his indulging in the luxury of
imagining his fate elsewhere - in the wilderness of Cherdyn,
to whose population he might have added another involuntary
inhabitant.

The last couplet of this third poem serves as a bridge to
the next cycle of the collection, 'Стансы':

> И хотелось бы эту безумную гладь
> В долгополой шинели - беречь, охранять.   (I No.310)

He 'would wish' to envelop the whole of the forest region in
the Red Army soldier's 'protective' greatcoat; absolute
military control could alone guarantee the proper functioning
of labour camps and organisation of re-settled populations.
Mandelstam addresses a malicious eulogy to the cut of the
greatcoat:

> Люблю шинель красноармейской складки,
> Длину до пят, рукав простой и гладкий   (I No.312.2)

He always maintained that 'Стансы' (I No.312) was written in
a spirit of reconciliation (N.Ya.III), yet the acrimony and
virulence of these verses rivals that of his bitterest poems.
Again on the subject of the greatcoat, he launches a rancor-
ous attack on the Red Army, in recognition of its service to
him in separating him from the mainstream of life:

> Проклятый шов, нелепая затея
> Нас разлучили.   (I No.312.3)

Like a neatly cut-out thundercloud over the Volga, the greatcoat holds the threat of the storm to come. When summer
arrives, however, it is rolled up and stored for future use
- but no glimmer of summer light could be seen on the
political horizon of spring 1935. One of the rough drafts,
dated May, begins the cycle with this stanza (N.Ya.III), but

this was thought too risky a step, so he buried it in the
main body of the group in later versions. Since he seriously
intended the poems for publication he also changed the last
line of what became the preceding stanza in the finished text
(I No.312.2), which was originally written down separately
from the others and ended: 'Земного шара первый часовой'
(N.Ya.III). Mandelstam's innocent belief that he had thus
removed all damaging material from the group is truly remarkable. The same lack of realism shows in his pathetically
hopeful letter to Nadezhda Yakovlevna in Moscow:

> Для Москвы условие: <u>все</u> или ничего. Широкий показ цикла.
> Хорошо бы в Литгазете. Все варианты окончательные. Только
> в начале 'Стансов' могут быть изменения, но давай так.
> (Letter No.57, III p.264)

In the end, however, he manages to throw off the menace of
the greatcoat, that is, the lies, denunciations and slanders
of the 'клевещущих козлов' - the soldiers noisily playing at
dominoes ('козла'); 'goat' is a term of abuse which he often
hurled at his enemies, as for example in 'Слово и культура'
(II p.223) or 'Четвертая проза' (II p.179). In a vivid
phonetic representation he also contrives to jeer at informers - 'стукач' even by then being the time-honoured design-
ation for such persons - as he rids himself of their
attentions:

> Харчи да харк, да что-нибудь, да враки -
> Стук дятла сбросил с плеч. Прыжок - и я в уме.
> (I No.312.4)

The leap back into sanity had its basis in reality. Suffering
from delusions of persecution Mandelstam jumped out of a
hospital window in Cherdyn to escape the secret police who,
he was convinced, were pursuing him. Mercifully he only
injured one arm (N.Ya.I pp.59-63). He had tried to cut his
wrists during his incarceration in the Lubyanka (N.Ya.I p.81)
but in Cherdyn it was rather fear of pursuit and not suicidal
despair which drove him to jump. The subject of suicide was

raised later, in 1937 - the worst year of their exile, but Mandelstam would hear nothing of it. For one to whom the human body and the humanisation of the surrounding world meant so much, suicide would have been unthinkable had he not been in a deranged state.

Sanity returned slowly, together with his poetic 'слух', and by the end of the spring of 1935 the pattern of his new future was clear to him. In 'Стансы' he twice repeats the phrase 'я должен жить' from the affirmative 'Чернозем' cycle:

> Я должен жить, дыша и большевея,
> И перед смертью хорошея
> Еще побыть и поиграть с людьми.   (I No.312.3)

- a reference to the third line of Tyutchev's 'Играй, покуда над тобою Еще безоблачна лазурь', where people are again of paramount importance: 'Играй с людьми' (S p.300). Mandelstam once remarked to Nadezhda Yakovlevna that the victory of the Bolshevik Revolution owed much to a happy choice of party name - one which was bound to inspire confidence and success with its associations such as 'сам-большой' or 'большой человек' (N.Ya.III). Thus in 'День стоял о пяти головах' (I No.313) the word 'большак' was no accident. 'Большеветь', that is to say 'хорошеть', constituted Mandelstam's goal for the future and it was in this respect that he considered 'Стансы' to be verses of reconciliation. Soviet machines were hammering away in the Arctic - 'стук' slips in again; he was prepared to start tapping on his own Soviet 'машинка', fulfilling his quota two-fold by dint of defying his inner ear: 'Работать речь, не слушаясь, сам-друг' (I No.312.7). A vain assurance: few poets can have been less capable of composition by the deliberate exertion of will than he. Once again his vocabulary betrays him with the perfidious Lorelei, the executioner-gardener figure of Hitler whose resemblance to Stalin was becoming more and more obvious, and even the word 'садовник' itself, not far removed from 'сажать в тюрьму'.

In spite of avowals that he will ignore his inner ear,
within seconds the truth is out:

> Как Слово о полку, струна моя туга,
> И в голосе моем после удушья
> Звучит земля – последнее оружье   (I No.312.8)

The whole context of battle, of resuming the fight after
defeat by barbaric tribes, applies to Mandelstam as to Prince
Igor. The reference to the *Слово о полку Игореве* was occasioned by some verses written by a certain Dligach, in which he
promised to recognise class enemies by one sound of their
lyres alone, mentioning the *Слово* (N.Ya.I p.94). Mandelstam
could now, like the poet-enchanter of the epic, lay his magic
fingers on the taut, living strings and those strings would
thunder glory of their own accord, again as in the *Слово*.
A noun which occurs with some frequency there is 'туга',
and there can be little doubt that Mandelstam intended a
dual meaning in his poem, his own poetry being heavily laden
with sorrow: 'тугою взыдоша по Руской земли' 'а древо с тугою
к земли преклонилось' 'А въстона бо, братие, Киев тугою'
(*Слово о полку Игореве*). The close association of this line,
'струна моя туга' with 'последнее оружье' may also derive
from the same source: bows and arrows were the weapons both
of Igor's forces and of the Polovtsy, engendering some
striking imagery: 'идти дождю стрелами с Дону великаго' 'Се,
ветри, Стрибожи внуци, веют с моря стрелами' 'Тъй бо Олег
мечем крамолу коваше и стрелы по земле сеяше' (*Слово о полку
Игореве*). Converted from their normal use into a weapon for
combat, the strings of Mandelstam's poetic instrument thunder
out against the enemy. It may have been his last weapon, but
it was also his most effective. His own country had struck
him down with a bolt:

> Но возмужавшего меня, как очевидца,
> Заметила – и вдруг, как чечевица,
> Адмиралтейским лучиком зажгла.   (I No.312.6)

He narrowly escaped being consumed by the flames and was now rising from the ashes to retaliate.

In the first draft of 'Стансы' there were only seven stanzas of which the third began:

Лишь бы страна со мною говорила,
И на плечо в полпальца мне давила,
Товарищески ласкова и зла,
Мирволила, журила, не прочла   (N.Ya.III)

The changes made to this before the final version emerged indicate a hardening of attitude in Mandelstam. In the draft the implication is that a 'friendly' warning, a tap on the shoulder before the annihilating thunderbolt, might have been heeded or, even if disregarded, would at least have forearmed him; whereas the final version reveals a complete lack of communication on the human level in his relationship with his country, a dialogue long since abandoned. Throughout the land all links have been severed between those whom the state considers its enemies, in the knowledge that unity and organisation alone make for strength. The 'проклятый шов' has succeeded in tearing him away from the focus of his life, Moscow: 'И ты, Москва, сестра моя, легка' (I No.312.5). In this possible allusion to Pasternak's *Сестра моя жизнь* the central position occupied by Moscow in Mandelstam's world is clarified: Moscow is life, life away from Moscow is a form of death.

The first stanza of 'Стансы', as is clear from the rough drafts, appeared at the very end of the group's composition and accords ill with the rest of it. Seldom did Mandelstam contrive to produce anything so half-hearted, so lacking in conviction and so patently untrue as:

Но, как в колхоз идет единоличник,
Я в мир вхожу, и люди хороши.   (I No.312.1)

The intention that this avocation would redeem the cycle in the eyes of publishers is effectively sabotaged by the stanza's opening lines:

Я не хочу средь юношей тепличных

Разменивать последний грош души (I No.312.1)

In earlier versions modern youth was characterised by the
epithet 'архивных' (N.Ya.III), borrowed from Pushkin's unflatt-
ering description of the youths who crowded round Tatyana in
the Moscow of *Евгений Онегин*. The interests of this set, who
worked in the Moscow archive of the Ministry of Foreign Affairs
in the early 1820's, lay in literature and social problems,
in particular with the work and the ideas of Schelling and
the Romantic poets. On Mandelstam's part this was a sarcastic
hint to Rudakov, who was continually pestering them, insisting
that he must work in the same room with them and thereby
interfering with Mandelstam's own work. At this time Rudakov
was dabbling in 'архивные' research projects, studying poets
like Kantemir, Kapnist and other poets whose names began with
the letter 'k'. In summer a timely attack of scarlatina
removed Rudakov to hospital (N.Ya.III). However, Mandelstam
considered even 'архивных' too positive a concept to be used
of the youth of the 1930's and substituted the much more
damning 'тепличных' to describe the *jeunesse dorée* of the
Komsomol.

In 'Чапаев' (I No.311) Mandelstam's counter-attack
gathers momentum. While Nadezhda Yakovlevna was in Moscow in
April 1935 he had gone on his own to see the Vasilev brothers
film, based on Furmanov's novel of that name. Mandelstam's
poem concentrates on the 'psychological attack' on Chapaev's
cavalry by Admiral Kolchak's officers (I p.523). The Whites
foster the illusion that the losses suffered by their camp are
immaterial -'Начихав на кривые убыточки' - by Furmanov's
strategy of showing rank upon rank of supporting troops rising
up to replace fallen men. In an indubitable 'перекличка' with
his earlier prose Mandelstam reveals exactly what this camp
stands for:

С папироской смертельной в зубах (I No.311)

Мы стреляем друг у друга папиросы и правим свою китайщину, зашифровывая в животно-трусливые формулы великое, могучее запретное понятие класса. 'Четвертая проза' (II p.179)

He is defending the forbidden concept of class, the very basis of the *ancien régime* of nineteenth-century Russia, which so appealed to the love of hierarchy he had expounded in the 1910 essay on Villon (II p.301-9). This helps to explain the presence of the Chapaev film at the end of 'День стоял о пяти головах' (I No.313); the reading of Pushkin conjured up the past and the old, civilised order, as the train took Mandelstam deeper into the Urals, further away from the last remnants of that order. And his companions were none other than Chapaev's heirs.

Past loves

A break followed the 'Чернозем' and the 'Урал' cycles. During this time, from the end of April to the end of June, Mandelstam was working on his radio broadcast 'Юность Гете' (III pp.61-80). He was also absorbing the news of Olga Vaksel's death in Oslo (N.Ya.II p.272). The dual motivation of the June poems results from a combination of these two elements.

Among their subjects the poems of June 1935 include Goethe (I No.316), Schubert (I No.315), a dead woman (I No. 314) and a female violinist (I No.298). The connecting thread is far from discernible unless reference is made to the text of the radio broadcast:

Чтобы понять, как разворачивалась жизнь и деятельность Гете, нужно также помнить, что его дружба с женщинами при всей глубине и страстности чувства, была твердыми мостами, по которому он переходил из одного периода жизни в другой.   'Юность Гете' (III p.75)

Mandelstam follows this with quick character sketches of the three most important women in Goethe's life, Friederike, Lotte and Lili. He had completed these portraits before Nadezhda Yakovlevna's departure for Moscow in April, but one of the last additions to the text was this introductory

sentence in which he appraises Goethe's women friends as
measures of his maturity, step by step. Quite naturally, then,
he reacted to the news of Olga Vaksel's death by retracing
his own development, recalling the women of various stages in
his own life. His immediate reaction, however, was the
recollection of Pushkin's lines about the death of a former
love (N.Ya.III). These beg quotation at length:

> Из равнодушных уст я слышал смерти весть,
> И равнодушно ей внимал я.
> Так вот кого любил я пламенной душой
> С таким тяжелым напряженьем,
> С такою нежною, томительной тоской,
> С таким безумством и мученьем!
> Где муки, где любовь? Увы! в душе моей
> Для бедной, легковерной тени,
> Для сладкой памяти невозвратимых дней
> Не нахожу ни слез ни пени.[1]

Mandelstam expresses these thoughts more tersely: 'Я тяжкую
память твою берегу' (I No.314). Olga Vaksel had been his
wife's only serious rival for his affections during their
married life. He found the remembrance of his longing to
elope with her to the South echoed in the Goethe which he was
even now studying, in the poem 'Mignon':

> Kennst du das Land, wo die Zitronen blühn,
> Im dunkeln Laub die Gold-Orangen glühn...
> Kennst du es wohl? Dahin! Dahin
> Möcht ich mit dir, o mein Geliebter, ziehn.

Hence Mandelstam's affectionate endearments 'Дичок, медвеженок
Миньона' (I No.314), clarified yet further by comparison with
the text of the broadcast:

> Маленькая дикарка с арфой – Миньона... Гете в мчащейся
> карете шутит с пугливым зверьком, самолюбивой, маленькой
> арфисткой...   'Юность Гете'   (III р.78)

Goethe was then leaving Germany, heading South to Italy:

> Тра-та-та-та! Тра-та-та-та! Труби, почтальон на высоких
> козлах!
> Прощай, неуклюжая, но все-таки милая Германия...
>   'Юность Гете'   (III р.77)

---

[1] Пушкин, vol. 2, p.74.

This illuminates the last lines of Mandelstam's poem:

> Но мельниц колеса зимуют в снегу,
> И стынет рожок почтальона.   (I No.314)

- the postman's horn which appears in Schubert's *Die Winterreise*:

> Von der Strasse her ein Posthorn klingt.
> Was hat es, dass es so hoch aufspringt, mein Herz?

Mandelstam has to bid farewell to Germany on his own account and, more generally, bid farewell to European civilisation and cultural values. There will be no journeys to Italy for him: with the death of Olga Vaksel his last links with the outside world are broken.

Schubert springs readily to mind with the idea of Romantic Germany, its great rivers and its water-mills. His other great song-cycle, *Die Schöne Müllerin*, was also based on the poetry of Wilhelm Müller, and Mandelstam's image of water-wheels wintering in the snow was born here. It was of Schubert that he was thinking when he wrote, in his broadcast: 'Хриплая бродячая шарманка лучше концертной музыки' (III p.77) - for this is the 'Leiermann' of *Die Winterreise*: 'und sein kleiner Teller bleibt ihm immer leer'. Mandelstam had made the connection between Schubert and Goethe as early as 1917, in the poem 'В тот вечер не гудел стрельчатый лес органа':

> Нам пели Шуберта - родная колыбель.
> Шумела мельница, и в песнях урагана
> Смеялся музыки голубоглазый хмель.   (I No.96)

A few lines further on he refers to the 'царь лесной', the 'Erlkönig' of Goethe and Schubert. He once remarked that Schubert often made use of songs previously performed by organ-grinders or sung to the accompaniment of the barrel-organ (N.Ya.III). All these associations are kaleidoscoped in an impressionistic collage from Mandelstam's second poem on the subject:

> Шарманщика смерть и медведицы ворс...
> И Шуберта в шубе застыл талисман -
> Движенье, движенье, движенье...   (I No.315)

Mingled together are the ideas of death, journeys, growing cold from death, 'застыл', or from winter, 'в шубе'.

Music had been foremost in his thoughts since a concert given in Voronezh in Nadezhda Yakovlevna's absence at which the soloist was the violinist Galina Barinova (N.Ya.III). The death of Olga Vaksel, with her composer-violinist ancestor A.F.Lvov (S p.299) - 'И прадеда скрипкой гордился твой род' (I No.314), prompted him to write 'Скрипачка' (I No.298) of which Barinova is the subject. There are hints at the content of the concert programme, which may have included an arrangement of Schubert's 'Trauerwalzer', originally for piano:

> Иль вальс, из гроба в колыбель
> Переливающий, как хмель.   (I No.298)

Very probably Paganini's instrumental composition 'Carnival of Venice', based on the air of a popular Venetian tune, was among the items:

> За Паганин длиннопалым
> Бегут цыганскою гурьбой...
>
> Мучным и потным карнавалом   (I No.298)

It becomes apparent, however, that Barinova herself had produced a profound impression on Mandelstam apart from her virtuoso playing. This was chiefly because of a strange coincidence: she bore a striking physical resemblance to one of the first women in his life, Marina Tsvetaeva (N.Ya.III):

> Девчонка, выскочка, гордячка...
> На голове твоей, полячка,
> Марины Мнишек холм кудрей   (I No.298)

Whether Tsvetaeva's hair as a young woman was curlier than later photographs would suggest or not, in Mandelstam's poems of 1916, the year of his affair with her, he identified himself with Dmitri Samozvanets and Tsvetaeva with Marina Mnishek. This was partly because she was then showing him historical Moscow. He saw the Moscow cathedrals through her and as part of her - even the fur coat here is hers, as he analyses the cultural influences present in the cathedrals:

С их итальянскою и русскою душой
Напоминают мне явление Авроры,
Но с русским именем и в шубке меховой.　　　　　(I No.84)

In 1935 the poetess and the violinist merge in his consciousness, the Italian musical heritage of Paganini, seen through
the Slav Barinova, with the Italian architectural heritage of
Fioravanti, Solario and Alevisio, seen through the Slav
Tsvetaeva. In another echo from the 1916 'Tsvetaeva' poems
Mandelstam, half-jokingly, half-seriously, characterises the
three important women in his life - Tsvetaeva, Olga Vaksel
and Nadezhda Yakovlevna - not as something sacrosanct and
mystical, like the original idea of the three Romes (I No.85),
but as their exact opposite, devils incarnate:

Три черта было, - ты четвертый:
Последний, чудный черт в цвету!　　　　　(I No.298)

　　　Although Mandelstam had been deprived by death of his
past loves and by exile of his freedom of movement, he shares
the pleasure of those who, like Goethe, have enjoyed both:

Римских ночей полновесные слитки,
Юношу Гете манившее лоно　　　　　(I No.316)

Моглиа твоя в скандинавском снегу
И Гете манившее лоно　　　　　(Draft of I No.314, S p.299)

Even here Mandelstam has an answer for the forces of repression. Enjoyment of life may be illicit for him, but as an
outlaw he has every intention of pursuing it in areas which
the law cannot touch, his inner life and his poetry, for
example:

Пусть я в ответе, но не в убытке -
Есть многодонная жизнь вне закона.　　　　　(I No.316)

Stones, soldiers and pilots

In July Nadezhda Yakovlevna returned to Voronezh after a
second fruitless expedition to Moscow. Although she had come
back empty-handed, figuratively speaking, from her quest for
work for either of them, she did bring with her a souvenir of
the past, a small bag of stones from Koktebel (N.Ya.II p.528).

News of Kirov's death and rumours about the identity of his
murderer also came with her. Mandelstam heard this with
gravity, realising it to be but a foretaste of the future
Terror (N.Ya.III). His mood remained sober for several days,
and this subdued frame of mind is reflected in his July poems

The Koktebel stones evoked quiet nostalgia for the South:

> В опале предо мной лежат
> Морского лета земляники –
> Двуискренние сердолики
> И муравьиный брат – агат   (I No.318)

Double meanings are exploited here: 'опала' alludes as much to
his disgrace as to the precious stone before him. In this
'опала' he sees a reminder of past summers, as depicted in
'Путешествие в Армению':

> Однажды в Абхазии я набрел на целые россыпи северной
> земляники.
> На высоте немногих сот футов над уровнем моря невзрослые
> леса одевали все холмогорье. Крестьяне мотыжили красно-
> ватую сладкую землю, подготовляя луночки для ботанической
> рассады.
> То-то я обрадовался коралловым деньгам северного лета.
> 'Путешеситвие в Армению' (II pp.150-1)

He prefers to live in the present, however, and affirms his
predilection for the more prosaic pebbles from the sea:

> Но мне милей простой солдат
> Морской пучины – серый, дикий,
> Которому никто не рад.   (I No.318)

References to the military are never long absent from the poem
of 1935; here the unlovable soldier in his grey greatcoat
becomes almost an object of affection, so dingy is he in
comparison with the exotic and unattainable world of the semi
precious stones. The memory of rank upon rank of soldiers from
the film on Chapaev is added to the picture of the stones,
which capture the movement of the sea, to form a new synthesi

> Бежит волна – волной волне хребет ломая,
> Кидаясь на луну в невольничьей тоске   (I No.319)

Mandelstam was beginning to see the soldiers as victims rather
than oppressors, as vassals in the power of oriental-style

despots, with their exotic retinues of janissaries and
eunuchs:

> И янычарская пучина молодая...
>
> И с пенных лестниц падают солдаты
> Султанов мнительных – разбрызганы, разъяты, –
> И яд разносят хладные скопцы.   (I No.319)

As the huge wave breaks on hitting the sand, and disintegrates,
the soldiers are broken up into drops of spray: they bear the
brunt of the damage in attack, not their masters who willed it.

All this appears as in a vision of the future:

> А через воздух сумрачно-хлопчатый
> Неначатой стены мерещатся зубцы   (I No.319)

The poem is allegorical, since it was inconceivable that its
fundamental subject, the Five-Year Plans, should be mentioned
by name. The waves of each plan, succeeding each other, were
making little impression on the sand, merely destroying the
forces which made up their strength, in the useless attempt
to reach for the moon which exercised a fatal attraction over
them: 'Кидаясь на луну в невольничьей тоске'. In the second
stanza the idea of building upwards is added to the imagery
of forcible aspiration; no tangible wall had so far appeared,
but the builders were continually falling from the 'пенных
лестниц' of the rearing waves, crashing to the ground and to
their deaths. Enormous 'зубцы' were already apparent in the
solid line of the waves. Mandelstam often spoke of the
futility of fixed plans and goals, and despised the pseudo-
military vocabulary of plan-fulfilment, realising as well as
anyone that the better the plan was fulfilled, the worse
living conditions became in reality (N.Ya.II, pp.190-1).

This period of brooding was protracted by another
national disaster, the death of two test pilots in a plane
crash. One of these was the son of V.Kuibyshev, and the
dedication of the poem 'Не мучнистой бабочкою белой' (I No.
320) is to him. Mandelstam saw in the pilots' charred bodies

an omen for himself and again voiced his longing for immortal
ity of any sort. The idea of the complete destruction of the
physical body, with no trace remaining, was abhorrent to him:

> Я хочу, чтоб мыслящее тело
> Превратилось в улицу, в страну –
> Позвоночное, обугленное тело   (I No.320

With his new-found sympathy for the common soldier he intimat
that they share a common destiny in the hostile vacuum of the
skies, where the pilots had met their death:

> Шли товарищи последнего призыва
> По работе в жестких небесах   (I No.320

This poem prefigures the 'Стихи о неизвестном солдате' (I No.
362) of 1937 where the probability of an impending war and
the importance of its aerial as well as its terrestrial
character is foreseen. This was originally the basic poem
around which a whole cycle about crawling and flying creation
collected; it included, for instance, lines about 'черепахи'
and tanks (N.Ya.III). Only the first line of its final text
bears any relation to this theme, in its concern with the
man-made equivalent of the butterfly, the aeroplane:

> Не мучнистой бабочкою белой
> В землю я заемный прах верну   (I No.320

Both these aerial dwellers lead lives of extreme brevity;
butterflies, like dragonflies and other insects, symbolise,
as usual, life's transience. As far as his fellow-victims,
the simple soldiers of the previous two poems, are concerned,
death is imminent and violent. Thousands of men, armed with
the new weapons of the heavens, are passing by:

> Шли нестройно – люди, люди, люди –
> Кто же будет продолжать за них?   (I No.320

The cycle as such did not come to fruition. Mandelstam's
life at this time was very disorganised. Journeys in search
of work, plus a 'командировка' with some Voronezh writers
around the district's prize industrial and agricultural
landmarks, interfered with work on the cycle. The 'командиров

was intended to provide material for poetic tributes to the
achievements of the new economic system: needless to say,
none was forthcoming on the part of Mandelstam.

However, a twin poem to 'Не мучнистой бабочкою белой'
did emerge: ' - Нет, не мигрень, но подай карандашик ментоловый' (I No.317) was written in July (not April-July, as in
I), on old paper, on the back of which were the rough drafts
of 'Волк' (I No.227). It has, notwithstanding, no thematic
or linguistic connection with the 'Волк' cycle, whose imagery
- that of wood, of Novgorod pails, of the North - is totally
different. Conclusive evidence that it dates to 1935 and not
to 1931 is furnished by the line 'Да коктебельского горького
чобру пучок положи мне под голову' (draft on same sheet, N.Ya.
III), which could scarcely have predated the bag of stones from
Koktebel, brought back by Nadezhda Yakovlevna in 1935.

The pilots' death in the air had led Mandelstam to
consider, not for the first time, the physical details of his
own death, and thus, in retrospect, his own life. Especially
interesting in this connection is the first draft of the poem:

> Нет, не мигрень, но подай карандашик ментоловый -
> (сонным обзором я жизнь) воскрешаю,
> Сгинь, поволока искусства. Мне стыдно, мне сонно и солово.
> (N.Ya.III)

This autobiographical reminiscence is expanded in the final
version:

> Жизнь начиналась в корыте картавою мокрою шепотью
> И продолжалась она керосиновой мягкою копотью. (I No.317)

For Mandelstam life began with the strange non-language spoken
by his father:

> У отца совсем не была языка, это было косноязычие и
> безъязычие. Русская речь польского еврея? - Нет. Речь
> немецкого еврея? - Тоже нет. Может быть особый курляндский
> акцент? - Я таких не слышал. *Шум времени*   (II pp.66-7)

Perhaps his recollection of his own early 'шепоть' was tied
up with this memory. Life continued for him with the sputter-
ing of kerosene lamps throughout his childhood at home:

Керосинка была раньше примуса. Слюдяное окошечко и откиднс
маяк... Больше всего у нас в доме боялись 'сажи' - то есть
копоти от керосиновых ламп. Крик 'сажа' - 'сажа' - звучал
как 'пожар', 'горим' - вбегали в комнату, где расшалилась
лампа.   *Египетская марка*   (II pp.25-6)

There followed holidays in Finland, where his family had a
summer dacha:

Зимой, на Рождестве, - Финляндия, Выборг, а дача -
Териоки.   *Шум времени*   (II p.62)

Где-то на даче потом, в лесном переплете шагреневом,
Вдруг разгорелась она почему-то огромным пожаром сиреневым
   (I No.317)

Life 'flared up' suddenly for him through a chance remark by
one of his numerous governesses who, on listening to his
childish efforts at literary composition, declared that 'there
was indeed something there' - one of the high points of his
childhood (N.Ya.III). Another vivid impression was also an
early one. Mandelstam had appropriated one of the coloured
lanterns hung in the streets as part of the celebrations for
Nicholas II's coronation in 1896, and would play with it for
hours, letting the sun shine through it to scatter myriad
colours over the ground and the trees:

... разламывал в детстве шестигранные коронационные
фонарики с зазубринкой и наводил на песчаный сосняк и
можжевельник - то раздражительно-красную трахому, то
синюю жвачку полдня какой-то чужой планеты, то лиловую
кардинальскую ночь.   *Египетская марка*   (II p.21)

Дальше, сквозь стекла цветные, сощурясь, мучительно вижу
Небо как палица грозное, земля словно плешина рыжая...
   (I No.317)

Now, looking at the world through glass of any colour, all he
saw was the threatening sky of the future. He had come to
identify it with hostile space, cold, uncomprehended, alien
'пространство', lacking form, gender - or indeed any attribu
of life and living beings, such as its former merry colouring
'Ни поволоки искусства, ни красок пространства веселого'.

Not only his eyes but his nose warns him of impending
danger; he smells the 'смола' with which his enemies will

smear him, and stinking blubber-oil: 'Пахнет немного смолою
и тухлою ворванью'. At this point he may well be recalling
the lynching episode from *Египетская марка*, when:

> Петербург объявил себя Нероном и был так мерзок, словно
> ел похлебку из раздавленных мух.
> Они воняют кишечными пузырями... (II p.20 & p.17)

In both the first and the final versions the images of
menthol, gauze and carbolic are continually repeated. At the
time of the test pilots' accident attempts to give first aid
were made at the crash, but the charred bodies were beyond
help (N.Ya.III). The detailed nature of these images derived
from visits which Mandelstam made to Nadezhda Yakovlevna when
she lay ill in the Botkinskaya Hospital in May 1932. She noted
how he was struck by the smell of carbolic, which filled the
building. It seemed to increase his awareness of his own sense
of smell and the smells around him (N.Ya.II p.439), and was
reflected in his 1932 notebook in references to soap - 'кусочек
земляничного мыла' (III p.151 & p.152) and the linden trees -
'липы пахнут дешевыми духами' (III p.154). This served as a
starting-point for the menthol stick in the 1935 poem, the
clinical smell which characterised for him the 'холод пространства бесполого', empty and sterile.

The first Voronezh *Тетрадь* closes here, with threads
pulling towards the Unknown Soldier of 1937, in which Mandelstam's death in the 'небо как палица грозное' would be
envisaged in yet more concrete terms.

4. *НОВЫЕ СТИХИ: ВТОРАЯ ВОРОНЕЖСКАЯ ТЕТРАДЬ*

December 1936 - February 1937

Mandelstam's last winter in Voronezh proved to be the most terrible period of his whole exile. In the summer of 1936 he had managed to spend a short time away from it, but his situation was worse on his return than at any time during the previous two years.

Six weeks of the summer had been spent at a dacha in Zadonsk, a little town on the Don heights, famous for its monastery and in particular for its association with Tikhon Zadonsky. This respite was made possible only by the generosity of Anna Akhmatova, Pasternak and Evgeny Yakovlevich Khazin (Nadezhda Yakovlevna's brother), who all contributed to the Mandelstams' expenses (N.Ya.I p.212). From the point of view of Mandelstam's deteriorating health the break was of some importance. His heart had caused him trouble from an early age and about this time his heart attacks were becoming both more frequent and more severe. At the end of 1935 he had written to Nadezhda Yakovlevna from the Tambov Nerve Sanatorium:

> Температура у меня по-прежнему немного подпрыгивает. Мерил вчера вечером: 37,2. Возбудимость сердца велика. Пульс иногда ускоряется. При этом я вполне бодр, хочется гулять. Но встречи с людьми волнуют. Разговоры утомляют. Чтение - тоже.   (Letter No.61, III p.269)

This condition was always aggravated by her absence, a fact he himself recognised but could do nothing to alter. In a letter to his mother-in-law, written at the time of composition of the third Voronezh *Тетрадь*, he asks her to come and stay with him, confessing that:

Как только уезжает Надя, у меня начинается мучительное нервно-физическое заболевание. Оно сводится к следующему: за последние годы у меня развилось асматическое состояине. Дыхание всегда затруднено. Но при Наде это протекает мирно. Стоит ей уехать – я начинаю буквально задыхаться.
(Letter No.71, III p.277)

In Zadonsk Mandelstam's health seemed at least not to be deteriorating; he was happy and able to relax during this last holiday.

However, ominous news of arrests and impending trials began to figure in radio broadcasts. Nadezhda Yakovlevna recounts the occasion on which it was announced that the murderers of Kirov had been 'found' (N.Ya.I p.212). The Mandelstams went out onto the monastery road to discuss the significance of this news and Mandelstam, pointing out traces of horses' hoofprints in which the previous evening's rain had collected, likened them to the recesses of the memory. During the winter which followed this brief interval of calm the memory of that day, preserved in the sound of the announcer's voice and in the image of the water-filled hoofprints, drove him to take steps to protect himself, however little success they might have.

When they returned to Voronezh it seemed that all doors were closed to them and the vivid sense of isolation returned in full force. One redeeming feature was the room found for them in the house of a theatre dress-maker by the local theatre manager. The house stood on a hill above the river and the move did much to raise Mandelstam's spirits. He accepted that the winter of 1936-7 was his last opportunity to write freely and gave himself over entirely to poetry. For this reason the second *Тетрадь* comprises some of the most energetic and the most defiant poems of his exile, notable for their freedom from duress and their affirmation of life at one of the most apocalyptic moments in Russian history. The more severe the external restrictions imposed on him, the greater became the

necessity to preserve his inner freedom as a refuge from the
horror of everyday life. The ever-present fear of starvation,
through being denied work, his own illness, as well as the
monotony of the Voronezh landscape, forced him to draw extensively on his own inner resources. Yet one of the outstanding
features of this collection is its wonderful range of colouring, its sense of breadth and space and movement, deriving
from an enthusiasm and faith in life which permeate the whole
collection.

The opening poem

The opening poem, 'Из-за домов, из-за лесов' (I No.322),
stands in the same relation to the *Тетрадь* as had 'Твоим узким
плечам' (I No.296) to the previous collection. Both supply
epigraphs to the main body of the work by stating their
dominant themes: in 'Из-за домов, из-за лесов', amazing as
this would seem in the circumstances, Mandelstam sees himself
as the mouthpiece of Soviet cities, voicing their thoughts
and feelings:

> Гуди, старик, дыши сладко
> Как новгородский гость Садко,
> Под синим морем глубоко...
> Гудок советских городов.   (I No.322)

Already there are obvious references to his difficulty in
breathing, a quite literal difficulty which appears either in
such allusions or in rhythmic representation throughout the
poetry. Mandelstam draws a parallel between himself and Sadko,
the minstrel-merchant of *bylina* fame. Mandelstam-Sadko, the
poem implies, will by his own methods and with his own weapons
thwart the forces of evil in their attempt to exact tribute
from him. Like Sadko's 'гуселки яровчаты', his poetry brings
him success, but is also the cause of his downfall. Sadko, too
accomplished musically for his own good, had delivered himself
into the clutches of the 'царь морской' in exactly the same
way as Mandelstam's disgrace at the hands of his own 'царь'

had come about - through too effective a use of his art. In
his poetry Mandelstam had none the less the certainty of a
future life, precisely through his poetry - 'Гуди протяжно
вглубь веков', and glorified the inspiration which filled the
nights with poetry - 'Гуди за власть ночных трудов' (N.Ya.III,
preferred reading of line 3). The spectacle of him working
alone at night, secure in the knowledge that he was expressing
the feelings of the inarticulate masses on their behalf arouses
a mixture of admiration for his faith and pity for his self-
deception. He believed whole-heartedly in poetry as a force
comparable in strength with political or military power.
During Anna Akhmatova's visit to Voronezh at the beginning of
the winter he mentioned this belief to her, nor did she
dispute it: 'Поэзия - это власть'. Mandelstam's assertion
that, because of this, the poet had a right to a place of
honour in society was as unlikely to gain a sympathetic
audience in the Soviet Union of the 'ежовщина' as the content-
ion that the poet's contribution to society was of intrinsic
value. Akhmatova saw the situation rather more realistically
in her poem on this visit to Voronezh:

> А в комнате опального поэта
> Дежурят страх и Муза в свой черед,
> И ночь идет,
> Которая не ведает рассвета.[1]

The 'Рождение улыбки' and 'Щегол' cycle

Notwithstanding its irrelevance to actual circumstances, the
right of the poet to a recognised place in society is proclaimed by Mandelstam with a confidence no less heartening for
being utterly misplaced in the cycle based on the poems
'Рождение улыбки' (I No.342) and 'Щегол' (I No.324), the
second and fourth respectively in the collection. As so often
in his work, a concrete instance provided the starting-point

---

[1] Ахматова, vol. 1, p.236.

of the poem: the baby son of one of his Voronezh acquaintances
the writer Olga Kretova, was beginning to smile (N.Ya.III) -
'Когда заулыбается дитя' (I No.342). The transitional poem
which links the cycle's two subjects - the smile of the child
and the goldfinch - sets out clearly the path of Mandelstam's
thoughts on this innocent smile:

> Но улыбка неподкупна,† как дорога,
> Непослушна, не слуга.   (I No.323)
> †'неподдельна' in S p.301

Although this quatrain, 'Подивлюсь на мир еще немного', began
merely as a desultory variant of the main 'smile' poem, Mandelstam felt it essential that his readers should grasp the
point it makes: creative freedom, like the unforced smile of
a child, cannot be faked, nor bought with bribes, nor enslaved.
For this reason he included the quatrain in the main text,
having earlier thought it too obvious and unsubtle (N.Ya.III).

In 'Рождение улыбки' the analogy between the infant smile
and creative freedom is emphasised by the elaboration of their
common function, cognition - 'Для бесконечного познанья яви'
(I No.342). Cognition of the surrounding world appeared to
Mandelstam as a constant miracle, involving the full and
imaginative use not only of the five senses, but also of the
sixth sense, whether this goes under the name of the inward
eye, the inner ear or simply intuition. Internal clues link
this poem with the 'Восьмистишия' of pre-exile days, where the
same type of image denotes the process of cognition:

> На лапы из воды поднялся материк -
> Улитки рта наплыв и приближенье -
> И бьет в глаза один атлантов миг:
> Явленья явного в число чудес вселенья.   (I No.342)

> Шестого чувства крохотный придаток
> Иль ящерицы теменной глазок,
> Монастыри улиток и створчаток,
> Мерцающих ресничек говорок.   May 1932 (I No.278)

Circles and arcs, such as characterise a snail's shell or the
eye of a primitive animal form, appear in both. In 'Восьмисти-

шия' the curves of rainbows and billowing sails, of cupolas
and arc-like bends enhance the sense of roundness:

И дугами парусных гонок
Открытые формы чертя   July 1935   (I No.275)

И вдруг дуговая растяжка
Звучит в бормотаньях моих.   November 1933   (I No.276)

Как бы дорогой, согнутою в рог, —
Понять пространства внутренний избыток
И лепестка и купола залог.   January 1934   (I No.279)

An identical series of images - rainbows, back-bones, mountain
ridges - echoes in 'Рождение улыбки':

И радужный уже строчится шов...

Хребтом и аркою поднялся материк,
Улитка выползла, улыбка просияла,
Как два конца их радуга связала   (I No.342)

All these instances of involution and convolution are in effect
ancillary metaphors for one of the most central in Mandelstam's
work, namely the poet's curved lips, invariably equated with
his poetry. Lip movements are as basic a feature in the
composition of poetry as in its performance. In the way that
a child begins to smile before it learns to talk, in its first
attempts to convey its reactions of pleasure mixed with bitterness - 'С развилинкой и горести и сласти', the poet's muttering lips likewise express his primary reactions, and in their
configurations lies the basis of the finished poem's words
and phrases.

The evolution of the final version is interesting, in
that both the third and fourth stanzas were never fully
admitted into the poem. Even in Samatikha and Kalinin Mandelstam hesitated between including them or including only the
first two stanzas in the finished text. The first two versions
in fact make no mention of the present second stanza:

Когда заулыбается дитя
С прививкою и горечи и сласти,
Концы его улыбки, не шутя,
Уходят в океанское безвластье.

И свет и вкус пространство потеряло,
На лапы из воды поднялся материк,
(second version: На лапы задние поднялся материк)
Улитка выползла, улыбка просияла,
Как два конца их радуга связала
И бьет в глаза один атлантов миг.   (N.Ya.III)

9-11 December

In the last three versions the two opening stanzas are in
their present form, but the third appeared in the following
variants:

1 На лапы из воды поднялся материк,
  Улитки рта наплыв и приближенье -
  И бьет в глаза один атлантов миг
  Под легкий наигрыш хвалы и удивленья.   (N.Ya.III)

8 December - 17 January

2 На лапы из воды поднялся материк:
  Улитки губ - наплыв и приближенье -
  И бьет в глаза один атлантов миг -
  Явленья явное в улыбку превращенье.   (N.Ya.III)

9 December - 6 January

3 На лапы из воды поднялся материк -
  Улитки рта наплыв и приближенье:
  И бьет в глаза один атлантов миг
  Явленья явного чудесное явленье.
  (Ягненка гневного разумное явленье)   (N.Ya.III)

8 December - 9 January

The reference to the 'Raphael' lamb of 'Улыбнись, ягненок
гневный' (I No.321), which he wrote in January, but earlier
(2 January) than the completion of the 'smile' poem, reveals
the great diversity of phenomena which man can apprehend;
reference through the lamb to works of art alone imposed a
misleading limitation on human potential in the field of
perception, and so was abandoned in this connection. One
point at which the earlier version is clearer than the final
one is the explicit link between external phenomena and the
new-born smile - 'Явленья явное в улыбку превращенье': an
exact definition of the work of the poet.

The concept of evolution is of particular importance here.
It is no accident that the genesis of poetry should be shown
in terms of the genesis of man. This extended metaphor has

three stages of development: the emergence of a continent;
the appearance of the most primitive life-forms; the awakening of cognition in infant man. The highest stage of all is
yet to come - not so much cognition as recognition, the process
by which comparatively formless material is recognised as the
stuff from which the ultimate in structural formality, poetry,
will evolve. In the beginning there is 'океанское безвластье'
and limitless space, devoid of sense perceptions: 'И цвет и
вкус пространство потеряло'. The first significant development
occurs when the land mass hauls itself up on its hind paws out
of the water. In this action it has acquired both shape and
identity: it has become vertebrate. The primeval ocean throws
up a huge and ungainly life-form, but one at least equipped
with a back-bone. Reference to the much earlier poem 'Век'
(I No.135) indicates the importance Mandelstam attached to
the possession of a back-bone, site of the central nervous
system and thus of human sense perception:

> Тварь, покуда жизнь хватает,
> Донести хребет должна,
> И невидимым играет
> Позвоночником волна...
>
> Но разбит твой позвоночник,
> Мой прекрасный, жалкий век.   1923 (I No.135)

Life ceases when the back-bone is broken and the spinal cord
severed. In 'Рождение улыбки' the reverse process obtains;
with the acquisition of its back-bone - here the dual meaning
of 'хребет' is fully exploited - the unformed continent gains
contours and so becomes the object of the most basic kind of
recognition. This contrast between form and formlessness
applies even more to the snail. From one of the lower forms
of life, a shapeless invertebrate jelly, there evolves an
object of some beauty and complexity, a snail shell. Every
advantage is taken of the phonetic similarity of 'улыбка' and
'улитка'. Mandelstam was tireless in his condemnation of those
who advocated the separation of form from content, and this

poem demonstrates more clearly than most the impossibility of
such a separation, for the poem's content, in the sense of its
argument, lies, to a vital extent, in the actual sound of the
words. The ringing sound in the poet's ears from 'Ариост' (I
No.267) must by definition contain sense units in which form
and content are both implicit; otherwise the poet will be one
of those whom he called scathingly 'переводчики готового
смысла':

> Иначе неизбежен долбеж, вколачивание готовых гвоздей,
> именуемых культурно-историческими образами...

> Но выжать что бы то ни было можно только из влажной губки
> или тряпки. Каким бы мы жгутом ни закручивали концепцию,
> мы не выдавим из нее никакой формы, если она сама по себе
> уже не есть форма.
>
> *Разговор о Данте* (II pp.364 & 375)

From the most primitive forms the poem moves to the most
sophisticated form of life, man. When a child begins to smile
its origins in primeval chaos are clearly apparent:

> Концы его улыбки, не шутя,
> Уходят в океанское безвластье.   (I No.342)

At the same time its cognitive faculties undergo a process
of coordination:

> И радужный уже строчится шов
> Для бесконечного познанья яви.   (I No.342)

Mandelstam's scale of comparison - snail shells and rainbow
arcs, mountain ridges and the curve of the lips, is breath-
taking. The synthesising of these disparate phenomena is in
itself miraculous - 'Явленья явного в число чудес вселенья'.
He marvels at the compass of the human mind, its ability to
assimilate impressions and relate them one to another. This
gift, the ability to correlate and think creatively, to
construct a 'радужный шов', leads at its greatest refinement
to the composition of poetry:

> Углами губ оно играет в славе...
> Как два конца их радуга связала   (I No.342)

The transitional quatrain, 'Подивлюсь на мир еще немного'

(I No.323), with its declaration of artistic integrity, unites
the 'smile' poem with 'Щегол' (I No.324). Work proceeded on
both main poems simultaneously and resulted in a great number
of variants. Apart from their common themes there is a whole
complex of related images in the poems which came as by-products, as a result of which a definite cyclical form, with its
twin centre in the two main poems, can be discerned. Comparison
of their dates shows that the 'рождение' impulse slightly
preceded the 'щегол' impulse - 'Рождение улыбки' was written
between 8 December and 17 January, the variant (I No.325) from
9-12 December and 'Щегол' from 10-27 December. An early variant
of 'Рождение' was already finished in the days between 9-11
December. It was the troublesome third stanza which delayed
the finalising of the text.

Disobedience, one aspect of the maintenance of integrity,
is the chief characteristic of the poet and his 'подобье',
the goldfinch:

И есть лесная Саламанка
Для непослушных умных птиц!   (I No.327)

Я откликнусь моему подобью:
Жить щеглу - вот мой указ!   (I No.326)

The poet admires two other qualities in the goldfinch: colourful dandyism and alert intelligence. Although Mandelstam liked
to imagine that his voice was that of the Soviet cities,
this consideration did not prevent him from seeing himself as
the literary bureaucracy saw him - a colourful dilettante,
whose work was at best irrelevant, at worst a slander on
Soviet reality. Comparison with the dazzling goldfinch, surrounded as they both were by their grey-brown fellows, clearly
amused him:

Хвостик лодкой, перья - черно-желты,
Ниже клюва в краску влит -
Сознаешь ли, до чего, щегол, ты,
До чего ты щегловит?   (I No.324)

It was perhaps inevitable that the colours yellow and black,

with all their attendant associations of Judaism for him,
reappear at this point in his poetry. His was the classic
destiny of the diaspora Jew: to live in exile, ostracised by
an alien society, a natural target for persecution. He shares
with the goldfinch an instinct for self-preservation in the
face of antagonism:

> В обе стороны он в оба смотрит - в обе!
> Не посмотрит - улетел.   (I No.324)

Both are endowed with an indomitable resilience, although on
the surface life appears intolerable. Mandelstam realises
that his anger is as impotent and as ludicrous as the goldfinch's, though no less vigorous:

> Зимний день, колючий, как мякина,
> Так ли жестк в зрачке твоем?   (I No.324)

> Клевещет жердочка и планка,
> Клевещет клетка сотней спиц   (I No.327)

Although he was fully aware of the cage enclosing him, his
'forest Salamanca' gave him the freedom of the cultural world
his extensive knowledge of world literature, the comfort of
music and his own poetry afforded a refuge to which he could,
like all disobedient birds, fly away. As in the first *Тетрадь*
he affirms that exile by no means eliminates the possibility
of living to the full - 'Есть многодонная жизнь вне закона'
(I No.316).

As Nadezhda Yakovlevna points out, the thematic framework
of the cycle is contained in the closely-knit complex 'мякина
(жевать мякину, поймать птицу на мякину, колючая мякина),
улыбка, щегол-щеголь', with the ideas of obstinacy and disobedience running throughout (N.Ya.III). The lines in which the
child and the bird are linked by this association of ideas
through their common attribute, 'мякина' (variant, I Nos.325
& 326), showed the connection between cognition, in its
earliest form, and stubborn insistence on continuing to foster
cognition as each individual comprehended it, whether this
involved seeing the world through the eye of a goldfinch or

the eye of a poet:

Детский рот жует свою мякину,
Улыбается, жуя.   (I Nos.325 & 326)

This 'птичья свобода' in defiance of all the rules causes the
poet to promulgate his own 'указ' to the goldfinch; there is
only one law and that is to live (I No.326).

A combination of ideas - reminders of childhood through
the smile of Kretova's son and through Vadik, their landlady's
boy, who organised the bird market in which the original goldfinch had figured, the colours black and yellow, and the
issuing of decrees - unexpectedly aroused reminiscences of
Leningrad, or rather the Petersburg of Mandelstam's school
and student days. The absence of change in his image of the
city is striking. Since he felt that at the Revolution it had
died a spiritual death (N.Ya.II p.121) he preferred to cling
to the memory of childhood impressions. In the epithet 'желторотый' from 'Нынче день какой-то желторотый' (I No.329) the
child's mouth from 'Улыбка' develops in a new direction. Its
primary meaning is its most obvious one: the near-idiocy and
lack of sense in the day. In addition to this, however, the
yellowness always associated with Petersburg's Italianate
architecture, the yellow mist, yellowish snow and the lemon
colour of the Neva from past poems are relived:

Над желтизной правительственных зданий
Кружилась долго мутная метель   1913   (I No.42)

Рыбий жир ленинградских речных фонарей!
Узнавай же скорее декабрьский денек,
Где к зловещему дегтю подмешан желток.   1930   (I No.221)

И над лимонной Невою...   1931   (I No.222)

In a variant the words 'желтый туман' appear and the final
version contains a similar reminder of the mist which covers
the city in winter:

И глядят приморские ворота
В якорях, в туманах на меня.   (I No.329)

Летит в туман моторов вереница   1913   (I No.42)

Только злой мотор во мгле промчится   1920 (I No.118)

In the second quatrain the black of the canals complements
the yellow of the day:

> И каналов узкие пеналы
> Подо льдом еще черней.   (I No.329)

The pencil-box is the same 'детский чернильный пенал' as had
featured in similar reactions to the city during Mandelstam's
stay in a completely different city, Tiflis, in 1930 (I No.
201), and is closely linked with another reference to children's drawing more specifically concerned with Leningrad: 'Не
потому ль, что я видел на детской картинке Лэди Годиву' (I No.
222). Consistency of viewpoint mattered very much to Mandelstam during the thirties; his unchanging attitude to the city
is a very minor illustration of one of his major principles.
The poem conveys his feeling for the misty, unreal Petersburg
of Russian literature as he had found it before and just after
the turn of the century, in the decade before the final
catastrophe overtook the city. He said of this poem that Blok
would have envied him it (N.Ya.III), and there is a marked
resemblance in tone and subject to one of Blok's better-known
poems. Indeed the authors of both poems must have shared
similar emotions at the sight of warships making their stately
way into harbour:

> Тихий, тихий по воде линялой
> Ход военных кораблей.   (I No.329)

> Ты помнишь? в нашей бухте сонной
> Спала зеленая вода
> Когда кильватерной колонной
> Вошли военные суда.[1]

With thoughts of flying away to freedom came ideas of the
promise of travel and excitement beyond the 'приморские ворота'
of Petersburg, which had existed since the early poem in which
the Admiralty was depicted as a sea-going frigate, sailing

---

[1] А.А.Блок, *Собрание сочинений в восьми томах*, (8 vols.,
Moscow-Leningrad, 1960-3), vol. 3, p.136.

away into an element where spatial restriction ceases to apply:

> Нам четырех стихий приязненно господство;
> Но создал пятую свободный человек...

> И вот разорваны трех измерений узы
> И открываются всемирные моря.   1913   (I No.48)

The sea, with the ebb and flow of the tide, permeates the cycle. The 'океанское безвластье' (I No.342) from which great continents arose displays tidal movement akin to the ebb and flow of the sounds in the poet's ear. The sea metaphor of Mandelstam's attempt to describe a certain stage of poetic composition in the poem 'Не у меня, не у тебя - у них' (I No. 328) is bound up with a synthetic conception of the world, where the sea and human blood are of similar composition - as is the case in Odysseus' narrative from the *Divine Comedy*:

> Это песнь о составе человеческой крови, содержащей в себе
> океанскую соль. Начало путешествия заложено в системе
> кровеносных сосудов. Кровь планетарна, солярна, солона...
>   *Разговор о Данте*   (II p.388)

The common element of salt corresponds to the tidal movement of the nameless sounds made by the waves on the shore and by poetry in the poet's ear. In this poem are gathered all the imagery and phonetic material of 'Рождение улыбки', but this is the most refined stage in cognition which has, as the identity of imagery testifies, evolved directly from the first cognitive act of the infant. The 'улыбка/улитка' metaphor for the curve of human lips reappears:

> И с благодарностью улитки губ людских
> Потянут на себя их дышащую тяжесть.   (I No.328)

In the same way the essence of the 'их' who are the subject of the poem is described as 'хрящ', like that of the snail; the configuration of the lips in a smile - 'развилинах' - expresses the same 'наслажденья', while the surging of primeval waters dominates the whole. The difference lies in the object of the exercise: the infant takes delight in the world around it by and for itself, whereas the poet apprehends

reality 'для людей, для их сердец живых' (I No.328). His work
is not exclusively for his own benefit, the voices in his ears
are not for him alone:

> Значит, 'они' – это нечто, существующее вне поэта, те
> голоса, та гармония, которую он пытается уловить внутрен-
> ним слухом для людей...   (N.Ya.I p.214)

In struggling to externalise these sounds and to give them
existence as audible entities, the poet's lips undertake a
task which, although welcome, is also exacting - 'дышащую
тяжесть'. Much that is implicit in the inner voices - 'Вся
сила окончаний родовых' - has to be given outward form, but
the reward is a rich one:

> Войди в их хрящ,
> И будешь ты наследником их княжеств.   (I No.328)

A somewhat more sinister by-product of 'Рождение улыбки'
emerged simultaneously (10-26 December) but entirely separately
from 'Не у меня, не у тебя – у них'. The transition from
infancy to maturity was now complete, but a further state is
envisaged in human development - the grown man becomes an idol
in 'Внутри горы бездействует кумир' (I No.330). In this connection the various stages of composition have a certain relevance. Although the poem should have been placed third in the
order of writing, the usual chronological arrangement was
upset by Mandelstam's uncertainty as to the identity of the
personage portrayed therein. This so delayed its completion
that other poems begun at the same time quickly replaced it.
The earliest extant variant was dictated to Nadezhda Yakovlevna on 13 December and appears as I No.331, with the exception
of the first stanza, which had not yet come. The second stanza
remained constant at all stages and most of Mandelstam's
effort was directed towards the third stanza. Before dictating
the supposedly finished version of 13 December he declared
that he had guessed the subject of the poem: 'Я догадался –
это Шилейко' (N.Ya.III). At this point he was sure that the
famous Assyriologist, Egyptologist and numismatist, endeared

to him by association with Anna Akhmatova, had been in his
mind while he was composing the poem. He supported this theory
by citing the lines which had made their first appearance in
this version:

Он улыбается своим широким ртом
И начинает жить, когда приходят гости.   (I No.331)

Having made a few minor alterations in keeping with the
character of the kindly scholar (See also I No.428) - 'широкий'
became 'тишайший', and it may be that its traditional use as
the fixed epithet of Peter the Great's father, Tsar Alexei,
has some significance - Mandelstam still felt that the subject
and its poetic realisation remained at variance. Despite
Shileiko's interest in the pyramids, in mummified idols and
the worship of rulers, the man himself should really be dissociated from his interests. It then became clear to Mandelstam that his own preoccupation lay rather with certain
aspects of Egyptology and Assyriology than with their exponent.
In this case the worship of pagan idols and the contemporary
parallel in the near-deification of Stalin - the present-day
'Assyrian' - engaged his interest against his will. Most of
the work on the poem has not survived, but the one draft of
the third stanza which has ends with the line: 'И исцеляет он,
но убивает легче' (N.Ya.III). At this point any connection
Shileiko may originally have had with the poem vanishes
completely. The change to the present form of the final line
was brought about by the realisation that the idol was still
a man, although this was an unpalatable truth: 'И вспомнить
силится свой облик человечий' (I No.330). Similarly the
epithet 'счастливых', relating to the idol's 'покоях' in the
first stanza, was abandoned, as Mandelstam insisted that the
sleep of an idol such as Stalin could be neither natural nor
happy, but only 'хранимых'.

This portrait of the idol inside the Kremlin - 'внутри
горы' - equals the 1933 epigram (I No.286) in malice, not

least in the way it dwells on the repulsive physical characteristics of Stalin: 'А с шеи каплет ожерелий жир' (I No.330)
accords with the earlier description of his fingers, as fat
and fleshy as worms. As with everything associated with
eastern religions, the idol has reached a state of complete
inertia:

Внутри горы бездействует кумир
В покоях бережных, безбрежных и хранимых   (I No.330)

Stalin's progress from childhood onwards is traced, in an
attempt to explain how this final stage in his career was foreshadowed and achieved. In general, the whole cycle is concerned
with the ages of man, from the smiling child through the adult
man to the figure of the idol. In the case of Stalin the
process begins in the idyllic Georgia of his boyhood, with its
rainbows, its exotic birds, its earthenware pots:

Когда он мальчик был и с ним играл павлин,
Его индийской радугой кормили.
Давали молока из розоватых глин
И не жалели кошенили.   (I No.330)

Only the last line jars. Cochineal, made from the bodies of
crushed ants, was an appropriate foretaste of the blood of
human beings which, having long been accustomed to the colour,
Stalin drinks like milk. Obsession with crushed bodies dominates his later life - 'Он мыслит костию и чувствует челом'.
Mandelstam demonstrates how effective and automatic are the
reflexes of cruelty. The idol has long since done nothing, as
he has become completely ossified, but the machinery of terror
has been set up and now operates by its own impetus. The still,
wide-mouthed smile of the idol strikes fear into the beholder
- especially the reader who remembers the enchanting first
smile of the child - because he knows the thoughts lurking
beneath the surface.

There are thirteen lines in the poem, a fact which Mandelstam regarded as significant. Any poem which had seven,
eleven or thirteen lines in its final version caused him to

wonder if some new form might be evolving in his work, but in
retrospect he saw that the instances of this were isolated,
and their significance limited to the individual poems concerned. In 'Внутри горы бездействует кумир' he had written a
potentially fatal poem on the most dangerous subject of all,
in which unambiguous physical description of his subject
replaces the more normal type of oblique allusion. Thus the
thirteen-line form took on a special aura, and the poem written
in its wake, 'А мастер пушечного цеха' (I No.333) is over-
shadowed by a presentiment of certain death, followed by the
last step in the development of man, his apotheosis in a
monument - the epitome of stasis. The 'мастер' who forges the
poet's monument for him - 'Уж мы сошьем тебе такое' - is also
called a 'памятников швец'. This phrase arose from Mandelstam's
amusement at the figures standing on plinths with their arms
extended, thus dragging the entire sleeve of the jacket up
their arms, instead of the arm being able to move freely in
the sleeve, as in well-tailored garments. He complained about
his own discomfort in these 'Москвошвейные' jackets and was
delighted to find it enshrined in official monuments.

A return to the present

The first poem which does not belong to the cycle of ages,
reminiscences and presentiments was written simultaneously,
but is set firmly in the present. 'Сосновой рощицы закон' (I
No.335) was begun one day later than the other poem which
describes Mandelstam's stay in Zadonsk, 'Пластинкой тоненькой
жиллета' (I No.334), but since the latter took definitive
shape only two weeks later, he considered its place to be
later in the collection (N.Ya.III). On a hillock in front of
their house in Zadonsk stood a clump of pine trees which lay
open to all the winds, and in the first poem his imagination
strays back to these trees, and to the music made by the wind
sweeping through them in winter. Although in Voronezh, he

could none the less hear the sound of viols and harps, and pictures the trees as the musical instruments played by the wind, their branches the strings, their trunks the resonating chambers:

> Стволы извилисты и голы,
> Но все же арфы и виолы
> Растут, как будто каждый ствол
> На арфу начал гнуть Эол   (I No.335)

The desolation of the as yet snowless winter in Voronezh pervades these memories of summer in Zadonsk, whereas the second poem (I No.334) depicts the Don heights at the zenith of summer, unmarked by the poet's intervening experience. Its inspiration was slightly bizarre: on leaving the public baths in Voronezh, he caught sight of a cart with hay in it and looked fixedly at it for some moments, to Nadezhda Yakovlevna' annoyance, since she wanted him to rest from the poetry whose imminent arrival was visible in that stare. He noticed this and said that nothing could be done to halt its arrival. When they arrived home he spread out the watercolours she had done of the area on the floor, and walked up and down among them - they were all of corn stooks and hills (N.Ya.III), hence the reference to the work of Ruisdael: 'Честь рюисдалевых картин' (I No.334). The corn stubble of the poem was that of her water-colours:

> Пластинкой тоненькой жиллета
> Легко щетину спячки снять -
> Полуукраинское лето
> Давай с тобою вспоминать.   (I No.334)

Harvesting and the hills beyond the Don both feature prominently in this recollection. An interesting image creeps into their description, suggesting that the poetic idyll was not entirely free from the unpleasant aspects of the present:

> Его холмы к далекой цели
> Стогами легкими летели...
> Над желтым лагерем жнивья   (I No.334)

None the less the memory of the hills, the trees lining the

monastery road - 'А тополь встал самолюбиво' - and the
'деревья-бражники' outside their house, leading down to the
willows by the Don, was all that lightened the 'бремя вечеров'
in Voronezh when night had fallen and the river, the fields
and the trees disappeared from sight.

The 'Темноводье' triad

Compensation from the cold of mid-December through memories
of summer gave way to the depiction of winter Voronezh in
the 'тройчатки' 'Эта область в темноводье' (I No.338), 'Вехи
дальнего обоза' (I No.340) and 'Как подарок запоздалый' (I No.
336). The last-mentioned names the key word 'запоздалый',
referring to the advent of winter with the first proper snow-
fall. Snow came late that year (N.Ya.I p.207), at the very
end of December, and the depressingly cold, dark, cloudy
weather usually associated with November seemed everlasting.
The landscape was bare - 'Степь беззимняя гола' (I No.338),
and the whole province was saturated - 'в темноводье' - by
the never-ending rain:

> Хляби хлеба, гроз ведро –
> Не дворянское угодье –
> Океанское ядро.   (I No.338)

The development of this poem can be traced in the unusu-
ally full fair copies of its drafts, of which the first dates
to 24 December, the day after work on the poem began:

st.1 Ничего, что темноводье,
   Ничего, что я продрог
   И что область хлебороба –
   Цепи якорной ядро.
   Thereafter as in I No.338, lines 5-12, except line 8:
   Тонких жилок не сочтешь

st.2 As in I No.338, except line 9:
   Трудный рай страны знакомой

st.3 Где я? Что со мной дурного?
   Кто растет из-за угла?
   Это мачеха Кольцова –
   Это родина щегла!
   Thereafter as in I, No.338   (N.Ya.III)

The second fair copy is dated simply 'December 1936' and is
identical to the above text except in respect of stanza 3,
line 2, which was altered to its present form, 'Степь беззимняя гола'; this alteration can probably be assigned to 25
December, since the dates 23-25 December appear at its foot.
Parallel with the composition of these versions ran variants
which never materialised into independent poems. Two of these
survived, the first of which, written down on 26 December,
appears in I as No.339, and the second, probably finalised on
27 December, appears in S pp.301-2, its dates of composition
therefore being 23-27 December. Further work after 25 December
was, as Mandelstam told Nadezhda Yakovlevna, preparatory to
the next two poems and not integral to the first, which was
to all intents and purposes finished by that date (N.Ya.III).

Since the weather in the province made it look like a
microcosm of the ocean, but one completely lacking in interest
or excitement, Mandelstam was driven to escape once again into
the world of memories. It was the illuminated plywood map of
the province hanging in the telegraph station a few steps
away from their house (N.Ya.I p.189), on which lamps lit up
to show which districts of the province were linked by the
telephone network (N.Ya.I p.206), which, with its life-giving
veins of human communication contrasting with the dead town
around him (24 December version), initiated the thoughts
expressed in the rest of the poem:

> Я люблю ее рисунок -
> Он на Африку похож -
> Дайте свет: прозрачных лунок
> На фанере не сочтешь...   (I No.338)

He repeats the names of the province's chief towns - 'Анна,
Россошь и Гремячье' - with some relish, since his inner vision
is already picturing the depths of the countryside as the
railway passenger would see it on his travels, under the light
white snow denied the province in reality:

Белизна снегов гагачья
Из вагонного окна. (I No.338)

His imagination wanders to the province's collective farms.
He had been commissioned to write poems in praise of them for
the Voronezh newspapers, and visited them in the summer of
1935. The tour began at the 'райцентр', the village of Vorob-
evko: here he states that he will never forget its 'райком'.
This very untypical declaration was on account of several meet-
ings he had with one of its members, a middle-aged man, sus-
piciously intelligent for one in his position. This official
had obviously shown too active an opposition to some plan or
someone in power, had paid for it dearly, and was accordingly
wary in his conversation. Yet in spite of his caution a bitter
intonation crept into his voice when he spoke of the liquidation of the kulaks and the agricultural reorganisation in
the province. This struck a chord in Mandelstam, who had seen
the aftermath of this policy in the Crimea in 1933, and knew
that he would never forget the misery of the *sovkhozy* which
were supposed to have been its crowning achievement:

Трудодень страны знакомой
Я запомню навсегда (I No.338)

With a bitterness equal to that of the administrator, he recalls another of his own journeys, this time 'abroad' to the
Tambov Nerve Sanatorium, although it was his heart condition
which was the subject of medical investigation:

Живем на высоком берегу реки Цны. Она широка или кажется
широкой, как Волга. Переходит в чернильно-синие леса.
Мягкость и гармония русской зимы доставляют глубокое
наслаждение. Letter No.60 (III p.267)

Здесь так плохо, что очень многие уезжают до срока:
неизбалованные работники районов... Чай без сахара. Шум.
Врачи - вроде почтовых чиновников...
Эти дни вроде дурного сна! Какой-то штрафной батальон...
Letter No.64 (III pp.271-2)

Въехал ночью в рукавичный
Снегом пышущий Тамбов,
Видел Цны - реки обычной
Белый, белый, бел покров. (I No.338)

The 23-27 December version of the poem indicates that the memory of his time there haunted him and was the subject of recurring nightmares:

> Сон первичный
> Соблазнителен и нов.
> Что мне снится? Рукавичный
> Снегом пышущий Тамбов etc.　　(S p.301)

In the poem's last stanza Mandelstam is compelled to face up to present reality, although he is unwilling to accept that something other than the weather is responsible for his depression. That this was so is shown more clearly in the version of 24 December:

> Где я? Что со мной дурного?
> Кто растет из-за угла?　　(N.Ya.III)

The subject of the last line, prefiguring the crawling creature of his January 1937 poem - 'И не ползет ли медленно по ним Тот...' (I No.350), is inevitably Stalin, the 'мачеха Кольцова'. A.V.Koltsov, a native of Voronezh, had written of the falcon who wonders why he is wasting his life sitting at home:

> Долго ль буду я
> Под окном сидеть,
> По дороге вдаль
> День и ночь глядеть?
>
> Иль у сокола
> Крылья связаны,
> Иль пути ему
> Все заказаны?
>
> Иль боится он
> В чужих людях быть,
> С судьбой-мачехой
> Сам-собою жить? [1]

In the final version of the poem this threat is immediately denied, as Mandelstam contrives to pass it off as a trick played on him by the gloomy shadows of the province, the 'родина щегла'. The poem is the culmination of his miserable

[1]　А.В.Кольцов, *Полное собрание сочинений* (St Petersburg, 1909), pp.125-6.

feelings induced by the sheets of bare ice where white snow
should be, about which Anna Akhmatova complained, in her poem
on her visit to them in Voronezh, that it made walking impossible:

> И город весь стоит оледенелый.
> Как под стеклом деревья, стены, снег.
> По хрусталям я прохожу несмело.[1]

Mandelstam spent the long nights writing poetry and looking
out on this 'гололедица', to the accompaniment of the electric
kettle noise - he drank endless glasses of tea at all times:

> Только города немого
> В гололедицу обзор,
> Только чайника ночного
> Сам с собою разговор   (I No.338)

The friendly hooting of passing trains in the distance emphasised in their companionable greeting his own isolation and
physical confinement. He was attracted by the peculiar mixture
of Russian and Ukrainian which he heard in Voronezh, especially
in the southern districts of the province, and ascribes this
'мова', the Ukrainian for 'speech', 'language', to the trains
calling at one another:

> Он чуял здесь вольный дух передовых окраин и вслушивался
> в южно-русский, еще не украинский говор. Вот почему паро-
> возные гудки заговорили у него по-украински.
>
> (N.Ya.I p.149)

> В гуще воздуха степного
> Перекличка поездов -
> Да украинская мова
> Их растянутых гудков.   (I No.338)

Predictably, all the main themes of the poem's finished
version are present from the moment when the first version
was written down - commital to paper happened only at a very
advanced stage in Mandelstam's work. The depression which
characterises the first four lines of the finished poem,
however, figures somewhat differently in the 24 December

[1] Ахматова, vol. 1, p.236

version. Instead of a generalised statement, impersonal in
its geographical detail, about the inundated province so
changed in aspect from the *chernozem* which had so delighted
him, this earlier version gives a more personal account of
the situation. Mandelstam, who had been soaked to the skin
time and again, felt vividly the practical consequences of
the rainstorms for one with inadequate protective clothing,
but here he shrugs it off. The compensation of the illuminated
map more than suffices; the contrast between the reality of
Voronezh and its outline on the map is lost in the final text,
as is the feeling of imprisonment suggested by the image of
the fettering anchor chain. He clings to his memory of the
province's fecundity as a grain-producing area throughout -
'Хляби хлеба' (24 December) and 'область хлебороба' (I No.338)
- but the substitution of 'трудодень' for 'трудный рай', the
sole alteration to the second stanza, reveals a shift in the
direction of the emotionally more neutral and more deperson-
alised final text. The same tendency is apparent in the
deletion from the third stanza of the potentially problematic
line 'Кто растет из-за угла?' and its replacement by the harmless and less self-indulgent 'Степь беззимняя гола'.

The second version (S pp.301-2) apparently seeks to
exorcise the Stalin nightmare by dismissing it. Its first
two lines summarise much of the content of the earlier version
- the nights of the last stanza, divided between writing
poetry and dozing off into a sleep in which bad dreams about
his recent journeys predominate. The absence of the Stalin
nightmare led to a greater concentration on the Tambov episode
and on the ominous sunflowers of the *sovkhoz*. In general,
however, reality seems to be slipping further away from him
in the course of the version:

> Кроме хлеба, кроме дома
> Снится мне глубокий сон:
> Трудодень, подъятый дремой,
> Превратился в синий Дон...   (S p.302)

Nadezhda Yakovlevna explains his hesitation in determining the final text by his desire to incorporate in it the 'optimistic' variant (I No.339), where the 'ведро' of unremitting storms eventually departs:

> Осторожно, грозно шло.
> Смотришь: небо стало выше –
> Новоселье, дом и крыша –
> И на улице светло!..   (I No.339)

He came to realise that this would have struck a false note. He had completely lost the sense of open, unbounded space – the trains are 'В гуще воздуха степного' – and was oppressed by the dark sky crushing him. A lightening sky , as the clouds lifted, was a mere fantasy, not only literally: figuratively speaking, the storm showed no sign of abating. The cloud of the 'темноводье' hangs over the 'гудок-щегол' poems and extended ultimately to the whole *Тетрадь*, a symbol of the approaching Terror. In the third poem of the 'тройчатки' Mandelstam accepted this peculiar winter as the precursor of storms to come:

> Хороша она испугом,
> Как начало грозных дел   (I No.336)

Only on 29 December did this sharp presentiment of catastrophe spring from the 'гроза-грозный' kernel to separate itself from the first poem and form an independent one. Between them came another, whose subject was again the horror of the Tambov sanatorium, 'Вехи дальнего обоза' (I No.340). From the 'особняк' in which Mandelstam felt forcibly confined, he saw the view described in his letter (III, Letter No.60). The frozen river and the snow-covered forest, whose trees could no longer be recognised, presented a motionless scene in which only the twitching of twigs as a train of sledges passed through the trees betrayed any sign of life, describing their passage in an indistinct script:

> Лишь чернил воздушных проза
> Неразборчива, легка ...   (I No.340)

'Проза' became the final element in the various lexical
motifs of the group, marked by their external similarity -
Nadezhda Yakovlevna points out how 'мороза-обоза- береза-
проза', together with 'совхозных-грозных', underly the sound
and sense structure of these poems (N.Ya.I p.208).

However, the development of the triad from the 24 Decembe
version of 'Темноводье' through to 'Вехи дальнего обоза' is
significant above all for the answer to the semi-rhetorical
'Кто растет из-за угла?' as the cycle develops. In the last
poems even the brash, aggressive raven quails before the
onset of this terrifying winter and its architect:

> Перед всем беслесным кругом
> Даже ворон оробел.   (I No.336)

> Природа ждала зимы, а люди в декабре 36 года уже знали,
> что им несет грядущий тридцать седьмой.   (N.Ya.I p.207)

Kashchei's cat; the angry lamb

Life was becoming increasingly lonely and hopeless. Only
Natasha Shtempel and actors from the local theatre dared to
visit or receive the Mandelstams (N.Ya.I p.189), there was nc
longer any opportunity to earn money (N.Ya.I p.146), and naturally neither of them enjoyed living on the charity of hard-
pressed friends and relatives. It was in the forlorn hope of
assistance, not only of a financial kind, that Mandelstam
sent the poem 'Оттого все неудачи' (I No.337), written betwee
9 and 30 December (not 20-30 as in I) to Tikhonov. He said
jokingly that since Kashchei was an expert golddigger - 'Камн
трогает клещами, Щиплет золото гвоздей' - he was in fact
sending Tikhonov a lump of gold in the very poem. Tikhonov's
telegram promising all possible aid was followed by silence
(N.Ya.I p.252). In the poem Mandelstam holds the avaricious,
feline eye - 'кошачий глаз' is a sort of quartz - responsibl(
for all his own misery. The descendant of stagnant weeds and
dealer in seaweed is clearly connected with the stagnation a

immobility of the idol inside the mountain. There is his reception of guests - 'Он на счастье ждет гостей', there is the idol's sleep - 'в покоях спящих', there is the mountain, whose booty is reflected in the cat's eyes - 'клад зажмуренной горы'. The 'кремль-кремень-камень' link postulated by Nadezhda Yakovlevna (N.Ya.I p.217) seems certain to have operated here: the stone of the mountain, the sparks of the pupils in the cat's eyes, as it might be from flintstone, would have led straight to the Kremlin with no difficulty. Although the folkloric aspect and the whole tone of the poem lack the deep seriousness of the main poem on the idol, their basic preoccupation is the same. Even the length of the stanzas, graduating to the last seven-line one, shows by its less strict form that the poem was relatively peripheral. Nadezhda Yakovlevna uses the poem to illustrate Mandelstam's ability to remember words he had heard or read in childhood many years later. The 'клешни' of Zhukovsky's poem about Kashchei,[1] which he had read as a child, becomes the 'клещи' with which Kashchei, instead of pulling out nails, 'щиплет зопото гвоздей', preparatory to extracting them. But the nails are another echo of childhood: in *Шум времени* Mandelstam recalls that when he was taken to visit his Riga grandparents he was deprived of his 'колючее богатство', the nails he was collecting, which were his pride and joy at the time (II p.68; N.Ya.II p. 621).

Only the cat's 'умоляющий' look connects this poem with that written on 2 January 1937 (not 9 January, as in I), 'Твой зрачок в небесной корке' (I No.345), since the reference to a cat in the Kashchei poem had made Mandelstam turn his

---

[1] 'Сказка о Царе Берендее, о сыне его Иване Царевиче, о хитростях Кощея Бессмертного и о премудрости Марьи Царевны, Кощеевой дочери', В.А.Жуковский, *Собрание сочинений в 4 томах*, (4 vols., Moscow-Leningrad 1959-60), vol. 3, p.161.

attention to their own domestic cat, a perfectly ordinary and
unsinister animal. So distasteful did Nadezhda Yakovlevna find
the proximity of these two completely different cats, that she
asked him to put the following poem, 'Улыбнись, ягненок гневный, с рафаэлева холста' (I No.321), between them; now she
has restored Mandelstam's original order (N.Ya.III). In contrast with the terrifying, rapacious eyes of Kashchei's horrible
pet, their own cat, a descendant of those idolised by the
Egyptians - 'обожествленный', and, in a different sense, idolised by the Mandelstams, spent its time making a detailed
appraisal of the world about it, 'вдаль и ниц', but with
reservation in its look:

> Защищают оговорки
> Слабых, чующих ресниц   (I No.345)

Mandelstam's fondness for the cat is apparent in his wish for
the unfathomable glance to be turned his way. He thinks the
cat has a quality of timelessness, an ability to see eternity
passing before its eyes, although this is hardly the sort of
quality which would be thought compatible with its normal
expression:

> Он глядит уже охотно
> В мимолетние века –
> Светлый, радужный, бесплотный,
> Умоляющий пока...   (I No.345)

Nadezhda Yakovlevna is not sure to which painting the
poem about the angry lamb (I No.321) refers. While the obvious
choice is Raphael's *Madonna Conestabile*, hanging in the Hermitage, she thinks that in certain undefinable ways it bears
a greater resemblance to Leonardo's *Madonna Litta*, which Mandelstam would also have seen there. Since they had no reproduction of either (N.Ya.III), the poem represents a general
longing for the riches of the Hermitage. Without being certain
which work he had in mind, it is still possible to appreciate
his delight in its lightness and colour:

> В легком воздухе свирели раствори жемчужин боль.

В синий, синий цвет синели океана въелась соль.
(I No.321)

His marvellous description of the Madonna's skirt is imbued
with the joy which makes him understand her wild happiness:
'Складки бурного покоя на коленях разлиты'. Recollection of
the painted sky's 'восхитительная мощь' particularly delights
him, given the absence of any such sky in Voronezh. It is
important that these three poems - this and the two on the
cats - radiate an energy and pleasure in life which seem
almost illicit in the circumstances. In the 'Темноводье'
group Mandelstam had just renounced an optimistic variant in
favour of dark predictions and, with the familiar swing of
the pendulum which characterises his changes of mood in these
collections, it was to these that he returned after a brief
interlude of pleasure.

The Koltsov twin poems

Of the 'двойчатки' which succeeded the triad, 'Я около Кольцова' (I No.343) was written on 9 January (not 1-9, as in I),
and 'Когда в ветвях понурых' (I No.344) was written on 9 and
10 January (not 6-10, as in I). In the latter the theme of
the disobedient bird, who refuses here to sing in late autumn,
returns:

Не хочет петь линючий,
Ленивый богатырь –
И малый и могучий
Зимующий снегирь.
(I No.344)

Mandelstam had every intention of remaining 'ленивый' - the
epithet, incidentally, is an example of the 'last word' which
often clinched a poem for him (N.Ya.I p.208). He was determi-
ned not to 'sing' in the way required of him, and so he sub-
mits to being carried off over the tree-tops by the sorcerer,
not inconceivably the Kashchei figure of the earlier poem,
and indeed seats himself on the sledge of the dead:

В сиреневые сани

Усядусь поскорей. (I No.344)

Death is envisaged in metaphors which are purely Russian in
origin - the sorcerer of folklore and the sledge of the dead
made famous by Monomakh's declaration in his *Поучение* that he
is 'в санях сидючи'. This comes as no surprise since, in the
second poem of the pair, it is the folk poet A.V.Koltsov
(1809-42), a native of the area, whom he associates with his
misfortune. It was therefore natural that death should present
itself to his imagination in traditional Russian guise. Koltsov's name provides the phonetic material for a display of
technical adroitness while dealing with a perfectly serious
subject, a *tour de force* not unique in Mandelstam:

> Я около Кольцова,
> Как сокол закольцован,
> И нет ко мне гонца,
> И дом мой без крыльца. (I No.343)

Like a ringed falcon, or the falcon with clipped wings of the
Koltsov poem (see p.166), he felt constricted in his diladpi-
dated dwelling, and the pine forest spread out around him
was as restricting to his movements as a ball and chain on
his leg. He was driven to contemplate the same solution as in
the first poem:

> В степи кочуют кочки
> И все идут, идут
> Ночлеги, ночи, ночки -
> Как бы слепых везут... (I No.343)

The sledge carries its blind passengers, whose eyes are
closed in death, over the uneven steppe land; they cannot see
but can feel the bumps. The distant steppe was always visible
from in front of the Mandelstams' house, and he became
familiar with this imaginary journey, deriving some comfort
from the fact that an end to misery was always at hand.

The ode to Stalin

At this point there is a completely new development in Mandelstam's work. Having foreseen the approaching cataclysm of

1937, Mandelstam was faced with the invidious choice between submitting meekly to his fate but continuing to write poetry the while or making an attempt to save himself (See N.Ya.I pp. 216-20 for all the factual information given here about the ode). On 12 January he decided to abandon everything and devote himself to the writing of an ode to Stalin. The ode form was one he had considered unsuitable for modern poetry even when he was engaged in the composition of 'Грифельная ода' in 1923, and his choice of it here indicates the artificiality of the whole project. He forced himself to sit down at their all-purpose table with paper and pencils and waited for something to happen. Since he had never in his life composed in this manner, and was wholly contemptuous of those 'писатели' who did, the ode was doomed to fail from the start. However, other poems materialised, unsummoned, from the mutterings he was unable and unwilling to suppress, as he played truant by walking up and down beside the 'ode' table:

> Это значило, что он не сумел задушить собственные стихи,
> и они, вырвавшись, победили рогатую нечисть...
> Искусственно задуманное стихотворение, в которое О.М.
> решил вложить весь бущующий в нем материал, стало маткой
> целого цикла противоположно направленных, враждебных ему
> стихов. (N.Ya.I p.217)

The 'ode' cycle comprises the rest of the second Voronezh *Тетрадь*, beginning with the 'двойняшки' of 12-18 January, 'Дрожжи мира дорогие' (I No.347) and 'Влез бесенок в мокрой шерстке' (I No.348). The pivotal word in the ode itself was 'ось' (N.Ya.I p.218), perhaps not unconnected with Stalin's christian name, in the forms 'мира ось' and 'сходства ось'. The word itself surfaced in the 'by-product' poems 'Влез бесенок в мокрой шерстке' (I No.348) and 'Вооруженный зреньем узких ос' (I No.367), while rhymes and assonances with the sounds 'o' and 's' are scattered throughout the cycle in the words 'окись-примесь, косит-просит, голос-боролись, Эльбрус-светлорус, мясо-часа, износ-разноголос' (N.Ya.I p.218).

The two opening poems began as one, in which both the 'дрожжи' and the 'бесенок' elements featured: this rough draft appears in I as No.346. Its genesis lay in the remark Mandelstam had made to Nadezhda Yakovlevna about the imprints of horses' hooves filled with rainwater, which he had pointed out on the monastery road in Zadonsk and had compared with memory (N.Ya.I p.212). In the first poem he elaborates on this remark and it becomes clear that in the comparison it is the memory of the poet which is the analogue:

> Словно вмятины, впервые
> Певчей полные воды,
> Подкопытные наперстки   (I No.346)

This developed into:

> В нищей памяти впервые
> Чуешь вмятины сырые,
> Медной полные воды.   (I No.347)

The coppery water of poetry lies in the thimble-like hoof-prints left by events in the memory. An image from the 'Щегол' group was carried over into this cycle with its significance unaltered: the 'начало грозных дел', arising from the rain-storms of December, recurs in the final version of 'Дрожжи мира дорогие' to give an air of menace to the driving rain:

> Ударенья дождевые
> Закипающей беды   (I No.347)

For this reason the water in the hoofprints is copper, not the precious silver of real poetry. Mandelstam asks from 'which ore' he can recover his lost genuine sounds; 'руда' here clearly derives from the ninth 'Восьмистишие', 'как руда из груди' (I No.279) by association with their common subject, the composition of poetry. In spite of the debasing of his poetic creation Mandelstam is still compelled to follow the imprints, to delve into his memory against his inclination:

> И идешь за ними следом,
> Сам себе не мил, неведом –
> И слепой и поводырь.   (I No.347)

The feeling of responsibility to poetry, which must never be

abnegated , had been expressed in this blind man - guide
metaphor in early drafts of 'Грифельная ода', but whereas
poetry was seen as blind and the poet as its volunteer rescuer
Mandelstam now combines both features in himself. The difference lies in his realisation that poetry, which he had always
thought of as an independent, external phenomenon, could be
debased into the deliberate versifying of the 'ode' type,
which the poet drags out of himself. The ode itself, or what
was completed of it, actually began with the words 'По нему
прошлось другое' (N.Ya.III). At its very inception he recognised its illegitimacy in relationship to 'мое родное':

> И уже мое родное
> Отлегло, как будто вкось
> По нему прошло другое
> И на нем отозвалось...   (I No.346)

The unthinkable - that something could go wrong with his own
poetry - was about to happen, and the ode would be a permanent witness to the moral degradation Mandelstam felt with
regard to it. Hence the violent resistance he put up to any
form of work on the ode and hence the immediate emergence
from the tainted water of new, genuine poetry:

> Дрожжи мира дороги –
> Звуки, слезы и труды   (I Nos.346 & 347)

With the appearance on the scene of the 'бесенок' he realised
that the original poem, now the variant, contained the material of two separate ones. He had always imagined the devil as
sitting in a thimble, gathering tribute, as he does here
(N.Ya.III):

> В подкопытные наперстки,
> В торопливые следы –
> По копейкам воздух версткий
> Обирает с слободы.   (I No.348)

Although this involves getting himself soaking wet, 'в мокрой
шерстке', the little devil none the less invades the water in
the thimble-like hoofprints and now sits levying tribute on
the air around him. Since Mandelstam believed that poetry

existed in the air, the seizure of this source by an evil,
alien power frightened him in earnest. This evil influence
working to take over his main joy and interest in life was
responsible for his going astray: from 'ось колеса', which
also came into the ode (N.Ya.III), there grew up the image
of the crooked, then the broken axle, symbolising the breaking down of the poet's resistance to the intrusion of evil
into his work. His subsequent unhappiness is in direct contrast to the laughter of the little demon:

> Колесо стучит отлого -
> Улеглось - и полбеды!
>
> Скучно мне - мое прямое
> Дело тараторит вкось:
> По нему прошлось другое,
> Надсмеялось, сбило ось!   (I No.348)

Mandelstam's sole consolation was that his very awareness of
what was happening in his poetry might guarantee that he would
not surrender his freedom and independence to the encroaching
forces.

During the work on 'Дрожжи мира дорогие' four poems on
different, but related, themes came to him, the result of the
same vigorous anti-ode impulse as the two main ones. 'Еще не
умер я, еще я не один' (I No.354) contains an energetic denial
that Mandelstam was meditating an unconditional surrender, or
indeed that the grounds for such an action even existed.
Together with his 'нищенкой-подругой' he could extract all
the enjoyment he required from his surroundings alone,
miserable though his circumstances might be:

> Я наслаждаюсь величием равнин
> И мглой, и голодом, и вьюгой.   (I No.354)

He ennobles and glorifies his own poverty - 'В прекрасной
бедности, в роскошной нищете' - since with it goes peace of
mind. He turns his isolation into a positive virtue, for in
his lonely work he finds the freedom and the honourable way of
life which were lacking in writers whose early capitulation

has earned them fame, adulation - and dishonour:

> Благословенны дни и ночи те,
> И сладкозвучный труд безгрешен.   (I No.354)

The last stanza is a magnificent denunciation of the capitul-
ator, who is shown to be the truly poor and unhappy figure:

> Несчастен тот, кого, как тень его,
> Пугает лай и ветер косит,
> И беден тот, кто, сам полуживой,
> У тени милостыни просит.   (I No.354)

Distaste at the prospect of becoming such a shadow, living a
fearful half-life at the mercy of a similar shade, the dictator, had conquered Mandelstam's temptation to regard Stalin
as the embodiment of evil, a superhuman figure, and those who
had made themselves subservient to him as enjoying a life of
security and comfort. These material comforts, which could in
any case be removed from them overnight, were as nothing in
comparison with the spiritual freedom they had forfeited.

The other three poems in the group develop the landscape
subject which had been only a small part of the first one.
Once the snow had fallen a sense of spaciousness in the flat,
endless steppe returned to Mandelstam. His obsession with
movement and action remained as strong as ever, and he did
acknowledge that in reality he was no less restricted than
before - he says of the frost: 'Он – никуда, я – ниоткуда'.
Nevertheless, he felt a new freedom to breathe, a new broaden-
ing of horizons, an illusion brought about by the expanse of
snow, but a comforting one withal:

> И все утюжится, плоится без морщин
> Равнины дышащее чудо.   (I No.349)

The sun had reappeared, crisp but wan, from the poverty they
had in common - 'в крахмальной нищете' - and this, added to
the image of the snow, blindingly white from its rays, is
immediately recognisable in view of its past associations as
a sign that the 'ode' force had been overcome:

> А снег хрустит в глазах, как чистый хлеб безгрешен.
>   (I No.349)

А белый, белый снег до боли очи ест   1922 (I No.127)

An untroubled conscience and obedience to duty preoccupied Mandelstam constantly, especially when he felt threatened. In the purity and whiteness of the snow he saw an example for himself, and in the snow-covered forest, with its trees standing rank upon rank - 'десятизначные леса' - he recognised something of the 'сад величин' from the eleventh 'Восьмистишие' (I No.285), namely an image for the ability to think in the poetic equivalent of mathematical powers, which distinguishes the poet from other men.

The amazingly rapid changes of mood which characterised Mandelstam's temperament are reflected in the third and fourth poems of this group which, with the preceding one, were written in the space of only one day, 16 January, and form another example of that rare occurrence in his work, 'тройчатки'. At one moment he was revelling in the boundless, open plains, in the next he discovered that they mirrored his feeling of suffocation caused by his illness and shortness of breath:

О, этот медленный, одышливый простор -
Я им пресыщен до отказа!
И отдышавшийся распахнут кругозор -
Повязку бы на оба глаза!   (I No.351)

The overwhelming snowy expanse blinded him and made him catch his breath. It also turned his thoughts to one of the places where he might now have been and where he would possibly have fared better:

Уж лучше б вынес я песка слоистый нрав
На берегах зубчатых Камы.   (I No.351)

His present restlessness made him long for the scenery of what had in fact been a nightmare journey, and demonstrated the lengths to which he was being driven by the reminders of his duty and the impossibility of salvation through the ode. All that he chooses to remember here is the picture of the 'жгучий ельник' (I Nos.308 & 309) and its fellows, whose acquaintance he had no time to make. Gone are the terror and the discomfort of the journey:

> Я б слушал под корой текущих древесин
> Ход кольцеванья волокнистый. (I No.351)

Behind this fanciful escape lies a very real fear, not mentioned until the final poem of the series, where the need to
flee the steppe plains is brought out into the open:

> И не ползет ли медленно по ним
> Тот, о котором мы во сне кричим, —
> Народов будущих Иуда? (I No.350)

Universal acceptance of the 'открытость' of the plains, to
which he is no exception, as the words 'распахнут, протяжным,
величием' indicate, is founded on illusion. The most characteristic quality of the plains is their 'убитость'. In reality
they are crushing and oppressive, since they are no more free
from the presence of evil than the rest of the country. The
sense of liberation had been a deceptive one. Again the force
behind 'убитость', Stalin's murderous nature, is not hard to
guess. The bitter cold, like that of Dante's Giudecca, still
harbours the subhuman reptile, slithering repulsively over
the steppe. The historical perspective which caused Mandelstam
to see him as the Judas not so much of present but of future
generations was seldom achieved by his contemporaries in 1937,
at the height of the Terror. No one could visualise the day
when an objective history would assign to Stalin the role of
arch-traitor to humanity, for their own safety from his
treachery occupied all their attention. Like Mandelstam, they
saw him crawling out of every corner.

By 18 January the hysteria seemed to have abated. Mandelstam's strength of purpose had gained the upper hand in the
struggle between his conflicting desires: to write an ode and
thus perhaps to survive, and not to betray his principles. He
could now review its vicissitudes with equanimity. 'Не сравнивай: живущий несравним' (I No.352) lacks the tension and drama
of its predecessors in the 'ode' cycle, and instead is perme-
ated with a sense of reconciliation: 'Я соглашался с равенством

равнин'. During the last few days he had been frightened by
the flat Voronezh steppe, he had been scared by the vault of
the sky, whose spaciousness had never previously worried him,
and all this because of his attempts to produce the ode. He
had foolishly expected the air to fulfil its usual task of
providing material for him to shape into a travesty of poetry
but nothing was forthcoming. He had prepared himself for the
poetic journey which had never begun:

> Я обращался к воздуху-слуге,
> Ждал от него услуги или вести
> И собирался в путь, и плавал по дуге
> Неначинающихся путешествий.   (I No.352)

He was cured of the 'illness' (N.Ya.I p.220) which, as he
later explained to Akhmatova, had possessed him. The ode, such
as it was, had been completed. More importantly he had found
his true relationship with the Voronezh steppe by finally
coming to accept its emptiness and its wide open heavens,
which would keep him wandering happily:

> И ясная тоска меня не отпускает
> От молодых еще воронежских холмов
> К всечеловеческим - яснеющим в Тоскане.   (I No.352)

The journeys which never took place were actual as well as
figurative. Italy, as Nadezhda Yakovlevna relates, existed
for Mandelstam in his Italian poets and in imaginary journeys
round, for example, the Baptistery in Florence (N.Ya.I p.215)
none of which could be taken away from him. He shared with
Chaadaev the achievement of returning to Russia and, more to
the point, staying there, after seeing the home of western
civilisation. Not only the treachery to his own country but
also an emotional attachment to the specifically Russian
provincial hills and to Russia's equally young civilisation
prevented him from seeking refuge in the ancient hills of
Tuscany, saturated with centuries of culture.

Nadezhda Yakovlevna thinks that the poem celebrating the
victory of true poetry over the evil which had tainted it,

'Как женственное серебро горит' (I No.353), probably split
off from the Tuscan poem. Its joyful sense of a completed
cure is especially appropriate when linked with the first
line of the latter: 'Не сравнивай: живущий несравним' (I No.
352), with its contrast between the half-life of the would-be
writer of the ode, and the full life of the poet now emancip-
ated from its bondage. The quiet, tranquil tone also extends
to this quatrain:

> Как женственное серебро горит,
> Что с окисью и примесью боролось,
> И тихая работа серебрит
> Железный плуг и стихотворца голос.   (I No.353)

The reference to base metals in the coppery water image is
picked up and developed, as is a much more longstanding one.
Since 1920 and 'Сестры – тяжесть и нежность – одинаковы ваши
приметы' (I No.108) in his poetry, and since 1922 and 'Слово
и культура' (II p.224) in his prose, he had written of poetry
as a plough, turning up the richest layers of the soil in the
process of recognition. In the 1937 poem, the honest iron of
the plough is silvered with work, the 'сладкозвучный труд
безгрешен' (I No.354). The purity of poetic silver remains
inviolate: no tarnish has succeeded in dimming its fire, no
admixture of alloys in debasing it. The poet's voice sounds
a clear note again.

This return to normality was succeeded by an apology for
poetry, paradoxical in that at this moment Mandelstam was
firm in the certainty that none was necessary and that poetry
was self-justifying. The sun sparkling in a cobweb - 'В
паутине световой' - exactly reflected his own joy in life, a
joy he would wish all to share:

> Народу нужен свет и воздух голубой,
> И нужен хлеб и снег Эльбруса.   (I No.355)

Air, colour, light, bread, the snows of Georgia were all lacking in drab, hungry Russia, as was the poetry which all these
images symbolise in Mandelstam's lexicon: 'Народу нужен стих

таинственно-родной'. This 'родной' is again opposed to the illegitimate ode, which had finally ceased to affect him, in a quatrain which became a separate poem:

> Как землю где-нибудь небесный камень будит, –
> Упал опальный стих, не знающий отца   (I No.357)

In this epitaph for the bastard verse the meteorite, a lifeless lump of burnt-out rock, furnishes another instance of the sterility and the absence of poetic impulse which doomed the ode at the outset. Instead, countless anti-odes sprang up one after another. It is not easy to comprehend why Nadezhda Yakovlevna thinks that the ode such as it was could have been instrumental in saving her from a fate similar to that of its author (N.Ya.I p.219), when the next poem actually formed a part of this ode (N.Ya.III):

> Уходят вдаль людских голов бугры,
> Я уменьшаюсь там – меня уж не заметят   (I No.341)

Mandelstam had little need to put the question 'Почему, когда я думаю о нем, передо мной все головы – бугры голов?' (N.Ya. I p.220) in connection with this poem, since the association of Stalin with executions had been with him at least since his journey to the South at the beginning of the thirties. The particular eloquence of this poem lies as much in his unemotional acceptance of himself as one of the mound of anonymous victims as in the absolute certainty of his future resurrection through his life-affirming poems:

> Но в книгах ласковых и в играх детворы
> Воскресну я сказать, что солнце светит.   (I No.341)

Professor Brown points out a similarity to Fet's 'Я пришел к тебе с приветом Рассказать, что солнце встало'.[1] Love of life, joy in all its manifestations already existed in Mandelstam's poetry, and future generations would hear his voice long after Stalin had disposed of his body.

---

[1] Clarence Brown, 'Into the Heart of Darkness', *Slavic Review*, XXVI (1967), 584-604.

The extent to which he had begun to think of himself as a
shade surrounded by real living people can be judged from
'Слышу, слышу ранний лед' (I No.358). He goes through all
the motions of everyday life in Voronezh, but as a spectral
observer. He hears the ice beginning to move along the river
bed, 'Шелестящий под мостами', but these are the bridges of
Leningrad. He sings of it as had Dante of his beloved Florence,
when the weariness of exile can be felt in his poetry. He
remembers the 'хмель' of his youth in Petersburg, but now the
true spiritual emptiness of the city behind its superficial
appearance is clear to him:

> Так гранит зернистый тот
> Тень моя грызет очами,
> Видит ночью ряд колод,
> Днем казавшихся домами.   (I No.358)

From the version of this poem of 21 January (its date is 22
January, not 21-22 as in I) it emerges that Mandelstam considered himself to have been in this state of semi-death for
the whole of his exile:

> Там уж скоро третий год
> Тень моя живет меж вами   (N.Ya.III)

The bitter bread of exile in the last stanza - an image of
which Nadezhda Yakovlevna makes frequent use in her memoirs
(as in N.Ya.II p.63) - is as poignant as the Akaki Akakievich
figure haunting the city, gnawing at it with its eyes. In the
pathetic shade seeking warmth from the pleasures of others
Mandelstam concentrates his desolation. Although he was
leading a life of sorts on the periphery of normal existence,
he was never accorded full rights:

> Иль шумит среди людей,
> Греясь их вином и небом,
>
> И несладким кормит хлебом
> Неотвязных лебедей...   (I No.358)

Much of the feeling of insubstantiality arose from the
knowledge that his heart disease was both a serious and an

incurable illness. He knew that an early death was in any
case inevitable and was already closing in on him. Part of
the immunity from fear and the imperviousness to threats
which characterised his conduct in the thirties must have
stemmed from this knowledge. His illness was present even in
his poetry. He said of the third line of 'Люблю морозное
дыханье' (I No.359) that anyone could see that the severe
frost exacerbated his shortness of breath:

> Люблю морозное дыханье
> И пара зимнего признанье:
> Я - это я, явь - это явь!   (I No.359)

Like its predecessor, this poem reveals an outward-looking
development in his post-ode poetry. Mandelstam had subjected
the firmest foundation of his existence, his poetry, to a
rigorous test and had not found it wanting. But the conflict
had been an inner one, and the searching self-analysis had
caused him to lose sight of the mundane world on which he
depended for his poetic material. Perhaps it was his shade
which yawned, sat up at night looking out of the window,
twiddled its thumbs and fed the swans, but it was a shade
healed from doubt and uncertainty and ready to observe the
everyday world as before. He was at odds with much of life -
'И я - в размолвке с миром' (I No.359) - but spectacles such
as the picture of small boys, including Vadik, the bird-catch
who had provided the subject of the goldfinch cycle, careerin
down the steep slope to the river on their sledges entranced
him. He often walked across to a vantage point outside their
house to watch them:

> И мальчик, красный как фонарик,
> Своих салазок государик
> И заправила, мчится вплавь.   (I No.359)

However, the poem 'Куда мне деться в этом январе' (I No.360)
illustrates the onset of another transient mood of depression
Winter in Voronezh sometimes delighted, sometimes depressed
him, and in this case he saw the cold and deadness of winter

as a reflection of his own situation. The wintry town gripped
him and pinned him to the spot. He felt himself losing his
reason as a result of its obsessive locking and fastening of
its doors against him:

От замкнутых я что ли пьян дверей? –
И хочется мычать от всех замков и скрепок.   (I No.360)

Voronezh was a town of fear and was not alone in this; its
inhabitants barricaded themselves against their terror and
fled from one corner to the shelter of another:

И прячутся поспешно в уголки,
И выбегают из углов угланы.   (I No.360)

In fact the subject of this withering portrait is not the
entire populace so much as one of its members in particular.
Mandelstam was desperate for a listener to whom he could read
his poems, from whom he could receive criticism, advice and
further stimulus, as he had from Bely, for example. Nadezhda
Yakovlevna and Natasha Shtempel were no substitute for a fellow
poet for this purpose, and so Mandelstam turned to a local
poet called Pokrovsky. At the end of January or the beginning
of February he and Nadezhda Yakovlevna went to seek Pokrovsky
out and found his flat in a wooden house at the foot of a
hill in Voronezh. Pokrovsky was not in, no doubt on account
of this very fear which prevailed in the town (N.Ya.III).
Contact with Mandelstam would do no good to any writer intent
on self-preservation. In the poem where this episode is
recorded Mandelstam watches rooks scattering in haste through
the 'мертвый воздух' as he hammers on the unresponsive door:

А я за ними ахаю, стуча
В какой-то мерзлый, деревянный короб:
Читателя! советчика! врача!
На лестнице колючей – разговора б!   (I No.360)

The period from 16 January to 10 February saw the most
concentrated and intensive poetic activity of Mandelstam's
life (N.Ya.I p.190). Nadezhda Yakovlevna was terrified that
his poetry was literally killing him through overwork, but it

was then that he silenced her protests: 'Не мешай, надо
торопиться, а то не успею' (N.Ya.III). There was no change in
the subject-matter: the ode, the battle against it, creative
freedom, poetic cognition, the defence of poetry, feelings of
doom and martyrdom all feature here. In 'Где связанный и при-
гвожденный стон' (I No.356) martyrdom is shown in the context
of classical Greek tragedy. In the person of Prometheus Mandelstam had found as early as 'Грифельная ода' (I No.137) the
epitome of one who suffered for having dared where others
would have fallen back, and had adopted the figure of Prometheus to point out the way in which he and his fellow poets
should follow. Mandelstam's gryphon-vulture is marvellously
fearsome and threatening:

> А коршун где - и желтоглазый гон
> Его когтей, летящих исподлобья?   (I No.356)

Classical tragedy had demonstrated the uniting of perfection
of form with depth of feeling which Mandelstam considered the
high point of Greek civilisation. His lament that it would
never return - 'трагедий не вернуть' - arises from a remark
made in a 1922 article that Innokenty Annensky was a born writer of tragedies, but was conscious of

> ...невозможности трагедии в современном русском искусстве
> благодаря отсутствию синтетического народного сознания
> - непререкаемого и абсолютного - необходимой предпосылки
> трагедии...   (III, pp.34-5; N.Ya.II p.391)

National consciousness of an entire people was a quality
absent from Soviet Russia. Formal tragedies had thus become
an impossibility, but in the 'наступающие губы' of the poet
were concentrated all the tragic elements of Aeschylus and
Sophocles. Since 'трагедийное действие разворачивается не на
подмостках, а в повседневной жизни' (N.Ya.II p.394), the
former becomes a 'грузчик' and the latter a 'лесоруб'. Mandelstam did not explain even to Nadezhda Yakovlevna why he
chose these particular figures to represent the modern state
of tragedy, but she imagines that somewhere in Annensky or

Ivanov, probably in works connected with their translations
from the classics, he chanced upon a phrase or idea which
suggested this metaphor (N.Ya.III). If this is so, it is not
immediately apparent in these two authors. The tragic destiny
of the poet is the object of Mandelstam's praise and glorification: 'Он - эхо и привет, он веха, нет - лемех' - a sound
cluster reminiscent of the 'опыт-лепет' one which had earlier
described the poet's work in 'Восьмистишия' (I No.283). But
his vision of the poet ascribes to him more than just the
stereotyped ability to echo what he hears; it also includes
a capacity for going out to find and greet both poetry and
the poet's 'собеседники'. 'Лемех', like 'плуг', is of long
standing as an image in Mandelstam's concept of poetry. In
spite of the tragic role now filled by the poet, he still
yearns for the return of the conditions in which classical
tragedy flourished:

> Воздушно-каменный театр времен растущих
> Встал на ноги - и все хотят увидеть всех:
> Рожденных, гибельных и смерти не имущих.   (I No.356)

If all the audience in the spacious amphitheatre - his own
people in his own time - were to stand up, instead of crawling
or darting from corner to corner or flattening themselves
against walls in an effort to remain unnoticed, then everyone
could see clearly those closest to them and the lines of
communication would reopen. National consciousness, the pre-
requisite of a noble tragedy, from which the squalid murders
of the 'ежовщина' could scarcely be more different, would
then be born. The unity of principles and values which Stalin
had managed to eliminate with such success would be revived.

A Rembrandt Golgotha had found its way from Dorpat University to the Voronezh museum, where the Mandelstams were
often to be found, and in the poem 'Как светотени мученик
Рембрандт' (I No.364) Mandelstam writes about his own Golgotha
(N.Ya.I p.218). His martyrdom comes from having tried to

penetrate into the depths of his time, only to discover that
it is 'немеющее' and that his attempts to break the silence
will not go unpunished. No soldiers will guard his tomb, no
watchers will stand vigil in respect for his agony - 'резкость
моего горящего ребра'. Rembrandt himself, like all artists,
has suffered - 'светотени мученик' - but Mandelstam turns to
him as a marvellous example of craftsmanship and inspiration
above all else:

> Простишь ли ты меня, великолепный брат,
> И мастер, и отец чернозеленой теми.   (I No.364)

He asks forgiveness of Rembrandt for his crime, the sinful
ode of which he is the progenitor. In mitigation he cites the
circumstances of its writing: and here the words 'око сокол-
иного' lead straight back phonetically to the ode:

> Но око соколиного пера
> И жаркие ларцы у полночи в гареме
> Смущают не к добру, смущают без добра
> Мехами сумрака взволнованное племя.   (I No.364)

At all hours he expects an attack from the 'tribe' of evil-
doers, whose preparations bode no good. At the time of his
sin against Rembrandt and his fellow artists he was able to
think only of defending himself against these forces.

Prometheus and Greece led naturally to thoughts of the
Crimea and Transcaucasia, the surrogate for the 'civilised,
historical' world. Longing for the South, and in particular
for the sea, never left Mandelstam. He said of 'Разрывы круглых бухт и хрящ и синева' (I No.366): 'А меня нельзя удержать
на месте... Вот я побывал контрабандой в Крыму.' (N.Ya.I p.
214). Nadezhda Yakovlevna points out how the tempo is slowed
down in this poem: 'И парус медленный, что облаком продолжен',
and explains that time seemed to them to be rushing by at an
incredible speed, whereas Mandelstam felt that only in the
South would it proceed - or appear to be proceeding - at a
normal pace (N.Ya.I p.214). Condemned to live in places he
found unacceptable - 'горловой Урал, плечистое Поволжье,

Иль этот ровный край', he breathed in their air, taking what
poetry it would give, while nursing a desperate need for the
sweep of the blue horizon over the Black Sea:

> Разрывы круглых бухт и хрящ и синева...
> Что ж мне под голову другой песок подложен?   (I No.366)

He felt the eleven-line form of the poem to emphasise his
discontent. The air of the steppes, giving little inspiration
at this time, was held responsible for this malaise. In the
poem 'Пою, когда гортань сыра, душа суха' (I No.365) he asks
after the health of the South, almost as though wondering
anxiously whether the stirrings of Colchis in the blood still
existed as before:

> Здорово ли вино? Здоровы ли меха?
> Здорово ли в крови Колхиды колыханье?   (I No.365)

He had remembered the wine of Georgia from as far back as
1920 - 'Кахетинское густое Хорошо в подвале пить' (I No.115),
but the quivering in the veins, the excitement concomitant
with life, laughter and poetry, had always been with him. It
was the feeling of an encroaching poetic deafness and dumb-
ness which he most feared, the result as much of his physical
state of breathlessness as of his inimical surroundings:

> А грудь стесняется, без языка тиха:
> Уже не я пою - поет мое дыханье -
> И в горных ножнах слух и голова глуха.   (I No.365)

The possibility of being deprived of poetry occasioned as
fierce a defence of it as anywhere in his work, a defence
based on an unequivocally moral foundation:

> Песнь бескорыстная сама себе хвала,
> Утеха для друзей и для врагов смола.   (I No.365)

These two lines could stand as an epigraph to his entire
oeuvre. After the episode of the ode they acquire yet more
dignity and eloquence in relation to his previous poems than
they have in isolation. The phrase 'власть поэзии' had real
significance for Mandelstam, as for Akhmatova. In this poem
the general statement of principle gives way, typically, to

a specific instance; abstraction made him uneasy, as the unambiguous 'смола' illustrates. In the last stanza the 'песнь
одноглазая' refers to a particular event. During the Mandelstams' visit to Sukhumi in 1930 they happened to witness an
Abkhazian wedding ceremony whose ritual imitated the abduction
of the bride (hence the hunting and horse-riding allusions)
to the accompaniment of a plainsong chant sung by a choir
such as they had heard many times, singing the music of
Komitas in particular, in Abkhazia and Armenia (N.Ya.III):

> Одноголосый дар охотничьего быта,
> Которую поют верхом и на верхах,
> Держа дыханье вольно и открыто   (I No.365)

Mandelstam speaks of their free, hunter's life and their
breath control with anguish at the contrast with his lack of
both. This last stanza resembles the Crimean poem in the
length and breadth of its lines, relaxed and assured in a way
unthinkable in the tense January poems. The long 'o' and 'a'
sounds open out into space, instead of weighing heavily on
the ear.

However, the closest phonetic connection with the 'ось'
of the ode is to be found not here, but in another poem written on the same day, 'Вооруженный зреньем узких ос' (I No.367)
- 'Разрывы круглых бухт' and 'Как светотени мученик Рембрандт'
were both written on 4 February, not 8 February as in I. The
'ось' of the broken wheel which, less than a month earlier,
had blazoned its connection with 'Иосиф' in all the poetic
by-products of the ode, now took on a positive significance,
which perhaps derived more from its connection with Mandelstam's own christian name. When he had spoken of 'penetrating
into the essence of tragedy' and into the approaching silence
of his own times, his definition of the poet's task as given
here had already been foreshadowed in these earlier lines:

> Я только в жизнь впиваюсь и люблю
> Завидовать могучим хитрым осам.   (I No.367)

The wasps here stand in the same relationship as does 'лемех' to 'плуг', being for this purpose a synonym for the bees of poetry - the honey-bees of Persephone from 'Возьми на радость из моих ладоней' (I No.116). Professor Brown has painstakingly catalogued all the instances where 'ось' and its variants appear in the ode cycle,[1] but their most insistent reiteration is here. The poet wishes to reach the very core of the earth, on which all life is founded - 'Услышать ось земную' - to discover its motivating force and its pivot. For this he has recourse to the weapon - 'оружие мысли' - of long-distance sight which he had observed in the bird of prey, to the 'historical' sight found in Dante's shades and finally to the sharp, penetrating sight of wasps, here associated with their sting: 'сосущих ось земную'. Through his particular insight the poet reaches a relatively deep understanding of the world, but unlike the wasps has not reached its very centre. In this lies his task, not in the external embellishment of the world around him:

И не рисую я, и не пою,
И не вожу смычком черноголосым   (I No.367)

'Черноголосым, разноголос, черноволосой, ложноволосая' are all epithets associated with the activities in which Mandelstam does not participate. He will not draw portraits to order or sing paeans of praise, since there can be only one subject for them.

Rather than portray Stalin, he preferred to sketch out a portrait of himself, the poet, which reads more like an epitaph:

Были очи острее точимой косы -
По зегзице в зенице и по капле росы   (I No.368)

The mournful tone and sombre quality are due to a great extent to one of the many allusions in his work to the *Слово о полку Игореве*, here to Yaroslavna's early morning lament for Prince

---

[1] Brown, *Slavic Review*, XXVI (1967), 599.

Igor: 'Полечию – рече – зегзицею по Дунаеви'. The dewdrop of
early morning is also a tear shed for the poet's closed eyes,
which had once been sharper than a scythe-blade in gathering
the harvest of poetry. Cut off before his work was even
nearing its natural conclusion, he had scarcely learnt the
most elementary steps in cognition – 'Различать одинокое
множество звезд', the oxymoronic phrase indicating how identical, if physically separate, were the lifeless, meaningless
stars, in contrast with the earth, teeming with life and
purpose.

For Mandelstam the appearance of stars in his poetry was
an unwelcome one, since he saw it as signifying the death of
a poetic impulse (N.Ya.I p.215). In this case the feeling was
justified, since the influence of the ode, both positive and
negative, was on the wane. It did, however, still have the
strength to engender a brilliant poem, which stands out among
the mid-January to mid-February group with its description of
Tiflis, which bears comparison with that of any other Russian
poet, 'Еще он помнит башмаков износ' (I No.363):

> Подновлены мелком или белком
> Фисташковые улицы-пролазы,
> Балкон-наклон, подкова, конь-балкон,
> Дубки, чинары, медленные вязы.   (I No.363)

Even the listing of nouns is reminiscent of Pushkin, one of
the first to immortalise his love of Georgia in Russian
poetry. In his turn Mandelstam gives a vivid impression of
the white churches, the tree-lined, steep streets, twisting
with the sinuousness of their inhabitants, the horses and a
whole way of life on horse-back led by the mountain shepherds,
but above all the energy and upright character of the Georgian
capital: the streets are 'фисташковые', the adjective last
used in connection with the description of true poetry (I No.
264), and in which the twin concepts of the South and moral
rightness meet. Tiflis is full of noise and colour, both in
its streets and buildings and in its people, dark-haired and

vivacious, in its curly, feminine alphabet - 'букв кудрявых
женственная цепь' - and in the background to the picture, the
magnificent Mt Mtatsminda and its monastery, with all the
grandeur of the Caucasus as a backdrop. In his flight from
the flatness of Voronezh Mandelstam particularly remembers
the mountains around Tiflis and the shoe-leather he had worn
out in the course of his walks on them:

> Еще он помнит башмаков износ -
> Моих подметок стертое величье   (I No.363)

The allusion here is also partly to Dante and thus also to
poetry (N.Ya.I p.192). For Mandelstam movement, walking up
and down if in a confined space, or roaming unconfined around
town and country, was an essential precondition for the composition of poetry, forming an active element in the process.
He could not imagine that Dante's methods differed from his
own:

> Мне не на шутку приходит в голову вопрос, сколько подметок,
> сколько воловьих подошв, сколько сандалий износил Алигьери
> за время своей поэтической работы, путешествуя по козьим
> тропам Италии.   *Разговор о Данте*   (II p.367)

He remembers the 'моложавое, стареющее лето' of Georgia, whose
contradictory characteristics of youth and experience are by
no means irreconcilable; Dante, in the person of Brunetto
Latini, had long since reconciled them (II p.367), and Mandelstam draws fresh strength from this example. He bears no
malice towards Stalin's country of birth, since he had established his own relationship with it long before any such
unpleasant associations arose.

    Tiflis gave him, as it were, a transfusion of new blood,
and this enabled him to add a further group to the ode cycle
which he had considered as coming to a close. In 'Обороняет
сон мою донскую сонь' (I No.371) elation at his victory over
the unwholesome influences surrounding the ode leads to a
new battle-cry:

> И в бой меня ведут понятные слова

За оборону жизни, оборону
Страны - земли, где смерть уснет, как днем сова.

(I No.371)

The 'кремлевские слова' against which Mandelstam says later
in the poem that he is fighting may well result from a word-
play on this 'бой', since both the Kremlin chimes and the
words of the ode are the objects of his attack. His weapon is
the 'черепах маневры' - the lyre of poetry, first constructed
from a turtle's shell. The other meaning of the turtle, the
Roman battle formation, should not be discounted here. As he
prepares for battle, he recalls in 'Средь народного шума и
спеха' (I No.361) the consequences of the last such encounter:

Далеко теперь та стоянка
Тот с водой кипяченой бак -
На цепочке кружка-жестянка
И глаза застилавший мрак.

Шла пермяцкого говора сила...

Только шел пароход по реке.

(I No.361)

His journey up the Kama from Cherdyn returns in all its misery
even to details of the 'кружка-жестянка' from which he drank
water on the way (N.Ya.III). It is typical of Mandelstam to
have preserved the clearest memory of the scurrying crowds in
the stations and their noisy shouting, even in this situation:

Средь народного шума и спеха...

В говорливые дебри вокзала,
В ожиданье у мощной реки.

(I No.361)

Mandelstam acknowledged that the ode was written as a direct
reaction to the circumstances of deportation and exile as
described here and confesses his shame: 'Губы жарки, слова
черствы'. He feels nothing but self-loathing from this almost
personal contact with Stalin:

И к нему - в его сердцевину -
Я без пропуска в Кремль вошел,
Разорвав расстояний холстину,
Головою повинной тяжел.

(I No.361)

The Kremlin and Red Square of his imagination had conjured up
the frightening image of the May-day celebrations there which,

in a moment of fantasy, he saw himself as witnessing this
year, should his release come when it was due. The spectacle
of crowds mechanically chanting, with the Kremlin chimes,
slogans whose emptiness in 1937 must have chilled the heart
was a fearsome one:

> - Рабу не быть рабом, рабе не быть рабой!
> И хор поет с часами рука об руку.   (I No.371)
>
> Я обведу еще глазами площадь всей -
> Всей этой площади с ее знамен лесами.   (I No.369)

He had a presentiment that he would be present on this occasion, in spite of the fact that for many of his friends the
very hour of his writing this poem was a fatal one - 'Час
насыщающий бесчисленных друзей'. These thoughts about the
present day reflect others about time in general, as he shows
the whole century looking at 'века могучая веха' (I No.361).
Both poems came about from the idea of death in battle and
thus of the battle illustrated by Favorsky, with its waving
red banners on the field of Igor's defeat. In the banners of
this 1937 May-day celebration history parodied itself as,
through the 'дерево и медь - Фаворского полет' (I No.369) the
twelfth century and the twentieth meet 'Мы с временем соседи'.
The felling of trees in preparation for the work of the engr-
aver seems to Mandelstam to be like killing a living thing,
whose heart - 'сердце-сердцевина' - still pulsates after
death:

> А в кольцах сердится еще смола, сочась -
> Но разве сердце - лишь испуганное мясо?
> Я сердцем виноват...   (I No.369)

He himself had been cut down like a tree, but his poetry, to
be used as 'смола' for his enemies, remained. He was justified
in asking whether the heart was what he frequently felt it to
be, mortal flesh in fear of its life. He had feared for his,
and the defensive measures he had taken made him guilty before
poetry.

The final poem in the *Тетрадь* also emerged in response to

an external stimulus, in the person of two singers. Mandelstam
had heard Marian Anderson, the American singer then on tour in
Moscow, on the radio, and the day before 'Я в львиный ров и
в крепость погружен' (I No.370) was written, he had visited an
exiled Leningrad singer on hearing of her husband's second
arrest. The unfortunate singer was planning to follow him into
what she assumed would be exile rather than camp life, and by
singing would earn money and food. On his return home Mandelstam, exhausted by his extended period of intensive composition, lay on the divan, where he appeared to be dozing, and
then suddenly produced the poem (N.Ya.I, pp.192-3; N.Ya.III).
The low-voiced singers led him down and down into a lion's
den, into the depths of a fortress, by the very power of their
voices:

> Под этих звуков ливень дрожжевой –
> Сильнее льва, мощнее Пятикнижья.   (I No.370)

The yeast image gives the clue to the genuine art of the
singers, as do the metaphors of depth and breadth - the pearls
on the bottom of the sea, the distant Tahitian ladies of
Gauguin - in the description of their singing:

> Океанийских низка жемчугов
> И таитянок кроткие корзины   (I No.370)

He is also accompanying them with his own genuine art:

> Неограничена еще моя пора,
> И я сопровождал восторг вселенский
> Как вполголосная органная игра
> Сопровождает голос женский.   (I No.370)

The evil spirit of the ode had finally been exorcised; the
singer is free to descend into the lions' den, since her
voice can conquer the lion, escape from the fortress - Marian
Anderson's speciality was negro spirituals - and Mandelstam
in his own lions' den and fortress was now sure of the same
strength in his own poetic voice.

5. *НОВЫЕ СТИХИ:*
ТРЕТЬЯ ВОРОНЕЖСКАЯ ТЕТРАДЬ
March - May 1937

The turning point at which Mandelstam decided to begin a new
Тетрадь was when the 'Стихи о неизвестном солдате' (I No.362),
eventually placed sixth in the finished collection, came to
him. They clearly signalled a new impulse, totally unrelated
to the post-'ode' poems which coincided with the first month
of their composition. Only at the end of May was the definitive text of the 'Стихи' written down. Meanwhile a series of
poems on miscellaneous subjects was also evolving, and the
third Voronezh *Тетрадь* opens with them.

The opening poems
References to Rembrandt and Raphael in the previous collection
represent two of many excursions into the 'лесная Саламанка'
of Mandelstam's cultural experience (See I Nos. 321 & 364),
which enabled him to preserve a certain aloofness from the
turmoil around him. At the beginning of the new poetry came
a sober acceptance of the fact that his inner world differed
so greatly from the mundane world before his eyes that no
point of comparison could - or should - be found to relate
the two. In the opening poem, 'На доске малиновой, червонной'
(I No.375), he mentally transforms the Voronezh winter scene
into the artistic form which most readily suggested itself,
the world of an Avercamp or Breughel canvas, whose snowy
landscape is dotted with brightly-coloured, dwarfish figures,
the counterparts of the small boys sledging down the steep
slope opposite the Mandelstams' house to the river below.

At the same time, however, he realises that this comparison
adds nothing to either, and that attempts to collate life
and art are inappropriate and even confusing here:

> Не ищи в нем зимних масел рая,
> Конькобежного фламандского уклона,
> Не раскаркается здесь веселая кривая
> Карличья в ушастых шапках стая! -
> И меня сравненьем не смущая...   (I No.375)

All the energy of the scurrying little skaters and tobogganers
is vividly mirrored in Mandelstam's poetic palette: their
bustle is depicted in the poem's busy 'ш' 'щ' 'с' sounds and
its incisive 'к', which well convey the noise of sledges and
skates on the snow and ice. Nevertheless the reality of the
Russian picture barely corresponded to that of the Flemish
school; their subject-matter, admittedly, was identical, but
the overtones were inconsonant. In the first of the two stanzas
the poet gives the Russian version, with its own specific
colour and texture:

> В сбрую красных углей запряженный,
> Желтою мастикой утепленный
> И перегоревший в сахар жженный.   (I No.375)

The poem has its own vivacity in the images of fire and
warmth, its own energy and verve. Mandelstam, when reading it
aloud, would give full weight to both the 'н's in the final
word of each line in the first stanza (N.Ya.III). The effect
would be that of a rise and fall in the voice with the high
point on the 'он/ён' syllable and the fall down to the 'ной/
ный' ending, in imitation of the sledging children climbing
up and catapulting down the slope. Likewise the greater significance of winter in snowbound Russia, in comparison with
the relatively brief periods of real cold and snow on the
North German Plain, is reflected in the extensive use of the
'сн' element from 'снег', for example in the phrase 'занесся
санный, сонный'.

During the course of this particular winter Mandelstam's
presentiment that his own death was not far distant grew in

strength. In one of his letters to Kornei Chukovsky, where
he begs desperately for financial help, he relates the outright persecution he has suffered from the first year of his
exile onwards. Physical illness and the starvation which
refusal of work by the authorities was rapidly bringing about
would very soon account both for him and his wife, if the
temptation to suicide had not already done so:

> Вы знаете, что я совсем болен, что жена напрасно искала
> работы. Не только не могу лечиться, но жить не могу: не
> на что... Вы понимаете, что со мной делается?
>   (Letter No.72, III p.279)

It was to Chukovsky that Mandelstam sent a copy of his poem
of February 1937 'Если б меня наши враги взяли' (I No.372),
in which the death of whose imminent arrival he was so certair
is placed firmly at the door of 'наши враги', with their
recourse to methods more direct that those previously used
against him. Obviously it was impossible to send the poem
with its last two lines in their proper form, and so Nadezhda
Yakovlevna suggested 'будить' to replace 'губить' and the
alteration of the first word of the penultimate line to 'И'.
Chukovsky immediately spotted the inconsistency of these lines
and remarked that 'our enemies' were still unidentified by
the end of the poem. Mandelstam was delighted that Chukovsky
still had a nose for such things (N.Ya.III). He felt that
the poem was an exact formulation of the feeling of imprisonment and the total deprivation of basic human freedoms:

> Если б лишили меня всего в мире –
> Права дышать и открывать двери
> И утверждать, что бытие будет,
> И что народ, как судия, судит...   (I No.372)

Few more succinct statement of Mandelstam's philosophy of
life exist. In these four lines he includes breathing - rarely
to be taken in a purely literal sense, since the act of breathing in the surrounding air through the lips invariably constitutes a metaphor for poetic composition; his natural revulsion against all forms of cruelty and repression (N.Ya.II p.24)

combined with firm principles on the absolute necessity of
individual freedom; his belief in an indomitable life-force
which would survive his present existence; and finally faith
in the power of those whose very existence was being crushed
to rise up in judgement on their oppressors. The tone of the
poem is distinctly rhetorical, both as to its devices - the
use of anaphora with 'Если б' and 'И' - and as to the presentation of the poet's last resistance in the dramatic imagery
of the *Слово о полку Игореве*: 'Тогда пущашет 10 соколов на
стадо лебедей: которыи дотечаше, та преди песнь пояше':

> И раскачав в колокол стан голый,
> И разбудив вражеской тьмы угол,
> Я запрягу десять волов в голос   (I No.372)

Once again the means of defiance is the poet's voice. His
body resounds, bell-like, with a roar of fury and anguish.
Yet even here, at the death of liberty and human dignity,
there are allusions to an idealism and an optimism which in
the average man would long since have been forced out of
existence:

> Сжатостью всей рвущейся вдаль клятвы...
>
> Но на земле, что избежит тленья...   (I No.372)

Echoes of the solemn oath to the fourth estate from 1924,
'И клятвы крупные до слез' (I No.140), mingle with an incorr-
igible faith in the power of the earth to escape the clutches
of decay. It is especially amazing for its proximity to the
line which, even more than the 1934 epigram, constitutes a
searing indictment of Stalin and his works - 'Будет губить
разум и жизнь – Сталин'. The poem rests on the contrast and
conflict between the incarnations of two principles - the
poet with his affirmation of life and the dictator dedicated
to its destruction. When the last line appeared Mandelstam
was almost frightened by the recurrence of the 'ode' subject
- 'почему это опять выскочило?' (N.Ya.III). What had not been
plainly stated in the way of sheer insolence and defiance of

the tyrant at the time of the ode is amply made up for here.
Mandelstam's trust in the fundamental integrity of his fellow
men, for which no empirical evidence existed in 1937, is
movingly expressed in his reference to the 'океан братских
очей' of his fellow-sufferers and sympathisers. Nevertheless
there can be no question that it is the final dénouement of
the conflict which they are witnessing, and that the victory
of the forces of evil is for the moment assured. That Mandelstam was engaged in serious consideration of his ultimate
gesture of disobedience indicates how close he considered his
imprisonment and death to be. He never envisaged himself as
surviving a Stalinist labour camp.

In view of the necessity to make ready for this inevitable
deprivation of liberty and then of life, he began to review
his past and to bid a calm farewell to the landmarks in his
past life. His 1910-11 visits to France and Italy, his first
introduction to the physical setting of the western European
cultural tradition, exercised an influence over him more
profound and lasting than their brief duration would ever
have led to expect. In the three poems which lead up to the
'Стихи о неизвестном солдате' these two countries are evoked
with the surety of touch which so delighted Ehrenburg (See I
p.537) in a distillation of their highly individual distinguishing features. It is no surprise to find among the chief
of these features architectural and other artistic forms.
'Я видел озеро, стоящее отвесно' (I No.374) was given the
provisional title 'Реймс-Лаон' in an early manuscript (N.Ya.
III; cf.S p.303). The 'lake' in question is the torrent of
light from the rose window of Laon 'С разрезанною розой в
колесе' - Laon, because Rheims' rose window of 1235 is contained in a pointed arch, unlike that of the earlier cathedral
of Laon (1178-90) which is set in a rounded arch. Another of
the principal features belongs to the glorious west façade of
Rheims, with its three portals - of the Virgin, St Paul and

the Last Judgement - with their innumerable statues:

Глазели внутр трех лающих порталов
Недуги - недруги других невскрытых дуг   (I No.374)

Blending with these portals in the poet's memory is the
magnificent position of the many-towered cathedral of Laon,
which crowns the flat top of the hill known as the 'Rock of
Laon' - 'И башнями скала вздохнула вдруг'. The untamed physiological riot of those Gothic cathedrals, which had held Mandelstam in thrall since his first rapturous account of the
Parisian Notre Dame (I No.39), had not lost its fascination:
indeed he may well have had Notre Dame itself in mind here -
the rose window, the towers, the portals are paralleled there,
and Mandelstam's memory of the various cathedrals may have
blurred with time. In the poem the carved stone figures of
animals - lions, foxes, gazelles - leap, run and fight, a
counterpart to the tension and the harmony of the living
architectural structure which is their habitat - 'средь
ремесленного города-сверчка'. Fish also feature, with dual
significance; when scattered around in a cathedral their
iconographic meaning is obvious and traditional, but here
they also form part of the lake metaphor. In the flood of
light from the window small insets can be distinguished -
pictures of saints, angels, doves, prophets, like fish in
deep water. As the light pours into the building the 'shore'
of the stone-work is inundated, but none the less towers up:
'И влагой напоен, восстал песчаник честный'. The whole cathedral is engulfed and becomes a 'мальчишка-океан' straining
up to the heavens: 'И чашками воды швыряет в облака'.

Mandelstam's longing for France in the poem 'Я прошу, как
жалости и милости' (I No.373) contains both an element of
nostalgia and an urgent plea for practical assistance. France
is personified in the figure of Romain Rolland's wife, Maya
Kudasheva, the 'безбожница с золотыми глазами козы' in the
poem. Mandelstam knew her of old and hoped that in the course

of her visit to Moscow with her husband, which took place
in the early spring of 1937, she would intercede with Stalin
on his behalf, a hope he cherished even in Vtoraya Rechka
after his arrest and imprisonment (N.Ya.I p.399) - but this
time it was Rolland himself who was to be approached. He begs
Kudasheva to incline her head and heed his grovelling pleas:

И кривыми, картвыми ножницами
Купы скаредных роз раздразни.   (I No.373)

Nadezhda Yakovlevna does not remember her as having the particular speech defect suggested by the play on 'картавить',
so presumably the association is with France and the French
way of pronouncing the Russian 'r' which Kudasheva would have
acquired there. Otherwise the France of the poem is the France
of cathedrals, vineyards, honeysuckle - and revolutions:

Где бурлила, королей смывая,
Улица июльская кривая.   (I No.373)

Following as it does the 'prison' poem where Lenin 'прошелес-
тит спелой грозой' (I No.372), the allusion to 1830 is far
from unintentional. The Russian poem ends with the destruction
of life itself, whereas the French upheavals are succeeded by
something very different from post-Revolutionary Russia:

А теперь в Париже, в Шартре, в Арле
Государит добрый Чаплин Чарли   (I No.373)

City Lights, the Chaplin film to which these and the next
two lines refer, is not without resentment of social injustice
and the juxtaposition of two identically-motivated revolts,
both of which had Mandelstam's full sympathy in theory, points
a clear moral when their outcomes are considered together.
The whole cultural tradition of western Europe militates
against the excesses of brutality which characterised the
aftermath of the Revolution; indeed the July days in France
had subsided - but when Russia would achieve the stability
to emulate her civilised conduct and her crowning achievements in the cultural sphere, as symbolised by the Gothic
cathedral, remained a purely academic question:

Там, где с розой на груди, в двухбашенной испарине
Паутины каменеет шаль   (I No.373)

The last line could well have featured in any of the delicate,
fastidious poems of the early *Камень*, with their emphasis on
the fragility of patterned stonework. The lacy shawl enfolds
the 'human' body of the cathedral, warm, alive, breathing and
flexing its muscles. Among the more robust poetry of the
Voronezh period, these French reminiscences breathe an air of
luxury and pleasurable indulgence.

France had undergone no change in Mandelstam's memory,
but Italy, on the other hand, was in the grip of a force as
inimical to humanity as the Terror which was destroying Mandelstam's own country, and by now it was impossible for him to
recall the Italy of his youth while ignoring its present sub-
jugation by the Blackshirts. The 'Lamarck' theme of pre-
Voronezh days is revived in 'Рим' (I No.381) to express
precisely the same phenomenon as it had in 1932 - the human
race's descent to the level of the lower forms of life. Rome
becomes amphibian. The 'лягушки фонтанов' symbolise the
venality of the city, always ready to accede to the wishes
of the powerful:

Город, любящий сильным поддакивать,
Земноводной водою кропят   (I No.381)

Fascism is shown as a linear descendant of the rule of the
Caesars, but without their grandeur. Once again Rome, the
'убийства питомник', has nurtured petty tyrants:

Вы, коричневой крови наемники,
Итальянские чернорубашечники,
Мертвых цезарей злые щенки   (I No.381)

Sandwiched between the Caesars and the Fascists is a different
brand of power, 'Мощь свободная и мера львиная', the artistic
power of Italian painters, sculptors and architects of the
Christian tradition, now eclipsed by brute force: 'В усыпленьи
и рабстве молчит'. The city once dominated both architectur-
ally and spiritually by the dome of St Peter's - 'ласточкой

купола' has deliberately cast aside this heritage of Christia:
art:

> Древность летняя, легкая, наглая,
> С хищным взглядом и плоской ступней   (I No.381)

All the joy, the carefree boldness, the artist's freedom to
observe and create what his piercing eye and his spiritual
insight dictated were gone. Michelangelo's Moses and David
had become orphans overnight, a night 'сырая от слез'. Images
of water predominate - the croaking fountains, the yellow
water of the Tiber, the Spanish Steps tumbling down into the
square - 'В площадь льющихся, лестничных рек', the statue of
Moses, whose beard cascades like a waterfall. After writing
the poem Mandelstam quickly remembered that Moses actually
sat, rather than lay, but decided to leave 'лежит' (N.Ya.III)
The mistake could well arise from confusion of Moses, an old
man, with the Vatican statues of the river gods, the Nile
and the Tiber, reclining on their elbows, who are also old
men. The glorification of man in the city - 'Рим-человек' -
is epitomised in the rising steps: the footsteps of man
ascending them should be seen as a symbol of the human race
affirming its spiritual aspirations, in contrast with the
maimed humanity of imperial Rome and its heirs, 'Как морские,
ленивые губки'. Contemporary Rome was beginning to resemble
Russia in so many ways that only the topographical references
here distinguish its tradition of despotism, whose latest
manifestation is the idolisation of Mussolini, from that of
Russia and Stalin, a dictator equally deeply embroiled in the
massacre of innocent 'orphans':

> Ямы форума заново вырыты
> И раскрыты ворота для Ирода,
> И над Римом диктатора-выродка
> Подбородок тяжелый висит.   (I No.381)

Work on the 'oratorio' 'Стихи о неизвестном солдате' (I No. 362; N.Ya.II p.533) had begun early in February 1937 and continued for 2½-3 months, thus running parallel with the poems which precede and follow it in the collection. It is the basic cycle of the whole *Тетрадь*, around which supplementary groups, connected by theme and vocabulary with it, arose. Nadezhda Yakovlevna defines the 'oratorio' as 'посвященной будущей... войне и массовым гибелям, а также смерти Мандельштама' (N.Ya.II pp.533-4), and also observes that 'речь идет уже не о со-умирании, то есть, об упражнении в смерти, о подготовке к ней, а о гибеле "с гурьбой и гуртом", о том, что названо "оптовыми смертями"...' (N.Ya.II p.441).

She also traces its origins back to 1932. When Mandelstam visited her in hospital in that year the smell of carbolic soap, which filled the whole building, remained fixed in his memory and served as a starting-point for the 1935 poem '- Нет, не мигрень, но подай карандашик ментоловый' (I No.317) - of particular interest is the main source of inspiration, the idea of death in the cold, indifferent void, which is one of this poem's dominant features: 'холод пространства бесполого' (N.Ya.II p.439). 'Не мучнистой бабочкою белой' (I No.320) was also written as a result of the same flying accident and, with its allusion to foot-soldiers marching to their death and the poet's wish not to return his body to the earth as burnt ashes, also prefigured the 'Стихи' (N.Ya.II p.541). The apocalyptic theme, however - the disappearance from the earth of its centre, mankind - had featured as early as 1921 in the poems on desolate Petersburg, now a dead city (I No.124), and on the angel of death swooping down from the sky like an aeroplane to claim his booty (I No.133; N.Ya.II p.546). War and annihilation of man were therefore familiar enough among Mandelstam's constant preoccupations, and their reappearance at this point is only too natural.

Extensive rough drafts of the 'Стихи' survive, from which
it is clear that work on the cycle was marked by three distinct stages of composition. Since the cycle is the fundamental
group of the collection and since it is not included in the
Soviet edition it seems worth discussing these in detail.

In what is perhaps the first stage the intention behind
the poems is made explicit from the very start:

st.1 Этот воздух пусть будет свидетелем -
     Дальнобойное сердце его -
     Яд Вердена, всеядный и деятельный -
     Океан без окна, вещество.

st.2 Как лесистые крестики метили
     (Откупив океан боевой)
     Океан или клин боевой.

st.3 Недосказано там, недопрошено,
     Недокинуто там в сеть сетей...

st.4 Миллионы убитых подошвами
     Шелестят по сетчатке моей -
     Доброй ночи! Всего им хорошего!
     Это зренье пророка смертей.

st.5 И не знаешь, откуда берешь его -
     Луч пропавших без вести вестей -
     Аравийское месиво, крошево
     Начинающих смерть скоростей.
     Недосказано там, недопрошено,
     Недокинуто там в сеть сетей -
     И своими косыми подошвами
     Свет стоит на сетчатке моей.   draft 1 (?)   (N.Ya.III)

This draft is now preserved in TSGALI, to which access has
not been possible. The second draft may conceivably have
preceded the above one - all that is certain about it is its
date, 1 March:

st.1 Этот водзух пусть будет свидетелем -
     Безымянная манна его -
     Сострадательный, темный, владетельный -
     Океан без окна, вещество.

st.2 as I No.362.2

st.3 Аравийское месиво, крошево
     Начинающих смерть скоростей -
     Это зренье пророка подошвами
     Протоптаю тропу в пустоте.

Миллионы убитых задешево –
Доброй ночи! Всего им хорошего
В холодеющем Южнем Кресте.   draft 2(?) 1 March (N.Ya.III)

On the edge of the text is a 'corrected' first stanza in
Mandelstam's hand:

Этот воздух пусть будет свидетелем –
Дальнобойное сердце его –
Сострадательный, темный и деятельный –
Океан без окна, вещество...

The third draft in this first stage is dated 3 March:

st.1 as draft 1(?), st.1

st.2 Миллионы убитых задешево
Протоптали тропу в пустоте
Доброй ночи! Всего им хорошего
От лица земляных крепостей.

st.3 as I No.362.2

st.4 as I No.362.4, st.1, except for line 4:
Свет стоит на сетчатке моей.

st.5 Там лежит Ватерлоо поле новое,
Там от битвы народов светло:
Свет опальный – луч наполеоновый
Треугольным летит журавлем.
Глубоко в черномраморной устрице
Аустерлица забыт огонек,
Смертоносная ласточка шустрится,
Вязнет чумный Египта песок.

st.6 as I No.362.1, st.4

st.7 as I No.362.4, st.3

st.8 as I No.362.4, st.4   draft 3 3 March (N.Ya.III)

The second stage in the development of the cycle was beginning as the first drafts were being committed to paper. The
fourth draft is dated 2-7 March and is almost identical with
the text of 3 March. Only in the fifth stanza does it differ:

st.1-4 as in draft 3

st.5 Там лежит Ватерлоо поле новое,
Там от битвы народов светло:
Свет опальный – луч наполеоновый
Треугольным летит журавлем.
Для того ль должен череп развиться
Во весь лоб – от виска до виска –
Чтоб в его дорогие глазницы
Не могли не вливаться войска.

st.6-9 as in draft 3

draft 4 2-7 March (N.Ya.III)

At some point during the second stage the ten-line stanza 'Хорошо умирает пехота' (I No.362.5) and 'Наливаются кровью аорты' (I No.362.8) must have been written, for the third stage consisted chiefly in arranging the order in which the various parts of the cycle were to be placed. There are two variants of the order, the first being in Nadezhda Yakovlevna's hand:

```
st.1 = I No.362.1, st.1-3
st.2 = I No.362.1, st.4; 3, st.4; 4, st.2
st.3 = I No.362.4, st.3-4
st.4 = I No.362.2; 4, st.1; 3, st.1-3
st.5 = I No.362.6
st.6 = I No.362.5        draft 5        (N.Ya.III)
```

The second variant is in Mandelstam's hand:

```
st.1 = I No.362.1, st.1-3
st.2 = I No.362.1, st.4-5
st.3 = I No.362.4, st.3-4
st.4 = I No.362.6
st.5 = I No.362.4, st.1-2
st.6 = I No.362.5        draft 6        (N.Ya.III)
```

Irritated by his inability to decide how to break up his 'колбаса', Mandelstam almost resolved to abandon the third 'mathematical' section ('Сквозь эфир десятичноозначенный'), thus leaving seven sections in the finished text, a number he preferred to the more conventional eight. No decision was taken, even in Samatikha, where the rough drafts of the cycle, including two fair copies of the dubious third section, went with the Mandelstams (N.Ya.III).

In the primary stage of composition Mandelstam presents a characteristically eclectic account of warfare as the historical starting-point of his thoughts. War is seen initially at the time of the First World War, with its poison gas - 'яд Вердена', its shelling - 'воронки, насыпи, осыпи', and its trenches - 'небо окопное'; long-range guns were then an innovation, hence the epithet 'дальнобойное'. This leads back

to reminiscences from the nineteenth-century version of war,
to Napoleon, with his tricorne and his battle formations, to
Waterloo, Austerlitz and finally Leipzig ('битва народов').
In the TSGALI variant, however, there is an important moment
in the cycle's evolution when Mandelstam turns from the past
to the future: 'Это зренье пророка смертей' - the poem on
Fascist Rome was contemporary with this. In the second stage
of composition the nineteenth-century theme is greatly reduced
and cedes its place to the idea of the future and to a new
theme, that of the human skull: 'Для того ль должен череп
развиться Во весь лоб...'. In the third stage the place and
the meaning of the two stanzas about the swallow undergo a
change. In early variants, one of which is I No.362.3, st.4,
which should therefore be deleted from the final text, the
swallow is seen as the carrier of death - 'Вязнет чумный
Египта песок'. When the Napoleon-nineteenth-century-Egypt
thematic complex was abandoned the swallow was replaced by
the 'ласточка хилая, Разучившаяся летать', a reference to
aviation, in particular to the aeroplane crash and the dead
pilots of 1935 and hence, indirectly, to Mandelstam's own
death.

The description of the cycle as an oratorio might perhaps
be altered to that of a War Requiem, since the cycle laments
the death of men in war, both past and future. The earth
flung up to make craters and trenches is also thrown up to
dig graves, as man disappears from the face of the earth and
disintegrates in the air or moulders beneath the soil. Death
in the air leads to a no less final grave, perhaps even more
desolate in its separation from the earth and its emptiness
- 'воздушная могила' 'яма'. To the accompaniment of the
mourning 'хор ночной' the precious human body, systematically
annihilated, is laid to rest. The association of ideas which
came with the introduction of the human skull - and metonymy
is used here to indicate the whole body - dates from much

earlier in Mandelstam's work, to a jotting in his 1931-2
notebooks:

> В <u>хороших</u> стихах слышно, как шьются черепные швы, как
> набирает власти... рот и / воздуха лобные пазухи, как
> изнашиваются аорты / хозяйничает океанской солью кровь.
> *Записные книжки*   (III pp.155-6)

Poetry is endowed with a human physiology: but it is the close
connection of the skull with the organs of breathing in air
and the aorta which is of relevance here. War underlines the
physical frailty of man and the fact that it is all too possible for him to disappear leaving no traces behind. In 'Не
мучнистой бабочкою белой' (I No.320) Mandelstam had protested
that his 'мыслящее тело' should retain some element of immortality, and in the 'Стихи' he questions the meaning of life
if all traces can be so easily obliterated. The seamed skull,
the cupola, the 'thinking' body, represent the high point of
man's physiological, artistic and intellectual growth:

> Развивается череп от жизни
> Во весь лоб — от виска до виска, —
> Чистотой своих швов он дразнит себя,
> Понимающим куполам яснится,
> Мыслью пенится...   (I No.362.6)

The poet asks whether it could have been intended that the
development of this infinitely complex and sophisticated
entity should lead to its violent destruction:

> Чтоб в его дорогие глазницы
> Не могли не вливаться войска?   (I No.362.6)

The skull becomes that of Yorick, lifeless and empty, as
universal in death as had been happiness in life, exemplified
here by Shakespeare: 'чепчик счатсья — Шекспира отец' (I No.
362.6). The grave teaches the curved spine of man, 'горбатого'
or 'сутулого', how to lie rigid and straight, as had the
Nuremberg spring of rumour in the 1931 poem 'Рояль' (I No.234).
Nadezhda Yakovlevna writes of the will to self-destruction -
'И воздушная яма влечет' - as being a typical feature of those
who lived through the purges, but had no inner resources to

sustain their interest in life (N.Ya.II p.542). So in the
poem Mandelstam sees air, normally the purveyor of poetry,
in two aspects, both opposed to this creative function: as
the carrier of poison gas and as the cold, indifferent void
which lures men to death. Perversion of its true purpose was
not unknown to him: as recently as 18 January he had written
of his own attempt to subordinate it to a base end, the
production of a sycophantic ode to Stalin:

> Я обращался к воздуху-слуге,
> Ждал от него услуги или вести   (I No.352)

In the stanza 'Шевелящимися виноградинами' (I No.362.2) it
becomes clear that Mandelstam's individual failure to abuse
the air is a quite different matter from the cosmic scale of
its abuse in war. Elaborating on the menace of the gas-laden
air, he speaks of the 'золотые созвездий жиры'; in the distorted world of warfare the flying gas-shells appear as
constellations, loaded with the promise of destruction:

> И висят городами украденными,
> Золотыми обмолвками, ябедами –
> Ядовитого холода ягодами   (I No.362.2)

This destruction is expressed in terms of the degradation of
speech, similar to that of air. In the same way light is
perverted for the same ends - 'Свет размолотых в луч скорос-
тей'. The mathematical, scientific basis of war is condemned
in the image of 'velocities' turning themselves into the
light of exploding missiles and searchlights, both bringing
death with them. Mandelstam had first-hand experience of
watching them at work in 1919, when he spent a considerable
time at the window in Kiev, appalled by the spectacle of
shells flying through the air (N.Ya.III). This terrible light
had illuminated battlefields of which the Napoleonic Wars
provided neither the first nor the last example:

> Весть летит светопыльной дорогою –
> И от битвы вчерашней светло.
>
> Весть леити светопыльной дорогою –

Я не Лейпциг, не Ватерлоо,
Я не Битва Народов. Я - новое, -
От меня будет свету светло.   (I No.362.3)

In the new conflict Mandelstam predicts wholesale destruction
on a hitherto unknown scale, thanks to the greater efficiency
of war; trench warfare becomes war in the air, the wastage
of human life escalates accordingly:

Миллионы убитых задешево...

Неподкупное небо окопное,
Небо крупных оптовых смертей   (I No.362.4)

Even the watching stars are affected as they speed back to
the heavens stained with the blood gushing upwards from the
earth:

Чтобы белые звезды обратно
Чуть-чуть красные мчались в свой дом!   (I No.362.7)

The shedding of blood was more repugnant to Mandelstam than
to many other poets, since his physiological awareness was
more acute than that of most. In the last stanza, where he
allies himself with the herd, the exploited victims of conscription - 'с гурьбой и гуртом' - as they stand in serried
ranks declaring their ages, his aorta, like theirs, fills
with blood, the heartbeats quicken from fear, and the lips
become pale and bloodless:

Наливаются кровью аорты...
Я шепчу обескровленным ртом   (I No.362.8)

What Mandelstam goes on to whisper is his epitaph, foreseeing
the future glory which will be his through his poetry, however
undistinguished his death may be:

- Я рожден в ночь с второго на третье
Января в девяносто одном
Ненадежном году, и столетья
Окружают меня огнем.   (I No.362.8)

Nadezhda Yakovlevna had been away in Moscow for a couple of
days at the beginning of March, during which Mandelstam contrived to have himself X-rayed in connection with his heart
attacks. The heart was thus at the forefront of his thoughts.

The pounding heartbeats of his fellow conscripts, each with
an individual age and identity (Mandelstam would clutch his
passport to his chest as he read the line about his 'истертый
год рожденья', only partly in jest [N.Ya.I p.129]), are
caused by the certain knowledge that they are doomed to
become 'без окна вещество', marked only by 'лесистые крестики'
In his general reading Mandelstam had come across Leibniz's
terse description of monads: 'The Monads have no windows
through which anything could come in or go out.'[1] (N.Ya.III)
Although the monad image applies primarily to the ocean of
gas engulfing the soldiers, through which no air-holes can
be bored, the idea of these same soldiers making the Lamarck-
ian descent to basic matter horrified Mandelstam, especially
since their use as war material had not been a matter of free
choice (N.Ya.III). Should these men survive it would be with
a maimed body:

> И стучит по околицам века
> Костылей деревянных семейка   (I No.362.5)

No matter what their attitude to participating in the slaugh-
ter might be - the idealistic foolishness of a Don Quixote
with his 'птичьем копьем', or the ironic determination to
make the best out of a situation of a Schweik, the end result
is the same:

> Будут люди холодные, хилые
> Убивать, холодать, голодать,
> И в своей знаменитой могиле
> Неизвестный положен солдат.   (I No.362.1)

The sky cycle

The 'целокупное' sky and the 'оба неба с их тусклым огнем'
of the 'Стихи о неизвестном солдате' formed the initial
impulse for a new cycle of poems generated by the 'Стихи'
which developed parallel with a similar one, the 'antique'

---

[1] Leibniz, *The Monadology*, transl. R.Latta (Oxford, 1965),
p.219.

cycle, whose origins it shared. Since his 'Acmeist' days
Mandelstam's views on the relationship between the earth and
the sky had been firmly and consistently held. Starting from
an anti-Symbolist position, he propounded the view that the
earth was given to man by God and that man should be content
to live there without speculating on hypothetical better
worlds in or beyond the heavens (e.g. in 'Утро акмеизма', II
p.322). This was not merely a polemical expediency, but a
genuine conviction that the real world, in all its marvellous
complexity, had an intrinsic fascination quite sufficient to
satisfy all human needs. The wish for something more was
symptomatic of inadequacy on the part of those ingrates who
sighed for the world of their various ideals:

> И под временным небом чистилища
> Забываем мы часто о том,
> Что счастливое небохранилище
> Раздвижной и пожизненный дом.   (I No.376)

After considering the sky as the void towards which men are
fatally drawn, he had returned to his previous conception of
it and tried to shake off the idea that the sky, the benevolent
roof of the world, now represented a positive threat to life.
The question 'Заблудился я в небе... Что делать?' (I Nos.378
& 379) poses this dilemma; its formulation is particularly
clear in an early version of these poems' first stanza:

> Одинокое небо виднее, -
> Как недугом, я пьян им в судьбе,
> Но оно западня: в нем труднее
> Задыхаться, чернеть, голубеть.   (S p.304)

Finding a solution to this dilemma presented a difficulty
which Mandelstam compares with that of making the nine circles
of Dante's hell resonate and ring out like an athlete's discus.
He sees two alternatives ahead: the distasteful life of the
victor ludorum, crowned with laurels - 'остроласковый лавр',
or the disintegration of his body, to merge with the blue sky
in a disembodied sound, a fate he finds preferable here:

Лучше сердце мое расколите
Вы на синего звона куски.   (I No.378)

He reconciles himself with the sky to the extent that he has
conquered its emptiness with the sound of poetry, the task
of the creative artist as originally defined by him (II p.
323). At his death he will feel not only that this task has
been fulfilled and that he can speak of himself as 'отслужив-
ши', but that he will have succeeded as well in leaving some
trace of his mortal self behind, in the way the builders of
Gothic cathedrals had done:

Чтоб раздался и шире и выше
Отклик неба во всю мою грудь.   (I No.378)

Man as the centre of creation - literally and poetically
speaking - is another fundamental Acmeist tenet which retains
its pivotal position in Mandelstam's summary of the task he
has accomplished: 'Всех живущих прижизненный друг'. Friendship with his fellows came as a result of love of life in all
its forms, and he valued it above all else. Having once
established the possibility of filling the void with sound,
the sound of human voices, he elaborates on the process by
which the carefree play of the sky is achieved:

Достигается потом и опытом
Безотчетного неба игра.   (I No.376)

Reference to the 'Стихи о русской поэзии' (I No.263) and to
'Восьмистишия' (I No.283) reveals that this is precisely the
method by which poetry is achieved. As so often, the subject
of poetry lurks not far beneath the surface: the play of the
sky has not changed since his description of the carefree
disporting of Christian art - 'игра Отца с детьми, жмурки и
прятки духа!' ('Пушкин и Скрябин', II p.315).

'Тайная Вечеря' (I No.377) in its very title implies
death and martyrdom. Again it is the sky on which the poet's
imagination focuses in contemplating these solemn events:

Небо вечери в стену влюбилось —
Все изранено светом рубцов   (I No.377)

Even in the context of a specific event from a different age
and culture, it is the images associated with present-day
Russia which are employed in the description of the backdrop
against which the tragedy begins to unfold - the blood-red
sun and the 'тринадцать голов' bathed in it. In linking the
occasion of the Last Supper with his own position, through
the agency of the sky - 'мое небо ночное', Mandelstam lends
the utmost gravity to the theme of the martyr, whose religious associations had been mentioned previously only once in
his work, in the Golgotha poem of February 1937 (I No.364).
It implies no blasphemy or hubris on his part, but a serious
realisation that each must be prepared to suffer for his
faith, whatever that faith may be. The circumstances of such
suffering will always be the same:

> И под каждым ударом тарана
> Осыпаются звезды без глаз, -
> Той же вечери новые раны   (I No.377)

The eyeless stars are in keeping with Mandelstam's feeling
that life could not possibly exist on them: in this respect
they are also monads.

In connection with the heavens, he went on to explore a
supplementary theme, that of the 'луч-паучок' in the light
from the sky. He reverts here to his memories of French cathedrals and their stained-glass windows for an image to
describe the unbinding of the knot of life, with which he
was still obsessed. In the diffusion of the light pouring in
through the glass, the various colours glow in their separate
rays, but reunite in rainbow patches on the cathedral pillars

> Так соборы кристаллов сверхжизненных
> Добросовестный луч-паучок,
> Распуская на ребра, их сызнова
> Собирает в единый пучок.   (I No.380)

The rays of light now forming lines of unmatchable straight-
ness will one day merge, meeting in eternity. Eternity as a
concept is envisaged as being a thing of this earth, quite

unrelated to the heavens:

> Только здесь на земле, а не на небе,
> Как в наполненный музыкой дом.   (I No.380)

The heartfelt reservation which escapes Mandelstam's lips
when contemplating this prospect, 'Хорошо, если мы доживем',
was made in the reasonable certainty that there was no like-
lihood of his doing so. He said of this poem 'Это моя архитек
тура' (N.Ya.III) and it can indeed be seen as an illustration both of the foundations and of the decoration or adorn-
ment of his life, that is his 'добросовестный' view of the
world and of the place of art in it. As always, he asked
Nadezhda Yakovlevna to read the poem aloud to him in even
tones, without underlining the rhythm, checking it by ear as
she did so; here he asks her forgiveness for the misery to
which his 'architecture' had brought them both:

> То, что я говорю, мне прости,
> Тихо, тихо его мне прочти.   (I No.380)

In the final poem of the cycle Mandelstam is suddenly
possessed by a strange longing to blend with the rays of
starlight in their travels:

> О, как же я хочу –
> Нечуемый никем –
> Лететь вослед лучу,
> Где нет меня совсем.   (I No.384)

Known domestically as 'Звездочка' - in his letter of 8 May
to Nadezhda Yakovlevna he calls it this: 'твоя звездочка...
очень как хороша' (Letter No.84, III p.291) - the poem change
its form continuously. Mandelstam was embarrassed by what he
called these 'постельные стихи', feeling them to be too
intimate to be exposed to the outside reader (N.Ya.III). The
extent to which he was still writing poetry for others rather
than as a lyrical diary for himself is revealed in this emba-
rrassment. Another factor which dismayed him was fear of
being teased by Narbut, whom he hoped to meet after his
release: 'Осип шопотом штопает звезды' was the sort of remark

the caustic Narbut might well be expected to produce (N.Ya.
III) to mock these charming and earnest lines. Thus there
are variant versions of the poem in three-stanza form, although
Mandelstam's ideal was to keep only one stanza - the first -
to escape Narbut's teasing. One stanza, discarded early on
in the poem's composition, displays the light-hearted
vivacity which was patently one of Mandelstam's most attractive traits:

> Он только тем хорош,
> Он только тем и мил,
> Что будит к танцу дрожь -
> Румянец вещих† сил.　　　(Cf.S p.304)　　　(N.Ya.III)
> † звездных in S

His use of the three-footed line to the exclusion of all
others was a rare occurrence in his poetry of any period.
In the third Voronezh *Тетрадь* it appears only twice, here and
in two poems of January 1937 (I Nos.343 & 344) where it is
used to convey the bumpy movement of the sledge of the dead
over the steppe-land. 'О, как же я хочу' is something between
a love poem and a cadenza on the 'шепот-лепет' poetry theme,
an unusual combination of ideas, perhaps producing an unusual
form of expression. This is the only instance in which Mandelstam takes the stars at their face value, as giving off rays
of starlight, without wondering about their composition and
their meaning. Nadezhda Yakovlevna, the 'дитя' of the poem,
is entrusted to their care by his 'шепот', since in this
case the radiance of the stars is also that of his poetry:

> Он только тем и луч,
> Он только тем и свет,
> Что шепотом могуч
> И лепетом согрет.　　　　　　　(I No.384)

The power and warmth with which the starlight glows merge with
those of poetry, so that poetry becomes the source and the
strength of the light. In dealing with the heavenly bodies he
had always treated the moon as a joke (I Nos.58, 58a, 58б),
while ascribing immense significance to the sun (I Nos 82, 91

& 108) and the active, 'day-time' side of life, but this poem demonstrates his ability to find the positive side even of the 'dead' stars, in his concentration on their light, not their bodies.

The antique cycle

Parallel with the 'sky' cycle develped the 'antique' cycle, occasioned by visits to the Voronezh museum's holdings of Greek pots, taken from the same source - Dorpat University - as the Rembrandt of 'Как светотени мученик Рембрандт' (I No. 364). The 'Кувшин' (I No.383) in question belonged to the black-on-red type (late sixth century B.C.) in which the black colour was painted round the red terracotta figures, as opposed to the black figures being painted onto the red background, as in the other type: 'на твоем ободу черно-красном'. The Voronezh example, one of many such, depicted satyrs - 'козлята' - playing *auloi* - 'флейты', in an apparent fury - 'клевещут и злятся' - at the chipped or broken state of the rim of the pot:

> ...беда на твоем ободу
> Черно-красном — и некому взяться
> За тебя, чтоб поправить беду.   (I No.383)

An interesting aspect of Mandelstam's description is his transference of the qualities of the satyrs to the pot as a whole: it becomes the 'должник виноватый' of a long thirst - the length of the thirst being measured not in time but by the volume of the pot's contents needed to quench it. It is referred to in a semi-pejorative manner as the 'Мудрый сводни вина и воды', where the wisdom and licentiousness of the satyrs infects the background on which they appear.

Music, in the form of the 'flutes', initiated a new train of ideas which were slower to take shape than those in the first poem, and Mandelstam meanwhile continued his farewell survey of Greece and the classical world in 'Гончарами велик

остров синий' (I No.385). Again he makes use of transferred
epithets to describe Crete in terms of the colour of the sea
surrounding it: there was no traditional appellation for the
island at all similar to 'синий'. It is not without significance that images previously associated with each other in
the 'Армения' group recur in juxtaposition here:

> Гончарами велик остров синий –
> Крит веселый, запекся их дар
> В землю звонкую..

> В осчастливленной обжигом глине   (I No.385)

> В библиотеке авторов гончарных..   (I No.214)
> Над книгой звонких глин, над книжною землей,
> Над гнойной книгою, над глиной дорогой,
> Которой мучимся как музыкой и словом.   1930 (I No.215)

Cretan pottery of the prehistoric period represents the most
basic and fertile example of artistic expression in this
medium up to the time of the classical period:

> Это было и пелось, синея,
> Много задолго до Одиссея   (I No.385)

In this respect Mandelstam's identical vision of Crete and
Armenia is one of substance. Armenia's long cultural history
formed a great part of its attraction for him, through its
similarity to the Mediterranean and the classical lands no
longer open to him. He begs the island: 'отдай мне мой труд'.
The world of dolphins and flying fish, the dark blue water
'говорящая "да"', represent an ideal and an inspiration for
his work. In connection with the sky and stars which were
then occupying this thoughts, the very association of them
with Greece here suffices to rid them of any negative qualities they may ever have possessed:

> Выздоравливай же, излучайся,
> Волоокого неба звезда   (I No.385)

Bo-opis, the fixed epithet of Hera, is applied here to the
sky of Greece, the domain of gods translated into constellations, which is endowed with the majesty and dignity mostly
appropriate to the consort of Zeus. The collation of these

elements of the sky, the goddess, the Greek pot and Mandelstam's own work is most apparent in the central stanza:

> Крит летучий, отдай мне мой труд,
> И сосцами текучей богини
> Напои обожженный сосуд. (I No.385)

It seems probable that Hera was first worshipped in the form
of a cow, her epithet being a reminder of this early cult.
The idea of abundance and fruitfulness, in the image of the
milk-filled vessel, links the poet's work with the goddess
and thus with the Greek world, wherein lay the origins of the
cultural tradition in which he was following, fully sharing
its joy in life, as the words 'веселый' 'осчастливленной'
'излучайся' show. Conversely, he considers in 'Нереиды мои,
нереиды' (I No.297), written in March 1937 (not 1935 as in I)
that the classical world shares his own sufferings with him.
The fifty Nereids ('the wet ones'), who attended on the sea-
goddess Thetis, were both beautiful and benevolent. 'Рыданья'
the tears shed by miserable mortals, were as essential as
their food and drink to these ocean-dwellers, being composed
of the same substance 'Вам рыданья - еда и питье' (corrected
from I, where the erroneous comma destroys the sense). Even
if his sympathy is unnecessary to them theirs is by no means
so to him. It is not inconceivable that Nadezhda Yakovlevna
and Natasha Shtempel are to be imagined in this role.

Among the poems of the 'antique' and 'flute' groups there
were significant losses, either through the filching of
Rudakov, or through confiscation in the search at the time
of Mandelstam's second arrest. Nadezhda Yakovlevna remembers
certain isolated lines, the first three of which come from a
poem on the subject of composers:

> И маленький Рамо-кузнечик деревянный
>
> Чайковского боюсь - он Моцарт на бобах
>
> И пламенный поляк - ревнивец форте-пьянный (N.Ya.III)

The second individual line is from a poem dealing with the

theme of death, most probably the 'корабль смерти' here:

На этом корабле есть для меня каюта   (N.Ya.III)

The third lost poem began:

Но уже раскачали ворота молодые микенские львы

                              (N.Ya.III)

It also included the phrase 'рельеф из Саккара', but she does
not remember the connection between the young lions and the
finds from the Saqqara excavations. From the fourth she cites
lines which reveal how Mandelstam's thoughts were directed
not only towards the Europe and the classical world of the
past, but also towards present-day life abroad, from which he
was cut off:

В Париже площадь есть - ее зовут Звезда
          ... машин стада   (N.Ya.III)

It would have been interesting to know how Mandelstam continued his musings on Rameau and Chopin, whose names had never
vied with, for example, Mozart and Schubert for a place in
his work. As these lines stand, they resemble very much the
method of characterisation used in his earlier poems on Russian poetry (I Nos. 259 & 262), where each poet is delineated
in one stroke by one particular quality of his personality
or his work: here it is Rameau's methodical, rhythmic tapping
and Chopin's fiery ardour by which they are known.

Music, its composition and its performance, links the
lost poems with 'Флейты греческой тэта и йота' (I No.387).
This poem was written at the time of the flautist Shvab's
arrest (N.Ya.I pp.194-5), and thus to the themes of the *aulos*
and inspiration from the classical world is added a new,
terrible dimension - the death of the artist. The lost poem
on death doubtless arose from the same event. Mandelstam
speaks of the flute's music both in the past and in the present: in the past, since Shvab could no longer delight him
with his playing, in the present, since he understands the
creative work of the flautist to have close affinities with

the continuing work of the poet. Their efforts are distinguished by the same qualities, as both the sound of the flute
and the the recited poem are 'неизваянная, без отчета'. Mandelstam had castigated the ascribing of a 'sculptural' quality
to Dante's work - literary critics had presented Dante as
having conjured up a finished product without apparent effort,
or, at best, 'ему дают в руки резец и позволяют скульптурни-
чать или, как любят выражаться, "ваять"' (*Разговор о Данте*,
II p.384). By way of antithesis to this, he names in the same
breath as 'unsculptured' the carefree, irresponsible nature
of Christian art. A third distinctive feature is the inevita-
bility of such creative endeavours. They are completely
involuntary and impossible to avoid on the part of the artist.
Once the basic material is present it cannot be got rid of,
either by trying to express it artificially in verbal form
or by attempting to knead it into a different shape from the
one it wishes to assume:

> И ее невозможно покинуть,
> Стиснув зубы ее не унять,
> И в слова языком не продвинуть,
> И губами ее не размять.

> А флейтист не узнает покоя...   (I No.387)

The string of negative verbs indicates the relentlessness of
poetry or music, forcing itself on the attention whether it
is welcome or not. The flautist and the poet feel both the
uniqueness of the part they play and the particular nature of
the process, expressed in terms of the synthesis of the most
basic and honest elements of the physical world:

> ... он море родное
> Из сиреневых вылепил глин.   (I No.387)

Earth and water - the Aegean and the chill water of Lake Sevan
the clays of Greece and of Armenia - blend together in artistic form here: 'Комья глины в ладонях моря'. The stanza which
describes the actual performance of the flautist, and thus of
the poet, conveys exactly the way in which Mandelstam himself

composed (N.Ya.I pp.192-7):

> Звонким шепотом честолюбивым,
> Вспоминающим топотом губ
> Он торопится быть бережливым,
> Емлет звуки, опрятен и скуп.   (I No.387)

Relatively early on in his work 'звонкий' had come to be
associated with the resonant quality of embryonic poetry, as
in the 'двойчатки' I Nos. 131 & 132, while 'шепот' had very
recently been used to convey the noise in the poet's ears
(I No.384). The moral rightness of poetry needs no elucidation,
nor do the symbol of the poet's lips and the search for the
'lost word' which slips away to the underworld and into
oblivion (See I No.113). In all, the first half of the stanza
is a distillation of the vital elements in poetic composition.
Only the two final stanzas link the world of art with the
world of the Stalinist Terror:

> И когда я наполнился морем,
> Мором стала мне мера моя.   (I No.387)

Whenever Mandelstam was overtaken by inspiration - the sea
image is used with some insistence here - the whole experience
was now ruined by the remembrance of Shvab: 'И убийство на
том же корню'. He ends with untypical pessimism, consigning
the flute, whose ability to move in purely mathematical
spheres which defy ordinary mortals equals his own (See I No.
285), to the doom which he must acknowledge as its inescapable
destiny:

> И невольно на убыль, на убыль
> Равнодействия флейты клоню.   (I No.387)

On 18 March Mandelstam had written down a fair copy of
his poem on François Villon, which is preserved in TSGALI.
After 7 April, the date of the Shvab poem, this Villon poem
took on a political complexion. It was reduced to the eight
lines which comprise the second and fifth stanzas of 'Чтоб
приятель и ветра и капель' (I No.382); the remaining stanzas
given there belong, in their present order, only in the

TSGALI early draft, and not with the eight lines of the final
text (N.Ya.III). In this choice of the essential portions of
the draft version the impulse behind the poem emerges very
clearly. It lies in a stark contrast between the tyranny of
the monolithic Egyptian state and the impudent rebel and
scoundrel, who refuses to conform to the norms laid down by
authority. The link rests in the gulf between those who mete
out punishment and those whose lot is to receive it. Mandelstam concentrates his most withering comments in the phrases
describing the powerful, inhuman machine of Egyptian government: 'Египтян государственный стыд' 'паучьи права'. Egypt
and Assyria retained all their previous connotations in his
lexicon (See 'Девятнадцатый век', II p.283), not least in the
person of the 'Assyrian' of 'Путешествие в Армению': 'Ассириец
держит мое сердце' (II p.175). Villon's life of a thief also
condemned to be hanged as a murderer, well illustrates the
opposite pole. In his search for 'беззаботного права' he spits
on authority, in life as in both his *Testaments*. The conflict
is symbolised, not unexpectedly, in the architectural monuments of both states. In Egypt there is the useless pyramid,
filled with tributes to the vanity and power of the deceased
ruler, whereas the Gothic cathedrals of France are a wild
celebration of life, movement, lack of reverence for the
conformist integration of monolithic structures. Villon, the
'Наглый школьник и ангел ворующий', the 'Утешительно-грешный
певец', is the antidote to the atrophy of the Assyrian's
despotic rule and thus Mandelstam's ideal and hero - the sort
of 'разбойник' always so dear to him: 'И не разбойничать
нельзя' (I No.255). An isolated phrase about Saqqara from the
lost poem must have been connected with the idea of Egypt, as
one on death would have been with Villon, and those on the
young lions and Paris with the Gothic cathedrals.

Poems of death and resurrection

Nadezhda Yakovlevna left for Moscow in an attempt to clarify their position by discovering whether Mandelstam would be allowed back to either capital after his period of exile had officially ended. Inevitably she was also in search of money and the promise of work. Her mother, Vera Yakovlevna Khazina, stayed with Mandelstam, a fact for which he was immensely and touchingly grateful:

> Болезнь 'быть без Тебя' протекает довольно мирно (благодаря маме) но все-таки болезнь.
> Letter No.75   (III pp.281-2)

> Мама твоя очень помогает - всем своим существом, вплоть до раздражающих моментов...
> Letter No.76   (III p.282)

However, at some point during April, the realisation that Nadezhda Yakovlevna was shortly to be a widow struck with such horrific force that he was unable to restrain the tragic thoughts of her future without him from developing into the poem 'Как по улицам Киева-Вия' (I No.395, written in April, not May). Kiev, her home town, takes on the horrendous aspect of Gogol's supernatural monster, the form in which it had revealed itself in 1919, during the year in which the Mandelstams had met there: ·

> Под самый конец, когда большевики перед уходом расстреливали заложников, мы видели в окно... телегу, полную раздетых трупов. Они были небрежно покрыты рогожей и со всех сторон торчали части мертвых тел. (N.Ya.II p.26)

> Уходили с последним трамваем
> Прямо за город красноармейцы,
> И шинель прокричала сырая:
> - Мы вернемся еще, разумейте!...   (I No.395)

The connection with a repulsive monster derives from a poem of Gumilev's, 'Из логова змиева'. The remembrance of Gumilev's death - only one of the manifold horrors of the Civil War - must have made Mandelstam's own seem yet more vivid; he, after all, knew what it was like to survive an officially unacceptable poet:

Из логова змиева,
Из города Киева,
Я взял не жену, а колдунью...
И смотрит, и стонет,
Как будто хоронит
Кого-то, - и хочет топиться.[1]

Nightmares about what would happen to his widow must have
tormented Mandelstam beyond human endurance after his arrest,
considering that he had so vividly visualised them here. No
quarter, as he knew from long experience of the activities of
the 'шинель', would be given to the helpless relatives of
its victims, even if they avoided becoming victims in their
turn:

Ищет мужа не знаю чья жинка,
И на щеки ее восковые
Ни одна не скатилась слезинка.   (I No.395)

Only his own suffering beyond the point of tears could have
enabled him to envisage such a state. Significantly, he not
only returns Nadezhda Yakovlevna to the scene of many of the
worst atrocities of the Civil War but compounds the horror
for her by placing her in one of the most traditionally anti-
Semitic regions of the Soviet Union. Nadezhda Yakovlevna
herself avers that she has never been subjected to humiliation
on account of her Jewish origins - even in the Ukraine, but
for Mandelstam it was a very real fear in a world where not
only Kiev smelt of death. All his terror at the fate of
Shvab, at the idea of punishments in keeping with the Egyptian
nature of the regime, and at his imminent separation from his
wife are concentrated here. At one point he wished to end the
Тетрадь with it, but Nadezhda Yakovlevna thought the poem
about the resurrected dead (I No.394) more fitting, and he
concurred.

    Natasha Shtempel, the subject of the final poem, had

visited Mandelstam as often as possible during Nadezhda Yakovlevna's absence, after her long teaching day. Escapades such
as when he accompanied Natasha and her boyfriend on a nocturnal expedition to the Hotel Bristol, where they sat eating
oranges and drinking wine (See Letter No.82, III p.289), did
much to enliven the depressing days. On 2 May he wrote a half-
joking, half-serious poem after the manner of 'частушки',
whose import was that Natasha and Boris should marry. Certain
details of her background had to be invented for this poem:

Для общезначимости пришлось приписать Наташе старшего
брата и сестру и постулировать характер будущего мужа. Но
то, что я ее уговариваю выйти замуж, это вполне реально.
       Letter No.81   (III p.288)

The period when his existence was brightened by Natasha's
presence also produced the two humorous verses quoted by
Nadezhda Yakovlevna (N.Ya.I p.231), the second of which was
composed on the eve of the Mandelstam's departure from
Voronezh:

Пришла Наташа. Где была?
Небось, не ела, не пила...
И чует мать, черна как ночь:
Вином и луком пахнет дочь...   (I No.390)

Natasha's mother's concern is gleefully pictured, followed by
her anger at the junketings where food and drink of a rather
different sort from what she might have wished for her daughter had been offered. The desirability of Natasha's marriage
was treated equally lightly, in the imagery of the approaching spring and of folk custom, and in an appropriately folksy
style:

Спросит гром своих знакомых:
- Вы, грома, слыхали,
Чтобы грушу до черемух
Замуж выдавали?...

Свахи-птицы свищут почесть
Льстивую Наташе.   (I No.389)

A serious note was none the less struck in this whimsical
jesting, for three of its lines are echoed in the poem on

spring which follows it in the collection:

> Клейкой клятвой пахнут почки...

> И к губам такие липнут
> Клятвы...   (I No.389)

> Я к губам подношу эту зелень,
> Эту клейкую клятву листов   (I No.388)

Mandelstam saw spring as the herald of the leaves and flowers
of summer, as might be anticipated, but more cogently as the
herald of a new life for those whose own lives, like his,
were soon to be ended. The burst of energy in the sticky buds
and foliage arouses a like vigour in him, a love of life as
instinctive as that of Ivan Karamazov. Crazy impulses seize
him - he even feels a little in love with Natasha himself,
hence the adjective 'клятвопреступную' applied to the earth,
which he blames for his temporary aberration. The 'клятвы'
are of importance, however, but in their earlier sense as
representing the vows of fidelity to their ideals taken by
Herzen and Ogarev and, after their example, by Mandelstam
himself (See I No.140). In the season which promises new life
resides a hope which he had never abandoned completely and
which was now being artificially fostered by the prospect of
release. The Voronezh black earth, seen in 1935 together with
poetry as his last weapon against his oppressors, is taken
symbolically to his lips, as poetry is shown to take its
inspiration from the earth and its inhabitants. As to the
future, the 'Комочки влажные моей земли и воли' (I No.299)
and the mutterings of his 'губ шевелящихся' (I No.307), which
had served him so well in Voronezh, could no more be taken
away from him now than when he first arrived there. Dostoevsky's feeling for the powerful spiritual regeneration to be
found in the earth is paralleled in the new flow of life
felt by Mandelstam in the mere act of observing and learning
from the roots of trees alone:

> Погляди, как я слепну и крепну,
> Подчиняясь смиренным корням.   (I No.388)

A distant echo of 'Гринельная ода' can be discerned here (see the rough drafts[1]), where oak trees - the 'дубков'. of this poem - and the blindness of poetic inspiration were memorably linked. Now, spring seethes and thunders around the poet, assaulting his senses with its noise, smell and colour:

И не слишком ли великолепно
От гремучего парка глазам?   (I No.388)

The voices of the 'квакуши' 'сцепляются в шар', a unison chorus of rejoicing.

The atmosphere is almost one of violence. In 'На меня нацелилась' (I No.393) the two fruit-blossom fragrances launch an all-out attack on the unwary: 'Силою рассыпчатой бьет меня без промаха'. Through their 'сладость неуживчива' they battle for the hegemony of the spring air which collapses, battered by whole branches of perfume, subjected to their 'двоевластье' - neither rival's claim being satisfied. The cry 'в чьем соцветьи истина', sent up by the bewildered poet whose senses are overwhelmed by the assault of the 'двойного запаха', shows how seriously he is involved in the battle of the star-like blooms on the boughs, 'воздушно белыми'. Appreciation of this earth, a leitmotif in so much of Mandelstam, reaches one of its high points here. The poem turned out to be the last of his many on the lindens, the birdcherry, the poplars, and other trees which had lined his ways through city and steppe and had never gone unremarked.

A sharp change of mood can be discerned in the poem which most aptly closes the *Тетрадь*, 'К пустой земле невольно припадая' (I No.394), even though it was written on the same day as the previous one. Its subject, again Natasha, appears here in a context of solemnity quite different from the jocular poems at her expense. Faith in eternity radiates from this

[1] Jennifer Baines, 'Mandel'shtam's "Грифельная ода": A commentary in the light of the unpublished rough drafts', *Oxford Slavonic Papers*, New Series V (1972), 76.

poem and casts its light over the whole collection. The true
significance of spring is stated explicitly and with confidence. On the other side of the grave lies a new beginning,
and the process of death leading to eternal life becomes a
perpetual one through its earthly incarnation in spring:

> ... эта вешняя погода
> Для нас праматерь гробового свода,
> И это будет вечно начинаться. (I No.394)

Natasha's vocation, the mission she shares with so many other
women, is a sacred one, connected with the cycle of death
and resurrection:

> Есть женщины сырой земли родные,
> И каждый шаг их - гулкое рыданье,
> Сопровождать умерших и впервые
> Приветствовать воскресших - их призванье. (I No.394)

This exalted role is exactly that of the Petersburg women of
an earlier age - to gather up the traces of humanity and to
fill them with new life:

> Может быть века пройдут
> И блаженных жен родные руки
> Легкий пепел соберут. 1920 (I No.118)

Ahead of Mandelstam lay his second exile from Moscow,
his second arrest and his death in a transit camp near Vladi-
vostok on 27 December 1938 (See N.Ya.I pp.232-416). The poems
'Чарли Чаплин', whose text survives (I No.386), 'Черкешенка',
'На высокие утесы Волга хлынь', 'И веером разложенная дранка
Непобедимых скатых крыш', all of which have survived only in
title, were written in Moscow shortly after his release from
his Voronezh exile. Mandelstam considered them weak and in
any case they disappeared at Samatikha or with Rudakov. The
sole poem produced to glorify the building of the White Sea
canal, to which Mandelstam was sent on a 'командировка' from
Moscow, was thrown into the stove by Nadezhda Yakovlevna and
Anna Akhmatova during the war - an action which beyond all
shadow of doubt would have met with his approval (N.Ya.I p.
319). Thus the final poem of the third Voronezh *Тетрадь* was

in effect Mandelstam's last word. Seen in this perspective,
the hope which transforms it into an act of faith illuminates
not only the collection which it crowns but Mandelstam's
entire life and poetry - and not least the tragedy of his
death:

> Цветы бессмертны. Небо целокупно.
> И то, что будет - только обещанье.   (I No.394)

APPENDIX

ПЕРВАЯ МОСКОВСКАЯ ТЕТРАДЬ

NYa	Number I	S	Title/first line	Date in NYa
1	202	143	Куда как страшно нам с тобой	30 Oct.1930
2			Армения	16 Oct.-5 Nov.1930
1	204	129	Ты розу Гафиза колышешь	---
2	205	130	Ты красок себе пожалела	21 Oct.1930
3	206	131	Ах, ничего я не вижу, и бедное ухо оглохло	16 Oct.1930
4	207	132	Закутав рот, как влажную розу	25 Oct.1930
5	208	133	Руку платком обмотай и в венценосный шиповник	---
6	209	134	Орущих камней государство	---
7	210	135	Не развалины - нет - но порубка могучего циркульного леса	---
8	211	136	Холодно розе в снегу	---
9	212	137	О порфирные цокая граниты	24 Oct.1930
10	213	138	Какая роскошь в нищенском селеньи	24 Oct.1930
11	214	139	Я тебя никогда не увижу	---
12	215	140	Лазурь да глина, глина да лазурь	5 Nov.1930
3	201	---	Не говори никому	Oct.1930
4	216	142	Колючая речь араратской долины	Oct.1930
5	217	141	Как люб мне натугой живущий	Oct.1930
6	220	---	И по-звериному воет людье	Oct.1930
7	218	---	Дикая кошка - армянская речь	Nov.1930
8	219	---	На полицейской бумаге верже	Oct.1930
9	221	144	Ленинград	Dec.1930
10	222	146	С миром державным я был лишь ребячески связан	Jan.1931

NYa	I	S	Title/first line	Date in NYa
	Number		Title/first line	Date in NYa
11	224	145	Мы с тобой на кухне посидим	Jan.1931
12	223	---	Помоги, Господь, эту ночь прожить	Jan.1931
13	225	---	После полуночи сердце ворует	March 1931
14	226	147	Я скажу тебе с последней	March 1931
15	227	149	За гремучую доблесть грядущих веков	17-28 March 1931
16	230	---	Ночь на дворе. Барская лжа	March 1931
17	228	150	Жил Александр Герцович	27 March 1931
18	229	---	Колют ресницы. В груди прикипела слеза	March 1931
19	232	---	Нет, не спрятаться мне от великой муры	Apr.1931
20	231	---	Я с дымящей лучиной вхожу	4 Apr.1931
21	233	---	Я пью за военные астры, за все, чем корили меня	11 Apr.1931
22	234	151	Рояль	16 Apr.1931
23	235	153	Сохрани мою речь навсегда за привкус несчастья и дыма	3 May 1931
24	236	---	Канцона	26 May 1931
25	260	154	Полночь в Москве	May - 4 June 1931
26	247	156	Довольно кукситься! Бумаги в стол засунем	7 June 1931
27			Отрывки из уничтоженных стихов	
1	237	---	В год тридцать первый от рожденья века	---
2	238	---	Уж я люблю московские законы	---
3	239	---	Захочешь жить, тогда глядишь с улыбкой	---
4	240	---	Я больше не ребенок	6 June 1931
28	248 +249	158	Фаэтончик	June 1931
29	265 +250(157)	---	Сегодня можно снять декалькомани	Summer 1931
30	251	155	Еще далеко мне до патриарха	21 Aug.-19 Oct.1931

ВТОРАЯ МОСКОВСКАЯ ТЕТРАДЬ

NYa	Number I	S	Title/first line	Date in NYa
1	252	163	Там, где купальни-бумагопрядильни	May 1932
2	253	159	О, как мы любим лицемерить	May 1932
3	254	160	Ламарк	7-9 May 1932
4	255	---	Когда в далекую Корею (last stanza finished in Voronezh)	11-13 May 1932
5	258	162	Импрессионизм	23 May 1932
6	257	---	Вы помните, как бегуны	May 1932-Sept.1935
7	256	161	Новеллино	22 May 1932
8	259	164	Дайте Тютчеву стрекозу	May 1932
9	261	165	Батюшков	18 June 1932
10	262 -4	166 -8	Стихи о русской поэзии	3-7 July 1932
11	266	169	К немецкой речи	8-12 Aug.1932
12	271	---	Холодная весна. Голодный Старый Крым	May 1933
13	267	---	Ариост	4-6 May 1933
14	268	170	Ариост (Variant)	4-6 May 1933, July 1935
15	270	---	Не искушай чужих наречий, но постарайся их забыть	May 1933, Aug.1935
16	269	---	Друг Ариоста, друг Петрарки, Тассо друг	May 1933
17	272	---	Квартира тиха, как бумага	Nov.1933
18	274	---	У нашей святой молодежи	Nov.1933
19	273	---	Татары, узбеки и ненцы	Nov.1933
20	286	---	Мы живем, под собою не чуя страны	Nov.1933
21			Восьмистишия	
1	275	171	Люблю появление ткани	Nov.1933, July 1935
2	276	---	Люблю появление ткани	Nov.1933
3	280	---	Когда, уничтожив набросок	Nov.1933
4	277	---	О, бабочка, о, мусульманка	Nov.1933
5	281	172	И Шуберт на воде, и Моцарт в птичьем гаме	Jan.1934
6	283	---	Скажи мне, чертежник пустыни	Nov.1933

NYa	Number I	S	Title/first line	Date in NYa
7	282	---	И клена зубчатая лапа	Nov.1933-Jan.1934
8	278	---	Шестого чувства крохотный придаток	May 1932
9	279	---	Преодолев затверженность природы	Jan.1934
10	284	---	В игольчатых, чумных бокалах	Nov.1933
11	285	---	И я выхожу из пространства	Nov.1933
22	488	286	Река, разбухшая от слез соленых	Dec.1933-Jan.1934
23	487	287	Как соловей, сиротствующий славит	Dec.1933-Jan.1934
24	489	288	Когда уснет земля и жар отпышет	Dec.1933-Jan.1934
25	490	289	Промчались дни мои, как бы оленей	4-8 Jan.1934
26	287	---	Как из одной высокогорной щели	Dec.1933
27	288	173	Голубые глаза и горящая лобная кость	10 Jan.1934
28	289	174	10 января 1934	Jan.1934
29	291	---	Когда душе и торопкой и робкой	Jan.1934
30	294	---	Откуда привезли? Кого? Который умер?	10 Jan.1934
31	293	---	Он дирижовал кавказскими горами	Jan.1934
32	292	---	Ему кавказские кричали горы	Jan.1934
33	290	---	А посреди толпы - задумчивый, брадатый	Jan.1934
34	295	175	Мастерица виноватых взоров	Feb.1934

ПЕРВАЯ ВОРОНЕЖСКАЯ ТЕТРАДЬ

NYa	Number I	S	Title/first line	Date in NYa
1	296	176	Твоим узким плечам под бичами краснеть	1934
2	299	179	Чернозем	Apr.1935
3	304	181	Я живу на важных огородах	Apr.1935
4	305	180	Я должен жить, хотя я дважды умер	Apr.1935
5	301	---	Пусти меня, отдай меня, Воронеж	Apr.1935
6	300	---	Наушники, наушнички мои	Apr.1935
7	306	186	Да, я лежу в земле, губами шевеля	May 1935
8	303	---	Эта, какая улица	Apr.1935
9	302	185	Стрижка детей	May 1935
10	308 -10	182 -3	Кама	May 1935
11	312	187	Стансы	May-June 1935
12	313	---	День стоял о пяти головах.Сплошные пять суток	Apr.-June 1935
13	311	188	От сырой простыни говорящая	May-June 1935
14	307	---	Лишив меня морей, разбега и разлета	May 1935
15	314	178	Возможно ли женщине мертвой хвала	3 June 1935, 14 Dec.1936
16	315	177	На мертвых ресницах Исакий замерз	June 1935
17	316	---	Римских ночей полновесные слитки	June 1935
18	298	184	Скрипачка	Apr.-June 1935
19	319	---	Бежит волна - волной волне хребет ломая	July 1935
20	318	---	Исполню дымчатый обряд	July 1935
21	320	---	Не мучнистой бабочкою белой	21 July 1935
22	317	152	- Нет, не мигрень, но подай карандашик ментоловый	July 1935

ВТОРАЯ ВОРОНЕЖСКАЯ ТЕТРАДЬ

NYa	Number I	S	Title/first line	Date in NYa
1	322	189	Из-за домов, из-за лесов	6-8 Dec.1936
2	342	---	Рождение улыбки	8 Dec.1936-17 Jan.1937
3	323	---	Подивлюсь на мир еще немного	10-13 Dec. 1936
4	324	190	Мой щегол, я голову закину	10-27 Dec. 1936
5	327	---	Когда щегол в воздушной сдобе	Dec.1936
6	329	---	Нынче день какой-то желторотый	9-28 Dec.1936
7	332	---	Я в сердце века - путь неясен	Winter 1936
8	328	---	Не у меня, не у тебя - у них	9-27 Dec.1936
9	330	---	Внутри горы бездействует кумир	10-26 Dec. 1936
10	333	---	А мастер пушечного цеха	1936
11	335	---	Сосновой рощицы закон	16-18 Dec. 1936
12	334	191	Пластинкой тоненькой жиллета	15-27 Dec. 1936
13	338	192	Эта область в темноводье	23-5 Dec.1936
14	340	193	Вехи дальнего обоза	26 Dec.1936
15	336	194	Как подарок запоздалый	29-30 Dec. 1936
16	337	---	Оттого все неудачи	29-30 Dec. 1936
17	345	195	Твой зрачок в небесной корке	2 Jan.1937
18	321	196	Улыбнись, ягненок гневный, с рафаэлова холста	2 Jan.1937
19	344	197	Когда в ветвях понурых	9-10 Jan.1937
20	343	---	Я около Кольцова	9 Jan.1937
21	347	---	Дрожжи мира дорогие	12-18 Jan. 1937
22	348	---	Влез бесенок в мокрой шерстке	12-18 Jan. 1937
23	354	198	Еще не умер я, еще я не один	15-16 Jan. 1937
24	349	199	В лицо морозу я гляжу один	16 Jan.1937
25	351	---	О, этот медленный, одышливый простор	16 Jan.1937
26	350	---	Что делать нам с убитостью равнин	16 Jan.1937

ТРЕТЬЯ ВОРОНЕЖСКАЯ ТЕТРАДЬ

NYa	Number I S	Title/first line	Date in NYa
1	375 ---	На доске малиновой, червонной	6 March 1937
2	372 ---	Если б меня наши враги взяли	Feb.1937
3	374 213	Я видел озеро, стоящее отвесно	4 March 1937
4	373 212	Я прошу, как жалости и милости	3 March 1937
5	381 215	Рим	16 March 1937
6	362 ---	Стихи о неизвестном солдате	Feb.-March 1937
7	376 214	Я скажу это начерно - шепотом	9 March 1937
8	377 ---	Тайная Вечеря	9 March 1937
9	379 217	Заблудился я в небе... Что делать	9-19 March 1937
10	378 216	Заблудился я в небе... Что делать	9-19 March 1937
11	380 ---	Может быть, это точка безумия	15 March 1937
12	384 218	О, как же я хочу	27 March 1937
13	383 ---	Кувшин	21 March 1937
14	385 ---	Гончарами велик остров синий	March 1937
15	297 ---	Нереиды мои, нереиды	March 1937
16	387 ---	Флейты греческой тэта и йота	7 Apr.1937
17	382 ---	Украшался отборной собачиной	After 7 Apr. 1937
18	395 220	Как по улицам Киева-Вия	Apr. 1937
19	389 221	Клейкой клятвой пахнут почки	2 May 1937
20	388 219	Я к губам подношу эту зелень	30 Apr.1937
21	393 222	На меня нацелилась груша, да черемуха	4 May 1937
22	394 223 -4	К пустой земле невольно припадая	4 May 1937

REFERENCES

Ахматова, А.А. *Сочинения*. 2 vols., 2nd edn. of vol. 1. Washington, 1967-8.

Блок, А.А. *Собрание сочинений в восьми томах*. 8 vols. Moscow-Leningrad, 1960-3.

Гумилев, Н.С. *Собрание сочинений в четырех томах*. 4 vols. Washington, 1962-8.

Державин, Г.Р. *Сочинения*. 2nd edn. 7 vols. St Petersburg, 1868-78.

Достоевский, Ф.М. *Собрание сочинений в десяти томах*. 10 vols. Moscow, 1956-8.

Жуковский, А.В. *Собрание сочинений в 4 томах*. 4 vols. Moscow-Leningrad, 1959-60.

Кольцов, А.В. *Полное собрание сочинений*. St Petersburg, 1909.

Пастернак, Б.Л. *Собрание сочинений*. 3 vols. Ann Arbor, 1961.

Пушкин, А.С. *Собрание сочинений в десяти томах*. 10 vols. Moscow, 1974- .

Семенко, И.М. 'Мандельштам – переводчик Петрарки', *Вопросы литературы*, 10 (1970), 153-69.

Тютчев, Ф.И. *Полное собрание сочинений*. 2nd edn. Leningrad, 1957.

Baines, Jennifer, 'Mandel'shtam's "Грифельная ода": A commentary in the light of the unpublished rough drafts', *Oxford Slavonic Papers*, New Series V (1972), 61-82.

Brown, Clarence. *Mandelstam*. Cambridge, 1973.

Brown, Clarence, 'Into the Heart of Darkness', *Slavic Review*, XXVI (1967), 584-604.

Brown, Clarence, 'Mandelstam's Notes towards a Supreme Fiction', *Delos*, I (1968), 32-48.

Brown, Clarence, 'Четвертая проза', transl. and introduction, *Hudson Review*, (Spring 1970), 49-50.

Leibniz. *The Monadology*. Transl. R. Latta. Oxford, 1965

Mandelstam, Nadezhda. *Hope against hope*. Transl. Max Hayward.
New York, 1970.

INDEX

including variants, rough drafts and fragments